The Badminton Library

OF

SPORTS AND PASTIMES

EDITED BY

HIS GRACE THE DUKE OF BEAUFORT, K.G.

ASSISTED BY ALFRED E T. WATSON

SHOOTING

(FIELD AND COVERT)

12ᵗʰ November 1992

Happy Birthday,
From your two favourite
flatmates

Nick and
Emma
xxx
St Andrews.

PARTRIDGE DRIVING

SHOOTING

BY

LORD WALSINGHAM

AND

SIR RALPH PAYNE-GALLWEY, Bt.

Author of 'Letters to Young Shooters' ' Book of Duck Decoys' &c.

WITH CONTRIBUTIONS BY THE
HON. GERALD LASCELLES AND A. J. STUART-WORTLEY

FIELD AND COVERT

WITH NUMEROUS ILLUSTRATIONS BY
A. J. STUART-WORTLEY, HARPER PENNINGTON, C. WHYMPER
J. H. OSWALD BROWN AND G. E. LODGE

Sixth Edition

ASHFORD PRESS PUBLISHING
SOUTHAMPTON
1987

Published by   ASHFORD PRESS PUBLISHING 1987
                1 CHURCH ROAD
                SHEDFIELD
                HAMPSHIRE SO3 2HW

First published in 1900
Republished 1987

Introductory Note © 11th Duke of Beaufort 1985

British Library Cataloguing in Publication Data

Walsingham, Thomas de Grey, Baron
   Shooting. (The Badminton library of sports and pastimes).
   Field and Covert.
   1. Hunting   Great Britain   History 19th Century
   I. Title
   II. Payne Gallwey, Sir Ralph.   III. Series
   799.2'13'0941   FK185

   ISBN 0-907069-73-8

Printed and bound in Great Britain

Introductory Note

My great great-grandfather, the 8th Duke of Beaufort, was always proud to say that he had been instrumental in bringing about one of the great sporting achievements of this century. In 1882, he and his great friend, Alfred Watson, set about compiling The Badminton Library, a series of books that would attempt to highlight, examine and explain all of the many great sports that this nation enjoys. The aim was simple; the Library was to become an encyclopaedia of sport that would supply basic information to all amateur sportsmen.

As a result of their work some 23 volumes were published that covered all sorts of activities: Hunting, of course, a subject always very close to my family's heart; Fishing; Racing and Steeplechasing; Lawn Tennis; Shooting; Driving; Athletics; Football, and even Cycling and Motor Driving. For each volume the most influential specialists were asked to impart their particular expertise, and indeed many of these are still remembered today for their sporting achievements. I think particularly of Lord Brassey on Yachting, Lord Walsingham on Shooting and the 8th Duke of Beaufort himself on Driving and Hunting – but the list of names is endless and each has a claim to our attention.

The finest illustrators were also eager to add their contribution: Archibald Thorburn and A.C. Sealy are notable examples. And so a magnificent sporting library was born, created from the greatest talents and with the immense tradition of Badminton firmly behind it. As might have been expected, the Library was a huge success. During the years it has gained great respect and instant recognition all over the world, and the books, although somewhat rare now, are still very much sought-after.

My great great-grandfather was more than the notional editorial figure-head that some might wrongly imagine. He worked enthusiastically to cull the best talents available and vi

to edit them into a series of readable, entertaining volumes. He was rightly very proud of his part in commissioning and compiling the Library: it has remained one of his greatest achievements.

The reissue of the Library is long overdue; it could not have come at a better time. Far from losing its popularity, sport is now once again at its height. Television has had a major impact and modern day lifestyles have enabled many more people to participate in and enjoy sport at both amateur and professional levels.

At the same time, sport in its truest sense is threatened today by many evils that my great great-grandfather would never have imagined – hooliganism, financial influences, drugs, politics, and even terrorism. Let us hope that the best of sport will survive and that the reissue of the Badminton Library will remind us of at least some of what is best in sport.

The Badminton Library offers lifetimes of experience gained by a host of illustrious sportsmen, and provides a fascinating insight into the traditions and rites of the sports as they were enjoyed so many years ago.

It has now fallen to me to follow in the family tradition, and I take great pleasure in being able to help re-launch the Badminton Library. In introducing it I hope I have managed to convey just a fraction of the enthusiasm with which my family has always regarded these volumes.

I commend the Badminton Library to a new generation of sportsmen and women; hopefully they will gain as much pleasure from reading these volumes as I have; and undoubtedly they will increase their abilities by listening to the great mass of advice and anecdotes offered by such an esteemed selection of our great sporting forebears.

The 11th Duke of Beaufort
June 1985

DEDICATION

TO

H.R.H. THE PRINCE OF WALES.

—•◦•—

BADMINTON : *October* 1885.

HAVING received permission to dedicate these volumes, the BADMINTON LIBRARY of SPORTS and PASTIMES, to HIS ROYAL HIGHNESS THE PRINCE OF WALES, I do so feeling that I am dedicating them to one of the best and keenest sportsmen of our time. I can say, from personal observation, that there is no man who can extricate himself from a bustling and pushing crowd of horsemen, when a fox breaks covert, more dexterously and quickly than His Royal Highness ; and that when hounds run hard over a big country, no man can take a line of his own and live with them better. Also, when the wind has been blowing hard, often have I seen His Royal Highness knocking over driven grouse and partridges and high-rocketing pheasants in first-rate workmanlike-style. He is held to be a good yachtsman, and as Commodore of the Royal Yacht Squadron is looked up to by those who love that pleasant and exhilarating pastime. His encouragement of racing is well known, and his attendance at the University, Public School, and other important Matches testifies to his being, like most English gentlemen, fond of all manly sports. I consider it a great privilege to be allowed to dedicate these volumes to so eminent a sportsman as His Royal Highness the Prince of Wales, and I do so with sincere feelings of respect and esteem and loyal devotion.

BEAUFORT.

BADMINTON.

PREFACE.

A FEW LINES only are necessary to explain the object
with which these volumes are put forth. There is no
modern encyclopædia to which the inexperienced man,
who seeks guidance in the practice of the various British
Sports and Pastimes, can turn for information. Some
books there are on Hunting, some on Racing, some on
Lawn Tennis, some on Fishing, and so on ; but one
Library, or succession of volumes, which treats of the
Sports and Pastimes indulged in by Englishmen—and
women—is wanting. The Badminton Library is offered
to supply the want. Of the imperfections which must
be found in the execution of such a design we are

conscious.   Experts often differ.   But this we may say,
that those who are seeking for knowledge on any of the
subjects dealt with will find the result of many years'
experience written by men who are in every case adepts
at the Sport or Pastime of which they write.   It is to
point the way to success to those who are ignorant of
the sciences they aspire to master, and who have no
friend to help or coach them, that these volumes are
written.

    To those who have worked hard to place simply and
clearly before the reader that which he will find within,
the best thanks of the Editor are due.   That it has been
no slight labour to supervise all that has been written
he must acknowledge ; but it has been a labour of love,
and very much lightened by the courtesy of the Publisher,
by the unflinching, indefatigable assistance of the Sub-
Editor, and by the intelligent and able arrangement
of each subject by the various writers, who are so
thoroughly masters of the subjects of which they treat.
The reward we all hope to reap is that our work may
prove useful to this and future generations.

                                        THE EDITOR.

CONTENTS.

— ·◆·—

CHAPTER   PAGE

    I. INTRODUCTORY   I

   II. SHOOTING, PAST AND PRESENT 13

  III. HINTS FOR BEGINNERS . . . . . ' 31

  IV. A SHORT HISTORY OF GUN-MAKING . . . 48

   V. PRICES OF GUNS 71

  VI. THE CHOICE OF A GUN 82

 VII. SHOOTERS 121

VIII. PARTRIDGE SHOOTING 139

  IX. PHEASANT AND WOOD-PIGEON SHOOTING . . [180]

   X. REARING 231

  XI. RABBIT SHOOTING 259

 XII. VERMIN 273

XIII. KEEPERS 290

 XIV. POACHERS AND POACHING 299

  XV. DOGS AND DOG-BREAKING 314

 XVI. PIGEON SHOOTING FROM TRAPS . . . 335

      INDEX 347

ILLUSTRATIONS.

Engraved by E. Whymper, J. D. Cooper, G. Pearson
G. E. Lodge, R. B. Lodge, G. Ford.

———◇———

FULL-PAGE ILLUSTRATIONS.

	ARTIST		
Partridge Driving	*A. J. Stuart-Wortley* / *Harper Pennington*	*Front.*	
Partridges (*Vignette on Title Page*)	*G. E. Lodge*		
Modern Style	*A. J. Stuart-Wortley* / *Harper Pennington*	*to face p.*	26
Walking up Partridges	*A. J. Stuart-Wortley* / *Harper Pennington*	,,	144
A Rise of Pheasants	*A. J. Stuart-Wortley* / *Harper Pennington*	,,	184
'As high as you ever saw them'	*A. J. Stuart-Wortley* / *Harper Pennington*	,,	194
Elveden Range of Fixed Hatching-pens	*From a photograph*	,,	242
'Old' Watson	*From a photograph*	,,	290
Israel Buckle	*Sir R. Frankland*	,,	296
John Buckle	*From a photograph*	,,	298
Considerate Masters	*J. H. Oswald Brown*	,,	320
'Have a care'	*J. H. Oswald Brown*	,,	328

WOODCUTS IN TEXT.

	ARTIST	PAGE
SHOOTER IN WOOD	*A. J. Stuart-Wortley* / *Harper Pennington*	1
GROUSE FLYING DOWN WIND . . .	*A. J. Stuart-Wortley* / *Harper Pennington*	7
'OLD STYLE'	*A. J. Stuart-Wortley* / *Harper Pennington*	13
PARTRIDGES REARED BY HAND . .	*A. J. Stuart-Wortley* .	29
DANGER FROM A NOVICE . . .	*C. Whymper* . .	32
'TOO FAR' . . . . . ,	*A. J. Stuart-Wortley* / *Harper Pennington*	33
THE YOUNG SPORTSMAN . . .	*C. Whymper* . .	35
HOW TO CARRY A GUN	*C. Whymper* . .	37
'TOO NEAR'.	*A. J. Stuart-Wortley* / *Harper Pennington*	41
'THE OLD AND THE NEW'. . .	*C. Whymper* . .	48
ANCIENT AND MODERN GUNS, BY PURDEY	. . . .	49
COGSWELL AND HARRISON'S EJECTOR		55
PURDEY'S HAMMERLESS GUN (FIG. 1)		58
,, ,, (FIGS. 2, 3)		59
HOLLAND AND HOLLAND'S PATENT EJECTOR	. . . .	60
THE GUN-ROOM	*C. Whymper* . .	71
GRANT'S HAMMERLESS GUN		77
LANCASTER GUN (SECTION OF LOCK)		78
,, ,, (BLOCKING SAFETY BOLTS)		78
CHARLES LANCASTER'S EJECTOR		80
GAME BAG, GUN-CASE, ETC.		82
A WELL-SHAPED GUN BY GRANT		87
STOCKS OF GUNS (FIGS. 1, 2)		87
,, ,, (FIG. 3)		88

	ARTIST	PAGE
HOLLAND AND HOLLAND'S TRY GUN		88
COGSWELL AND HARRISON'S TRY GUN		89
BEESLEY'S SINGLE-TRIGGER GUN		93
COGSWELL AND HARRISON'S SINGLE-TRIGGER GUN		94
CHARLES LANCASTER'S SINGLE-TRIGGER GUN		95
CLEANING-ROD		120
THE RIGHT SORT	*A. J. Stuart-Wortley* / *Harper Pennington*	123
THE GENT FROM TOWN . . .	*C. Whymper* . .	125
THE WRONG SORT	*A. J. Stuart-Wortley* / *Harper Pennington*	127
'DOWN CHARGE'.	*J. H. Oswald Brown* .	139
'MARK OVER'.	*C. Whymper* . .	143
DIAGRAM		147
,, ...		149
,, ...		150
,, ...		151
,, ...		152
'KILLED AS HE TOPS THE FENCE' . .	*A. J. Stuart-Wortley* / *Harper Pennington*	161
DIAGRAM		163
BATTERY MADE WITH HURDLES . .	*G. E. Lodge* .	164
SHOOTER AND LOADER CHANGING GUNS, No. 1	*From a photograph* .	173
SHOOTER AND LOADER CHANGING GUNS, No. 2	*From a photograph* .	175
SHOOTER AND LOADER CHANGING GUNS, No. 3	*From a photograph* .	177
DIAGRAM		179
PHEASANT	*C. Whymper* .	. [180]
'BEATERS ARE COMING'.	*C. Whymper* . .	186

	ARTIST	PAGE
JAMES PINNOCK	*From a photograph* .	189
SHOOTING ATTITUDE—HIGH SIDE SHOT	*From a photograph* .	192
,, ,, —STRAIGHT OVER	*From a photograph* .	194
SHOOTING POSITION, NO. 1 . .	*From a photograph* .	197
,, ,, ,, 2 . . .	*From a photograph* .	198
DIAGRAM	. . . .	199
STANDING BACK IN COVERT. . .	{ *A. J. Stuart-Wortley* / *Harper Pennington* }	202
STURSTON CARR	. . . .	216
CHERRY ROW	. . . .	217
LORD LONDESBOROUGH'S COVERT . .	. . . .	218
WAYLAND WOOD	. . . .	220
,, ,, ALTERNATE PLAN . .	. . . .	222
MERTON HOME WOODS . . .	. . . .	223
STUFFED DECOY PIGEON ON BRANCH .	. . . .	226
FRESH DECOY ON GROUND . . .	. . . .	226
PIGEON TURNING	. . . .	226
NET-WIRED DECOY PIGEON . .	. . . .	229
NET-WIRE FOR DECOY PIGEON. . .	. . . .	229
KEEPER AND PHEASANTS . . .	*C. Whymper* .	231
KEEPER TESTING EGGS	*C. Whymper* .	237
HATCHING-PENS AT BRADGATE PARK .	. . . .	240
GROUND-PLAN OF HATCHING-BOXES AND PATHWAYS	*From a photograph* .	241
GROUND-PLAN OF HATCHING-PENS .	*From a photograph* .	241
PORTABLE SINGLE PEN	. . . .	245
THE FOSTER MOTHER	*C. Whymper* .	248
A NIGHT ALARM	*C. Whymper* .	249
AN INTRUDER	*C. Whymper* .	257
A DAY WITH THE FERRETS . . .	*C. Whymper* .	259
RABBITS	*C. Whymper* .	271
THE BLACK LIST	*C. Whymper* .	273
A REAL POACHER.	*C. Whymper* .	277

	ARTIST	PAGE
THE POACHING KESTREL	*C. Whymper*	281
THE KEEPER'S COTTAGE	*C. Whymper*	290
'SOVS. AND HALF-SOVS.'	*C. Whymper*	291
KEEPER WITH FIELD-GLASS	*C. Whymper*	293
HEAD-KEEPER'S LODGE, THIRKLEBY PARK	*From a photograph*	298
THE POACHER	*C. Whymper*	299
THE DAY POACHER	*A. J. Stuart-Wortley* / *Harper Pennington*	301
DRIVING POACHERS	*C. Whymper*	303
THE NIGHT POACHER	*C. Whymper*	309
HARE IN NET	*C. Whymper*	311
THE RETRIEVER	*From a photograph*	314
OFF HOME	*J. H. Oswald Brown*	321
A REAL TREASURE	*J. H. Oswald Brown*	325
'AH-H! YOU BRUTE'	*J. H. Oswald Brown*	327
'WARE CHASE, WILL YOU?'	*J. H. Oswald Brown*	327

CHAPTER I.

INTRODUCTORY.

NO apology need be offered for the attempt to produce a new and comprehensive work on the subject of Shooting. Several admirable books on sport with the gun have been written from time to time, notably the treatise of Colonel Hawker, to whom the young sportsmen of a former generation were so deeply indebted. Nothing could have been better than this at the period when it was published ; but in all that appertains to the pursuit of game by English methods a vast change has of late years taken place. The invention of breechloaders has tended much to revolutionise shooting, and, for reasons which we shall presently proceed to explain, the introduction of a new system of agriculture has actually changed the habits of game.

In former days a man went out with his pointers or spaniels and made his probably modest bag in a manner which everyone must admit to have been perfectly sportsmanlike, though—contrary to an opinion which prevails generally among persons who are not practically acquainted with modern shooting—the tasks he set himself were for the most part much more simple than the sportsman of to-day is called upon to accomplish. Shooting is now of necessity often carried on in ways that were unknown to our forefathers, and we are not aware that any endeavour has been made to cover the ground by describing in detail the modern developments of a sport which every year brings health to, and provides recreation for, so many thousands of Englishmen—to say nothing of the benefits which it incidentally confers upon that large portion of the community which finds employment about estates whereon game is more or less extensively preserved, or is connected with the sport in the making and selling of the innumerable articles and implements necessary to the equipment of the shooter.

It is proposed in this volume to take all connected with the sport as much in detail as possible, beginning with the guns generally employed for shooting game. When the guns and their accessories have been dealt with, the different birds and animals on which they are used will be considered, and the sport they show described, not omitting the methods by which such sport is best obtained.

That a work on shooting will not be without its uses is suggested by the fact of the curiously inaccurate descriptions often to be met with in print. Writers are even found to satirise what they imagine to be the cruelties of modern game and wildfowl shooting, and we may surely assume that they know little of the difficulty of bringing down birds which pass high overhead down wind, or of the skill that is necessary to successfully stalk the wildfowl that haunt our coasts. They innocently talk of the old-fashioned method of walking the game up in the woods and fields as the only true sport, not understanding why this is often practically impossible, and not discerning any difference between the art required in shooting birds flying sixty miles per hour high overhead towards the gunner, and the stupid simplicity of putting a charge of shot into the tail of a pheasant flopping slowly up before the gun.

It is now-a-days generally admitted among those who really know what shooting is, and should be, that driving is the neatest, most skilful, and most satisfactory way of killing winged game, and that it, above all, gives the birds a chance; for an in- different shot will not bring them down, and, what is more to the point, will not wound them, as he would be sure to do were they flushed under his nose to fly slowly away.

A pheasant ' battue '—the latter word a favourite one with the scribe, though it is not used by sportsmen—where slaughter, easy shots, and luxurious refinements reign supreme, is, we may say, of very uncommon occurrence in the British Islands. On the other hand, at the large majority of places where great numbers of pheasants are shot in a day, it is invariably the object of the host or his head keeper to send the game as wild, high, and fast over the guns as is possible. ' Pheasant shoot- ing,' a sensible writer says, 'affords a day's outing and pay to a number of labourers (as beaters) who immensely enjoy it, and it gives permanent employment to a large number of keepers. It provides thousands of middle-class people with pheasants at the price of chickens, or even less. For instance, during November, 1885, any number of fine cock pheasants could be bought in the London market at 2s. apiece, where, if there were no big days of pheasant shooting, pheasants would be a guinea a brace. It affords a subject of sarcasm for cockney artists and the writers of leading articles in the "sporting" papers. In short, there is scarcely a class in the community which is not benefited or amused by it.'

It is a common idea, ever before the imagination of those who ignorantly criticise shooting on a large scale, especially pheasant shooting, that the home-reared birds are as tame as chickens   Let us say that by the middle or end of November, at which date most shooting parties are formed, so-called tame birds cannot be distinguished from the purely wild ones, bred in the woods, which latter they equal in their power of flight if properly driven to the gun, and afford in consequence as great an exhibition of skill on the part of the shooter.

Even some of those who have the reputation of being trust-worthy guides on the subject of shooting are apt to lead their readers far astray.   In the last edition of a book on 'British Rural Sports,' published in 1886 by a writer ('Stonehenge') who is supposed to be somewhat of an authority on all connected with guns and shooting, we find the following :—

It is for the purpose of the 'battue' that pheasants are now reserved and preserved with all the formidable retinue of head keepers. . . . No one can deny the fitness of the pheasant for affording gratification to the *good* sportsman if the bird is *fairly found*, put up and shot ; but as well might mobbing a fox be called fox hunting as a 'battue' be considered genuine pheasant shooting. In the 'battue' nothing short of hundreds, or if possible thousands, of killed, to say nothing of wounded, will constitute a successful day.   The pseudo-sportsman, who should be tempted from his 'Times' and his fireside for anything under five brace an hour, would be inclined to complain, and would think, if he did not say, that his presence had been obtained under false pretences.   The mode usually adopted is as follows :—

First, get together eight or ten crack shots, who may, many of them, be in wheeled chairs or on shooting ponies. . . . Domestic poultry must be reared and killed, but who would admit the pleasure of wringing their necks or cutting their throats?   Yet where lies the difference?   The pheasant is not even a difficult shot.[1]

This nonsense, derived entirely from the imagination of its writer, who can of course have no practical acquaintance with the sport he endeavours to describe, is not worth disputing. He is welcome to think that pheasant shoots are always termed

---

[1] Certainly the pheasant is *not* a difficult shot if kicked up under-foot, and this seems to be what the author in the above quotation means by 'fairly found.'

'battues'; that dropping pheasants flying down wind at a tremendous pace is easy work and resembles mobbing a fox ; that
many are wounded ; that nothing short of hundreds, and usually
thousands, are killed during a day's pheasant driving ; that a
sportsman would not leave his fireside under so many brace
an hour ; that many shooters go out in wheeled chairs and
on horseback to shoot pheasants.

The sporting writer here quoted is, we say, welcome to his
opinions ; but we beg the reader to believe that English sportsmen do not act thus, and are never cruel for cruelty's sake,
though this stigma is thrust upon them by the critic.

It is true such criticism as this may not be very palatable
to the 'sporting writer,' but this is no affair of curs, as in these
pages we merely describe shooting *as it is*, and *not* as it is *supposed* to be.

In connection with criticism on shooting (driving against
walking) it is often lamented that the breed of pointers has
deteriorated. This is quite true ; but, on the other hand,
pointers have been replaced by an improved breed of retrievers.
The latter dog is, in our opinion, far superior to the former,
as a companion, for its intelligence, and for its value in regard
to finding wounded game.

Many old shooters love to speak of the way their pointers
found game in the days of thick stubble and close-lying birds,
and especially how they backed one another up in doing so. It
was a pretty sight, no doubt, unless the leading dog stopped
for any private reason of his own or stood a lark, as we have
often seen him do. But it was very dull, and in most instances
made shooting subservient to dog-training. The birds offered
easy shots, for the gunner was able to stalk right up to them
under his dog's nose. If he wished (as we have heard it said
of 'Grouse-shooting in Caithness') he had time to take a
pinch of snuff, so as to allow the birds to get out of the range
within which they would be blown to pieces. We admit that,
under a few circumstances, working with *perfectly* broken dogs
on wild birds such as grouse, or partridges late in the season,

is very interesting ; with dogs partially or even fairly well broken it is very much the reverse.

Before closing these prefatory remarks we will generally and briefly allude to grouse, partridge, and ground game, subjects which will afterwards be found fully dealt with in detail.

In Scotland grouse are usually walked up with dogs. The birds in that country lie well. There is better ground for them to do so than in England, nor are they in most parts of Scotland numerous enough to make driving them a necessity to reduce their numbers, as is the case in England. In the latter country they are commonly driven to the guns. The chief and by far the best English grouse moors are in Yorkshire. On these the birds have increased enormously during recent seasons, since driving was introduced, somewhere about thirty years ago, one of the earliest exponents of this system having been the late Sir Henry Edwards.

There are various theories to account for this increase, such as the old cocks getting killed by flying to the guns in advance of the others, but the matter has not as yet been quite satisfactorily explained. There is no doubt that as driving grouse became fashionable, and the birds so vastly increased in numbers, the moors were better looked after and protected year by year ; increased care was in every way bestowed, poachers in particular having been prevented from destroying the grouse in large numbers after the moors were deserted for the season by their owners. This they did both by 'shooting,' 'netting,' and by 'calling,' the latter a fatally successful method of poaching grouse.

If grouse lie well to dogs, as is commonly the case in Scotland, and notably so in the rough ground to be seen in Caithness, they give easy marks to the gunner ; if the birds are wild, much the reverse. But driving is the cream of grouse shooting, for every shot then offered is more or less a test of marksmanship. What may be termed an easy shot is an exception.

Grouse flying fast when driven down wind, frequently tax

the skill of even good shots, and are missed time after time by the average marksman. A man who is unaccustomed to grouse driving takes days of practice before he can secure one bird to his three shots, even though he be above the average at ordinary game shooting. Two grouse to every five shots, taken as they come one day with another, is first-rate work.

The phenomenal marksmanship attained by shooters such

Grouse flying down wind

as Earl de Grey, Lord Walsingham, Lord Huntingfield, Mr. F. Corrance, the Maharajah Duleep Singh, Lord Newport, Mr. A. Stuart-Wortley, Sir Frederick Milbank, Mr. Ward Hunt, or Mr. F. Fryer, men who will at all reasonable distances account for from forty to forty-five birds out of sixty fired at, whether grouse, partridges, or pheasants, is quite exceptional, and results from a marvellous power of judgment of pace and distance of flight, as well as from long and constant practice. A sportsman may privately regard himself as a brilliant shot, but when he first tries to kill driven grouse or partridges he is apt to be greatly

disappointed, not to say astonished, with his shooting, especially if there is a good breeze and the birds are strong on the
wing; and it will take him some years of practice before he
can make fairly certain of knocking down four birds out of a
pack of grouse, stringing past or overhead, with four shots from
his pair of guns, or, on the other hand, of regularly dropping
a right and left from a covey of driven partridges—a simple
feat to such shooters as we have named, and one they rarely
fail to achieve.

The number of double shots an ordinarily good—yes, and
very good—marksman will fire ineffectually at driven grouse,
for instance, at from fifteen to twenty yards distance will at first
strike him as being curious. There comes the bird; it can be
seen a quarter of a mile off or more. On it flies, straight for
the butt, apparently going neither one way nor the other. It
approaches, skimming over the heather, straight as a dart for
the shooter. He gets his gun ready—he fires. The bird does
not even swerve in its rapid flight as it passes. The occupant
of the butt is perhaps amazed. He hastily swings round and
fires another barrel at the retreating bird, but still on goes the
grouse, floating into the horizon. He must be hit ! he is
going to tower ! Not a bit of it; he is only topping a rise in
the heather just as he vanishes from sight.

How was the mistake made? Usually because the shooter
fired too soon; he saw the bird so plainly that it appeared
far nearer than it really was—we are speaking, of course, of one
who is unaccustomed to the sport. Had he waited till he saw
the colour of its plumage it would have been fully twenty yards
distant; and even at a lesser distance the bird might not be
injured by the charge, for many of the pellets will glance off
him when approaching the gun as from a stone, unless he be
struck in the wing. Judging distance is of the greatest importance in grouse and partridge driving, as it is in every other
kind of shooting, only, perhaps, here more so, for so many
side shots occur. By 'judging distance' we mean pulling
trigger when the gun aims so far in front of the object that

the latter and the shot meet one another. It is a common fault for young shooters to aim well in advance, but *not* to pull the trigger till the bird or beast has come in line with the gun. The aim then is just as much behind the object as it *ought* to have been in front. 'Aim high and in front' is nearly always a golden rule for a driven shot.

Partridge driving is very similar to grouse driving as regards the practice and skill required. It is a common argument amongst shooters as to whether it is the more difficult to kill a driven partridge or grouse. We do not think there is much difference, but confidently assert that more shots are thrown away at the former than at the latter. Grouse do not, it is true, often fly slowly, except against a strong wind, and as they rarely rise within so short a distance as a quarter of a mile of the butts, they are at full speed when they reach the guns. It is true they present larger marks than partridges, but then they are far stronger and have denser plumage, and so require more pellets to drop them.

On the other hand, a partridge, when a gun is pointed at him, will often swerve, which is not generally the habit of a grouse. The shooter, however, labours under the disadvantage of not being able to take a clear view of approaching birds from behind the sort of shelter usually made to serve for partridge driving; whereas a grouse shooter in his butt can see on all sides of him, and prepare for his game long before it reaches him. In Norfolk, Cambridge, and Suffolk driving partridges is the usual practice, the birds being so abundant that it is the best method of obtaining them, as also of increasing their numbers, by reason that the old birds, flying first, are well thinned off. In walking up partridges the reverse is the case; the old birds, rising first, generally escape. The result is that they fight and drive each other off the ground the next breeding season; those that remain also rear smaller broods.

Shooting partridges over dogs is very pleasant for men who only care for seeing their pointers work, and ignore the skill of shooting. If partridges lie so close that pointers can be

successfully used in finding them, they afford such simple shots
that there is little skill required in killing them. The perfection of shooting demands that the game shall spring up wild,
and so offer a test of true aiming. It is not real sport when,
the attitude of the dog showing that there is a partridge or a
hare squat under his nose, the shooter walks on cautiously
till he is close to it, kicks it up, lets it get a fair distance so as
not to blow it to pieces, takes steady aim as with a rifle, and
drops it at eighteen to twenty paces. If partridges are fairly
numerous, it is far more sporting to walk them up and afterwards find them with a retriever—a noble, skilful, and affectionate dog, and one whose work in the field is of the most
interesting character. In the above remarks we are speaking
of partridge shooting generally. Every rule has its exception.
It is very enjoyable to walk with a brace of pointers (*and* a
retriever) over an extensive range of wild ground (especially
if an odd duck or snipe is to be met), alone or with a friend.
In such case the birds would be missed unless found by
pointers ; but this is a different thing from searching a thick
field of turnips in which you *know* partridges are more or
less numerous, and spending half a day in finding them, and
walking up to the point.

When shooting hares—to glance briefly at the question of
ground game before ending these introductory observations—
the great object of the shooter should be not to wound. Of
course this is, we need scarcely say, equally the case in all kinds
of shooting, but a hare is more liable to be wounded on account
of his size than is other game.

A wounded hare is a pitiable, a distressing sight, and has
often haunted us from the beginning to the end of a day
when we have inadvertently failed to kill. Everyone can *hit*
a hare who is a tolerable shot, but not everyone can hit her in
the right place—that is, the head. Long shots at hares, especially when going straight away, prove the shooter to be a
cruel, reckless blunderer. A hare going straight from the
shooter should *never* be fired at if over thirty yards away,

because, if she is wounded, a second shot will only make matters worse, and a wound at forty yards is almost a certainty. A vital part can hardly be struck ; if struck, the wound will probably not be felt for some little time by the unfortunate animal, and it will presently die by slow degrees in the recesses of a wood or hedge. Even a hare coming directly towards a shooter cannot be easily killed, however simple the shot may appear; but in this case a second shot is, or ought to be, a *finale*. Hares crossing, if in fair range, there should be no difficulty about. Hares crossing outside a fair range it is better and more humane to leave alone. The number of useless *second* shots fired at hares throughout a day's shooting is always remarkable to a close observer.

In rabbit shooting the above remarks equally apply to rabbits going away—if possible they apply even more forcibly, as poor bunny, if wounded, will probably die underground, and will, likely enough, never be found in time to be of use as food ; so this is a question of waste as well as of cruelty.

To shoot rabbits neatly in covert is one of the best tests of marksmanship that can be suggested. It is snap-shooting, and usually means a kill or a clean miss. Some men are from constant practice wonderful adepts at this difficult sport. A rabbit has but to stir a leaf or move, and he is that instant stretched dead. This success is obtained by the shooter firing the instant his eye catches sight of the game, and by his *not* waiting for a better chance or a clearer view, the latter being a common fault with young shooters.

Shooting rabbits in the open is very pretty, but no test of skill when compared to shooting them in a covert, or especially in turnips. In the latter case, if a rabbit runs down a furrow, as is his custom, by stepping into the same furrow and getting in line with him he may often be killed. Killing rabbits in grass fields when turned out of their holes is a popular method of shooting them, and thirty to forty may be killed in succession by a skilful shot. It is also a good way of making them show sport of a kind, for rabbits are most difficult to manage in this respect, and very hard to manœuvre to the gun, though they may exist on an estate in thousands. The prettiest rabbit shooting is to be enjoyed in parks, such as there are many of in England, in which high bracken abounds; the chase at Wortley (Lord Wharncliffe's residence) is a very good example. Rides are cut, and the rabbits are killed in crossing these narrow open spaces or lanes. It requires very quick and true aiming to kill rabbits with any *certainty* as they dart across a narrow ride, and it can only be done by the shooter walking or standing, as the case may be, as near the cover on one side as he can, and so stopping bunny as he is just entering covert on the other side—in fact, making a diagonal shot. Otherwise a rabbit often flits across before the gun can reach the shoulder.[1] Some enormous (two to five thousand) bags of rabbits have been made in a day in warrens by turning them out of their holes, as well as by sending keepers with lanterns and dogs to parade their feeding ground for several nights before the shooting, so as to make them feed and lie out. It is a good method of obtaining them, and is much less cruel than ferreting. After all, they must be killed somehow or other, and when killed afford cheap and excellent food.

We have now briefly alluded to ordinary game shooting. Wildfowling will be found fully treated later on.

R. P. G.

[1] The late Sir Victor Brooke, Bart., who died at Pau on the 23rd of November, 1891, was one of our best rabbit shots. In the wild and beautiful deer park at Colebrook, Sir Victor's residence in Ireland, he killed, in the year 1885, 740 rabbits in a day to his own gun. Sir Victor expended exactly 1,000 cartridges, and shot from his right shoulder for one half of the day, and from his left the other half. The last shot fired killed a woodcock 'back' from the left shoulder.

'Old style.'

CHAPTER II.

SHOOTING, PAST AND PRESENT.

SHOOTING, as a national sport, may be said to have commenced
with the eighteenth century; the days of fairly heavy bags as
late as 1840. Shooting was not, however, general, and shooting at flying and running game was not the rule, till toward the
end of the last century. There are, nevertheless, many records
of the use of firearms for killing game in the fifteenth century.
It was at first thought almost an impossibility to make fatal
flying shots, with any certainty, as may well be imagined,
having regard to the construction and capacity of the earlier
flint fowling-pieces; consequently all the verbal and pictorial
illustrations of shooting in olden days represent the gunner
taking steady aim at motionless objects.

That the sportsmen of long ago, before aiming at flying birds
came into vogue by reason of improved guns, were close ob-
servers of the game they followed, we may rest assured; indeed,

they must needs have been so in order to make successful stalks, and so obtain sitting shots. Many records exist of shooting parties in the eighteenth century on the Continent, at which vast totals of game were obtained. But it must be borne in mind that on these occasions an army of men in different divisions with nets and dogs surrounded a large tract of country, and, preparing for the event many days beforehand, each circle of men gradually drove all the game into one wood. Each wood was then encompassed by high nets; the gunners—one cannot say sportsmen—entered its precincts, and, being provided with six guns or more apiece, as well as the necessary attendants to load them, slew all living things that were driven near them that escaped the nets. For example, in 1753, we have records of a ' chasse ' in Bohemia that lasted twenty days. The writer possesses one of the originally printed cards describing the affair, with the names of the shooters and what they killed thereon in full. Nothing can be fuller or more explicit than the details given in this interesting *aperçu*, which reveals the names of the twenty-three shooters—among whom the Emperor of Austria and her Imperial Highness the Princess Charlotte were included—also the number of shots fired, the amount and various descriptions of the game bagged, and the places and dates at which each day's shooting took place. The number of shots fired in the twenty days was no fewer than 116,231,[1] and the amount of game bagged 47,950 head, being at the rate of more than two killed to every five shots. The aggregate of this enormous bag is made up of stags, roedeer, wild boars, foxes, hares, pheasants, partridges, larks, quails, and ' other birds.' The last item, amounting only to fifty-four head, may be supposed to include such small fry as blackbirds and thrushes—from which foreign sportsmen, and especially our French neighbours, can never withhold their eager hands—and possibly a few wood pigeons. But it will also be seen with astonishment that this amazing list includes a total of 18,273

[1] Mr. Greener, in his book on the ' Gun,' quotes the number of shots fired as being 16,231, an error worthy of correction here.

hares, more than two thousand of which occasionally fell before the guns in a single day. Partridges appear to have been as numerous in Bohemia towards the middle of the last century as they are in Norfolk at the present time, seeing that 19,545 head of these birds were bagged in the course of a 'chasse' which lasted for twenty days. The pheasants killed amounted altogether to 9,499 head, the stags to 19 head, the roedeer to 77, the wild boars to 10, the larks to 114, and the quails to 353. There is no doubt that every possible method of killing and mobbing the game, both by night and by day, was employed to obtain such a vast total.

In the latter years of the eighteenth century, as sporting guns became gradually more trustworthy and accurate, this driving of game into nets and pretending it was shooting, because a small proportion of shots were fired, seems to have become less in vogue. We give the following, copied from an original letter written by Sir Ralph Payne, afterwards Lord Lavington :—

Memorandum of a Chasse in Bohemia.

Our party was at the *château* of Prince Adam d'Auersperg, at Schlep, and consisted of eleven guns, including General Plunkett and myself.

We were out the 9th and 10th of September, 1788, five hours each day. The first day our party fired 6,068 times, and bagged, or rather waggoned, 876 hares, 259 pheasants, and 362 partridges, besides quails, rabbits, &c. The second day we fired 5,904 shots, and killed 181 hares, 634 pheasants, and 736 partridges, besides other game ; and in addition to this there were picked up in the evening of the second day 42 more hares, 65 pheasants, and 103 partridges—in all 210, which could not be immediately found in the heat of the *chasse*. Our number, then, of shots in the two days was 11,972, and our game found and carried home 3,258. According to the printed list or *billet de chasse*, I fired 456 times the first day and 578 the second. I could not keep any account of the number of head I killed on the 9th, but my *ramasseurs* (loaders) said that of hares, pheasants, and partridges, I killed about 150, besides inferior game. On the 10th I shot and picked up 200 head. It is to be observed that neither on the 9th or 10th was any of the game driven nor any particular method taken to assemble it. The birds were perfectly wild and remarkably strong, and were all shot on the wing.

In the above it will be noticed that the proportion of kills to misses was just two in seven. Such large bags do not, however, as far as we can learn, appear to have been obtained in England till within the memory of sportsmen now living.

We will next give some extracts from our shooting library, showing what was considered good shooting and an abundance of game in the early years of the present century. The estates selected are, so far as possible, those which are now and have long been celebrated for the amount of game on them.

Rendlesham (Lord Rendlesham's).

This princely and hospitable seat in Suffolk has been lately open to the most celebrated shots of the present day, and *nowhere* could there be found a more abundant field for the entertainment of the sportsman.

The following is the amount killed in the last week of the campaign just ended :—

On Monday, at Butley, 70 pheasants, 46 hares, besides partridges, woodcocks, &c. On Tuesday and Friday, partridges only. On Wednesday, at Butley again, 80 pheasants with other game. On Thursday, at Whitmore Wood, 192 pheasants, with woodcocks. And on the last day, 195 pheasants, besides hares, &c. Over a thousand head of game were shot here within the week.—*Suffolk paper*, 1807.

Holkham (Lord Leicester's).

—	Par-tridges	Phea-sants	Hares	Rabbits	Wood-cocks	Ducks	Total
Nov. 5	20	54	244	205	—	—	523
Nov. 7	7	42	153	196	3	—	401
Nov. 9	20	65	196	267	4	4	556
Nov. 11	10	24	168	344	6	—	552
	57	185	761	1012	13	4	2032

(From MS. describing a shooting party at Holkham in 1810.)

The following accounts of some yearly bags made at Holkham nearly an hundred years ago are from the same source :—

Date	Partridges	Pheasants	Woodcocks	Hares	Total
1793	1349	262	114	358	2083
1794	1433	358	104	286	2181
1795	2594	323	93	616	3626
1796	2814	304	123	795	4036
1797	3800	396	102	1178	5476
1798	3965	519	201	1107	5792
1799	2895	349	132	889	4265
1800	3865	355	127	854	5201

Holkham, Season 1818–19.

Pheasants	Partridges	Hares	Rabbits	Woodcocks	Snipes	Various	Total
1227	1711	3176	3789	181	168	347	10,599

It will be seen from this how remarkably pheasants increased in numbers, and how greatly partridges diminished.

Hares appear to have been wonderfully abundant in former
times.   For instance, in 1806, complaint being made by the
farmers that hares were too numerous at Sir Thomas Gooch's
in Suffolk, there were killed in consequence, from February 1
to March 12, no fewer than 6,012—(MS.)

Here is an extract which shows the numberless vermin
that game preservers had to contend against in those days; it is
taken from a Suffolk paper, dated 1811.   The quotation is also
otherwise of interest :—

At the gamekeepers of this county's annual meeting, held on
December 9, for the purpose of awarding a large silver flask to the
keeper who should produce the certificates for the greatest quantity
of hares, pheasants, and partridges *shot at* as well as killed during
any six days from the 8th of October to the 8th of December,
Richard Sharnton delivered vouchers for the following list, and
obtained the prize.   The prize was given upon a comparison of the
sport, estimating the number of guns and the extent of land in

strict preserve. Sharnton's list averaged three guns, and his extent
of preserve 4,000 acres :—

				Killed	Missed
Cock pheasants	•	•	•	378	199
Hen pheasants	•	•	•	51	39
Partridges .	•	•	•	506	301
Hares •	•	•	•	177	94

Sharnton afterwards produced the account of the vermin and
birds of prey that he had destroyed in the last twelve months. He
has but two under-keepers :—

Foxes .	•	•	22	Hawks .	•	•	167
Martins	•	•	9	Field rats	•	•	310
Polecats	•	•	31	Brown owls	•	•	19
Stoats .	•	•	416	Cats .	•	•	7
Magpies	•	•	120				

As to the increase of game in England, it may be said that
pheasants, in the main, are what really form the immense
addition to our stock. From the extracts we have given it will be
seen that, till about 1820, pheasants were somewhat scarce on
a large sporting estate. From that date they have steadily increased in numbers. Since the Crimean War sportsmen have
settled more peacefully to a country life, and devoted much
more time and money to game rearing than was the custom
of their forefathers. The remarkable bags of pheasants that
have been so much denounced may be said to date from
about 1860, one of the first to startle the shooting world in this
respect having been the Maharajah Duleep Singh, of Elveden
Hall, Suffolk. Among other equally successful pheasant preservers may be named H.R.H. the Prince of Wales, the late
Lord Stamford, Lord Leicester, Lord Sefton, Lord Walsingham,
Lord Londesborough, Lord Huntingfield, Lord Rendlesham,
Lord Hill, Mr. Fellowes, Mr. Tyssen-Amherst, and many others
on a lesser scale.

On the estates of some of the above named the shooting
of a thousand pheasants in a day is no unusual occurrence ; [1]

[1] A few years ago, Lord Hill, of Hawkstone, in Shropshire, a very beautiful
estate in a county most suitable for and full of game, was said to have more
pheasants in his coverts than anyone else in England, not excepting the land-
lords of Norfolk or Suffolk.

sometimes as many as two thousand are accounted for, and from five to ten thousand in a season.

As being one of the earliest and at the same time one of the largest bags of game on record, we give the following which was made at Bradgate Park, the seat of the late Lord Stamford, in Leicestershire, in 1864 :—

			Jan. 4	Jan. 5	Jan. 6	Jan 7	Total
Partridges	.	.	1	—	2	1	4
Pheasants	.	.	690	1822	338	1195	4045
Woodcock	.	.	26	24	2	7	59
Snipe	.	.	—	—	1	1	2
Hares	.	.	328	258	220	54	860
Rabbits	.	.	812	225	2534	331	3902
Various	.	.	5	6	5	12	28
Total	.	.	1862	2335	3102	1601	8900
Guns	.	.	13	14	13	13	—

The quotation below is from Mr. Henry Stevenson's 'Birds of Norfolk,' and ably defends the heavy shooting common to Norfolk and Suffolk, each of which counties is truly a land of game, beyond any others in England. Mr. Stevenson says that the pheasants sent to London alone from Suffolk average 120,000 a season. He deals in such a masterly manner with the sporting critics of shooting of the present day, as applied to large bags, and so thoroughly endorses what is written herein on the question, that we cannot refrain from quoting what he says, as under :—

Few subjects of a like nature have excited warmer controversy or tended to the exhibition of more violent prejudices than the so-called 'battue,' and, as usual in such discussions, supporters and their opponents, in their bitter hostility, have been so given to exaggeration and the use of hard words that the true merits of the case must be looked for apart from the arguments of either faction.

Undoubtedly, so far as the pheasant shooting is concerned, if a large number of birds are reared for sport—and why should not landed proprietors provide such amusement for their friends at a time when partridge shooting is well-nigh over?—there is no means so effectual of obtaining an equal amount of shooting for several guns as the 'battue,' whilst the most inveterate opponent of the slaughter system (if a sportsman at all) will not venture to deny that pheasants, as well as running game in large quantities, can be shot down by no other means.

There is, however, every reason to believe that the majority of those writers who are loudest in their denunciation against the 'battue,' and can find no milder epithets than 'bloodthirsty' and 'unsportsmanlike' to mark their abhorrence of it, are either practically unacquainted with the working of the system, or are deficient themselves in that necessary coolness and skill without which even pheasants, big as they are, will escape from a perfect volley of double barrels. Such individuals seem wholly unable to associate the enjoyment of a 'heavy' day's covert shooting with skill in the use of firearms and physical endurance, quite overlooking the fact that amongst the sportsmen accustomed to congregate towards Christmas time at the country seats of noblemen and wealthy squires for the purpose of joining in these great 'battues' are some of the very best shots in the world—men for whom no day on the open moors or in the treacherous snipe marsh is too long, no sport in any part of the globe too hazardous, though pursued by them merely for pleasure and excitement. If such men as these— and there are many—can enjoy for a change a 'big day' in some well-stocked coverts (where hunting probably is stopped by the frost), one would scarcely term it an unsportsmanlike diversion, even though carried to excess in the number of head killed in a single day. There is not certainly much bodily fatigue, yet the necessity of being always on the alert, always ready for a chance shot in the 'thick' or in the 'open' during many consecutive hours, to say nothing of incessant firing from the shoulder for a like period, is somewhat trying to the head and nerves ; and if anyone is inclined to despise the amusement on the ground that pheasants are easy to kill, let him try his hand late in the season at a few old cocks flushed some two hundred yards from the post of the shooter, so that the bird is in full flight when he passes over. The pace is then tremendous ! In short, the truth is that the 'battue' affords every opportunity for the display of good as well as bad shooting, and he is no ordinary shot who can account satisfactorily in 'feathers' and 'felt' for one in every three of his empty cartridges, provided always that he shoots fair and does not pick his shots.

Again, if pheasant shooting is only the wholesale slaughter of tame pheasants driven up by the beaters like barn-door fowls, how comes it that on many of the more highly preserved manors only the best shots are invited? Is it no honour to be named for the outer ring at 'Holkham' to stop those 'rocketers' which only crack shots can hit? and even the 'bouquet' at a 'hot corner' requires for a successful personal result an amount of cool self-possession which might prove invaluable under more trying circumstances.

It is, of course, difficult for the world at large—we mean those who have little or no experience of shooting—to know what to believe, whether the sporting papers (so-called), or the sporting books (so-called), or the words of sportsmen themselves. Many papers are flooded with abuse of pheasant, partridge, and grouse driving, by writers who in every sentence betray the grossest ignorance of the subject. As an example, we may quote a ludicrous account of grouse driving which was sent as a test to a paper that had a short time previously published a leading article on the iniquity of shooting grouse and pheasants by driving them overhead, as being a simple and unsportsmanlike system of butchery. The account ran as follows :—

Grouse Shooting by Electric Light.

A few days ago a novel method of shooting grouse was carried out by Mr. —— on his moors at ——. A large party of shooters proceeded to the moor about twelve o'clock at night, to a spot where an electric light had previously been temporarily established. Beaters were sent out over the ground, and as the birds rose they flew straight for the light. The sportsmen shot several hundred by its means; and when their guns became too hot to hold from such rapid firing, the grouse were knocked down and killed with sticks (!)

The editor gravely added as a footnote to the above hoax :—

This account of grouse shooting is most curious, but we can really scarce call it 'sport.'

In a Yorkshire journal not long ago an account (also a hoax) appeared of 'a day's shooting,' including many impossibilities, such as a number of rats and water-hens, and a regret that the hampers of woodcocks ordered from Holland had not arrived in time for the day's sport—all seriously inserted in the news columns of the journal in question as if nothing unusual.

We have several cuttings from newspapers before us as we write. The one idea of the shooting critics who year by year indite leading articles for the 1st of September on partridge shooting for their respective papers (in the supposed interests of shooting readers) is pointers. They apparently have pointers on the brain. Take a score of articles written for the papers about September 1—they all run in precisely the same groove, and the burthen of them is :—

We (i.e. the critic and article writer), for ourselves, prefer ranging the *stubbles* with a brace of well-broken and steady pointers, and would deem it a disgrace to make one of a party who, instead of finding the birds in a fair and skilful way, and one necessitating good aiming, rather, as is the custom now amongst some people *calling* themselves sportsmen, choose to shoot in an idle and unsportsmanlike manner. We refer to driving the birds, which consists in frightening them all into one field by surrounding them with a mob of beaters, and subsequently slaughtering them, each shooter being armed with two or three guns.

Now, in the first place, there is scarcely a stubble field in England at this day (owing to close cutting) that would shelter a mouse. If a mouse in a machine-cut corn-field knew he was an object of sport he would not, unless a very foolish mouse, let a shooter get within range of him; as to partridges lying to dogs or guns in stubbles, *that* is too absurd to consider. It is because there is no covert in the stubbles nowadays that, if the shooters walked them, it would be a waste of time on their part, as the birds would rise at least a hundred paces off; hence driving has come into vogue as a necessity. And if the stubbles *are* walked by the shooters, it is only to drive the birds into covert, such as turnips ; if walked by beaters, it is to drive the birds over the shooters' heads as they stand far in advance waiting for shots. How the editorial ' we ' finds and shoots partridges in ' stubble,' with even the assistance of

his well-broken pointers, is a thing that would be worth knowing
—that is to say, if the 'we' in question ever does what is now,
in fact, an unheard-of proceeding.

The following extract from the late Mr. Bromley Davenport's book on modern shooting deals with these sporting
critics in a very amusing fashion. His words are so truthful
and to the point that we append them.

Here (he says,—after quoting some such remarks as those which
we have given)—is an example of cockney censure on the thing as he,
according to his cockney lights, assumes it to be done, combined
with cockney advice as to how it should be done, which, in spite of
its Wonderland English, terse and concentrated ignorance, soaring
bathos, attempted sublime and realised ridiculous, is copied ver-
batim from a leading article in a leading London journal only some
two or three years ago. After denouncing the effeminacy of the
modern pheasant shooter, this sporting instructor to the multitude
says : 'Sportsmen of tougher calibre, and more capable of exertion, unnerved by misty weather (*sic*), will seek out the "rocketer"
for themselves, and will decline to try their skill upon him when he
is driven past them, *ducking, calling*, and *chattering*, and as helpless as a young duckling making its way to the water.' These are
feats which no one ever saw the 'rocketer' perform. But on
another occasion my risibility was likewise gladdened to its inmost
core by a fierce reprobation, possibly by the same hand, of the
cruelty of 'partridge driving,' which process was described as
hemming the unhappy birds with multitudinous beaters into the
corner of a field, there to be 'butchered' in a mass without skill on
the part of the shooters or chance of escape for the game ; winding
up with a savage denunciation of those tyrannical landowners who
not only did not permit their tenants to kill the ground game
on their farms, but even forced them, under heavy penalties, to
preserve their eggs.

In the instructive passage above given, however, the impossible
is pointed out as the legitimate aim of the manly shooter. But
alone—manly or unmanly—he may as well try for the lost tribe as
the 'rocketer,' which I may at once define as a bird flying fast and
high in the air *towards the shooter*. His only chance would be a
pheasant that flusters up at his feet and flies straight and low
away from him : a tame and stupid shot even if he kills him dead,
which he probably will not do unless he 'plasters' him, but will

have to run after him and massacre him, winged, on the ground.
Much in the same strain, though not so grossly ignorant, is the
advice to the partridge shooter to range the stubbles with his
pointer, and kill his birds in the good old-fashioned style, not walk
them up or drive them with beaters out of turnips, the main difficulty of following such advice being that there are no stubbles to
range over which would shelter *a lark.*

The above are samples of many of the kind that might be
quoted. The competence of the class of critic to which
reference is made need not be further examined.

If pheasants have increased in England enormously during
the last forty years or so, they are almost equalled in this respect
by grouse, and, it is to be noted, grouse are not artificially
reared. They are purely wild birds, in every way rearing and
supporting themselves without the aid of man. The best grouse
moors are as under, viz.—The 'Bowes' moors near Barnard
Castle, in North Yorkshire, the 'Wemmergill' portion of which
has for many years been rented by Sir Frederick Milbank,
Bart., M.P., and the 'High Force' section by various sportsmen, including the late popular and well-known General Hall ;
Mr. Remington Wilson's at Bromhead, near Sheffield, the
Marquess of Ripon's near Ripon, the Duke of Devonshire's
near Bolton, Mr. Cunliffe Lister's near Masham, Lord Downe's
near Pickering, Mr. Gilpin Brown's at 'Arkendale' near Reeth
in Swaledale, and the Blubberhouse Moors near Harrogate,
Lord Walsingham's—all in Yorkshire. Perhaps the most famous
of all are the Wemmergill Moors (14,000 acres), on which
17,073 grouse have been obtained in *one* season (1872).

The largest bag of grouse ever made in a day by one
shooter was on the Blubberhouse Moor in 1872, when, on
August 27, Lord Walsingham killed 842 birds. The next
largest bag of grouse (728) on record to one gun was made
by Sir F. Milbank in the same season, and also in Yorkshire.
In the previous year Sir Frederick had made an extraordinary bag, which was the subject of some discussion ;
and in 1872, when a still larger number was killed, he sent to

The Field the following details of six days' shooting on the
Wemmergill Moors, North Riding of Yorkshire. It will be
seen that the total amounts to 3,983½ brace, or nearly eight
thousand birds. The number of guns varied from day to day,
as is shown by the blanks opposite some of the names. On
the 28th, when the smallest bag was made, the day was wet
and the wind high.

	Aug. 20	Aug. 21	Aug. 23	Aug. 27	Aug. 28	Aug. 30
	Brace	Brace	Brace	Brace	Brace	Brace
Sir Fredk. Milbank, M.P.	364	214½	129½	185	87	119½
Mr. M. W. Vane Milbank	195	144	86	—	—	—
Mr. Powlett Milbank .	163	73	81	140½	53½	80
Mr. Preston . . .	112	60	75	—	—	—
Lord Rivers . . .	75	—	94½	98	38	66
Mr. Coore . . .	—	—	—	149	46	63
Mr. Fairfax . . .	—	—	—	123	38½	43
Col. Straubenzee . .	—	—	—	68	28	53½
Collinson . . .	126	112	86½	141½	73	98½
Total brace 3,983½	1,035	603½	552½	905	364	523½

In sending these particulars, Sir Frederick said :—

I am aware that the amount killed may be open to question and
cavil, as last year. I therefore inclose a perfectly correct account
of the number of brace of grouse killed by each gentleman, and
also the number I myself killed at each drive. I shot with three
guns, and only on four occasions during the first day were two
birds killed at one shot. The first shot was fired at 8.20, and we
left off at eight.

Sir Frederick's bag of 364 brace, on the 20th, was made in
eight drives, as follows : first drive, 24 brace ; second, 38 brace ;
third, 46 brace ; fourth, 14½ brace ; fifth, 70 brace ; sixth, 95
brace ; seventh, 55½ brace ; eighth, 21 brace. The sixth drive,
in which Sir Frederick killed 95 brace, lasted only twenty-three
minutes, so that he must have averaged more than eight birds
a minute during that time.[1] The whole day's proceedings lasted

[1] An interesting incident in connection with this, the best drive, is worth
recording. A friend of Sir Frederick who chanced to be shooting on an
adjacent moor, and who had the same day succeeded in killing 55 brace of

nearly twelve hours ; but the actual time of shooting in the eight drives was not more than half an hour each on the average ; or a total of four hours' shooting.

The heaviest bag made by a party in a day was in the same extraordinary grouse season (1872), and was obtained by Mr. Rimington-Wilson and his friends, who shot 1,313 brace.

It was also in 1872 that 1,006 brace of grouse were killed in a day on Lord Ripon's moors, at Dallowgill, near Ripon. The first heavy bag of grouse made by one shooter was about the year 1858, by Mr. Campbell of Monzies, in Scotland, who killed 220 brace with his own gun in a day ; a mere nothing to the feat of Lord Walsingham or that of Sir F. Milbank, the latter gentleman, on the occasion of the six days' shooting quoted above, having picked up as stated 728 birds, his contribution to one day's sport, taking his chance with the other guns that were shooting with him at the time.   The Maharajah Duleep Singh has also made several noteworthy bags of grouse to his own gun in Scotland, on one occasion shooting 440 birds in a day himself, curiously enough just equalling Mr. Campbell's total above quoted.

It may be said that in England at the present time fifty to seventy brace of grouse to five or six guns shooting over dogs is an excellent day's sport, and over a hundred brace the exception.   In England a hundred brace of grouse obtained by driving is a moderate bag, a hundred and fifty to two hundred brace a fair day's sport on a large and well-stocked moor.   Two hundred and fifty to three hundred and fifty brace a good day, and anything over this very good indeed.   It is only in Yorkshire that such large totals as five to seven hundred brace, the result of one day's grouse driving, are obtained, and the moors on which such sport can be found may almost be counted on the fingers of one hand ; the most celebrated in this respect are those shot over by Sir F. Milbank, Lord Ripon,

---

grouse to his own gun in a drive, sent a messenger with a scrap of paper on which he had written ' 55 brace at one drive to my own gun.   Beat that if you can.'   Sir Frederick promptly did so.

MODERN STYLE

(Batteries of growing firs on Norfolk heaths)

Mr. Rimington-Wilson, Lord Downe, and Mr. Cunliffe Lister, before referred to.

In Scotland driving is little practised, as the birds are far less numerous and not nearly so strong and wild as in England. Grouse in Scotland lie to dogs long after August 12 ; in England they certainly will not do so. In the former country from thirty to forty brace of grouse in a day to one or more guns is considered average sport—anything approaching a hundred brace unusual.

In North Wales good bags are made over dogs, especially in the vicinity of Bala. In Ireland twenty brace is a very successful day, forty brace uncommon, and, as far as our experience goes, fifty to sixty brace phenomenal, if not indeed unheard of.

Partridge shooting is in some respects akin to grouse shooting, and the bags made of these birds are generally very similar in numbers to those of grouse. But partridges are nowadays hand-reared in many parts.

In the North of England large bags of partridges are not often obtained, the totals made in Norfolk, Suffolk, or Cambridge never being reached. Partridges, as far as we can determine, were generally as abundant in our islands at the end of the last century as they are now, with perhaps the exception of a few large estates in the eastern counties, whereon they have of late years been especially protected as well as hand-reared. The reason we hear of and obtain such large bags of partridges now as compared to former days is that, when pointers were in general use and when covert in the fields was much higher, affording better shelter, the shooting was slower. Now that partridge shooters walk straight away over miles of country, they cover much more ground, see and shoot at many more birds in a day, and by the aid of breechloaders get shots at every bird that rises before them within range; for in these days the shooter is nearly always ready with a loaded gun, and no birds go away without being fired at. Formerly, when muzzle-loaders were used, the sportsman was often in the act of charging whilst birds were rising. Forty brace of partridges to six guns walking up the birds is a fair day's sport in the north, south, and west of England or in Scotland; sixty to eighty brace very good indeed, and a hundred brace quite the exception. In the North of England there is no partridge shooting to compare with Lord Londesborough's, in Yorkshire. Taking the season of 1884 as an example, a party, averaging six guns, killed driving 1,540 birds in four days' shooting. One day's bag was 557.

The best day's shooting at partridges by one gun in the north of England was in 1884, when Earl de Grey obtained on the Studley estate 300 birds.

Several traditional and well-authenticated bags of partridges, consisting of forty to fifty brace in a day, have been made by one gun in England long before the days of breechloaders, notably by Mr. Coke, Mr. Osbaldeston, Lord Kennedy, and others, the totals having been the occasion of heavy wagering at the time, and doubtless as many birds were killed, and as favourable ground selected for the purpose, as was possible. Before the days of breechloaders, the present Sir Vincent Corbett once shot on his estate in Shropshire seventy brace of birds in *one* field of turnips to his own gun. But it rested with the Maharajah Duleep Singh to far surpass all previous records of partridge shooting. This he did on his famous sporting estate of Elveden, in Suffolk. The particulars of these days are annexed.

Elveden Hall, near Thetford, Norfolk.

1876								Partridges
September	1	.	.	.	.	.	.	230
,,	2	.	.	.	.	.	.	231
,,	4	.	.	.	.	.	.	151
,,	5	.	.	.	.	.	.	56
,,	8	.	.	.	.	.	.	780
,,	11	.	.	.	.	.	.	390
,,	12	.	.	.	.	.	.	182
,,	13	.	.	.	.	.	.	196
,,	15	.	.	.	.	.	.	314
		Total to one gun	.	.	.	.		2530

The bag of 780 birds is of course unprecedented, and far above whatever has been done, or for that matter is ever likely to be done again. On this occasion the Maharajah fired just a thousand shots, and it is notorious that he was one of the very 'quickest' shots in England, as well as one of the best. It is said by many competent to judge that no shooter then

Partridges reared by hand.

living could get his gun up to his shoulder and fire it in such a short space of time as did the Maharajah, and this power, when combined with very straight aiming, will of course add up a big bag very rapidly, provided always that the game is to be found.

In Norfolk, Suffolk, and Cambridge driving partridges is

practised on an extensive scale, and in these counties 250 brace
to six or seven guns in a day is nothing unusual.

The most extraordinary record of partridge shooting in existence is, however, contained in the gamebook of the 'Chantilly'
estate, and pertains to the last century. The Paris correspon-
dent of *The Field* newspaper, who has had the privilege of
carefully inspecting it, writing in 1885 says :—

It was kept under the Prince de Condé just a century ago
The volume in question, bound in red morocco and stamped with
the royal arms, was stolen from the château of Chantilly during
the Revolution, and has only recently been recovered by the Duc
d'Aumale. It relates to the whole of the Chantilly shooting, and
what strikes one most is the enormous number of partridges killed,
and the early period at which shooting commenced. Thus on
August 10, 1785, the Duc de Bourbon and six other guns killed
974 partridges ; on the 11th, 393 ; and on the 14th, 523. Upon
September 14, seven guns killed 1,500 head of game, of which 1,106
were partridges, while on the 16th they killed 829 partridges out of
a total of 1,181. Upon September 26, fourteen guns killed 1,889
head, including 1,101 partridges, and on Michaelmas Day eight
guns killed 619 partridges and 449 hares. The most remarkable
record in the book, however, is that of October 7 and 8, upon
which days the two Princes de Condé and the Prince Conti, with
twelve other guns, killed 2,580 partridges, 1,593 hares, 24 rabbits,
12 pheasants, 2 fieldfares, and 2 larks, making in all 4,213 head.

R P. G.

CHAPTER III.

HINTS FOR BEGINNERS.

WE need scarcely begin with the rudimentary directions usually to be found in books on shooting, designed for the guidance of young sportsmen, such, for instance, as : Do not bring a loaded gun into a nursery full of children. Do not point a loaded gun at anyone, especially (what a delightful addition !) if it is at *full cock.* Do not drag a loaded gun if at full cock after you through a thick hedge, holding it by the muzzle meanwhile.

We came upon a book the other day that had fifteen direc-·tions in it of this kind.

No ! We will not suppose even the youngest of sportsmen to be absolute idiots, or, if they are, that their parents or guardians would allow them to endanger their own and other folks' lives by flourishing loaded guns about in all directions. We will merely at present say on this head : be ever careful ; always treat a gun as if it *were* loaded, whether you be in or out of doors, and learn to handle it with skill and confidence, combined with absolute and unswerving caution.

You will not then get into difficulties. For when in the field with practised shooters, they will consider it as great a fault, and one almost as unpardonable, for a youngster to point his gun at a fellow-creature, as if he actually fired it off to the latter's injury.

For this reason coolness and complete self-possession under all circumstances out shooting is the best attribute and strongest recommendation in favour of a young shooter. If in a flurry when game rises, the young gunner is apt to think only of the *game* ; his one and absorbing idea is to kill *it.* In such case his eyes and mind lose touch of everything near him save himself, his gun, and the object he means, if possible, to bring down. Round goes his gun as he follows the bird or animal, for he cannot be expected to be a quick shot ; he sees nothing else, he does not know that he is covering with his weapon half a dozen friends and beaters, to say nothing of dogs, and creating consternation in the field generally. For this reason a young sportsman should always endeavour

to fire the instant the game rises, so long as it is clear of fellow-creatures or dogs, if at a fair range; if it springs too near him, then to keep his gun down till the moment he considers the object is far enough, and on *no account* to follow the mark with his gun in the hopes of getting a better aim. Putting safety out of the question, he will never become a neat and skilful shot unless he learns to drop his game the moment the gun comes to the shoulder. The only possible exception to this rule is when pheasants are passing straight and high overhead.

Although later on we propose to treat of *how* to fit a gun to a sportsman, we would here say a few words on the importance of doing so properly in the case of a young shooter. It is a common thing for a beginner to have any chance gun put into his hands ;

probably it is not of the right bend or length to suit him, still he uses it for years and so gets into a bad style of shooting, simply because the weapon does not fit his shoulder. It therefore does not come readily on to the object when mounted, with the probable result of not only deferring the time when a shooter should have become a fair shot, but possibly getting him into a habit of poking after his game while aiming. For these reasons we have known of many instances where the young sportsman never had a fair chance from the first.

More accidents happen by *following* game with the gun than by any other means. The rules of etiquette to be observed

'Too far.'

in the field when out shooting all tend to ensure safety. A jealous shot is never a safe one, and jealousy out shooting is tabooed by common agreement.

If you shoot safely and in good style, it is more a subject of favourable comment than is the obtaining a dozen more birds than the neighbouring guns. It is only by going out with and closely observing an experienced sportsman that the young shooter can learn how to handle and use his gun, as well as to respect the many unwritten laws of the field. From the beginning of the day to the end the novice will have something new to learn, and this too from the moment he takes up his gun to load it, to the moment when he finally extracts the cartridges on reaching home. Nor is this the lesson of one day, but rather the result of careful observation during a season's shooting.

The beginner will have to learn that his gun must invariably be made safe from accidental discharge on every occasion on which a slip of the foot is a bare possibility, such as when crossing a hedge, a ditch, or a piece of slippery ground ; not so much for his own safety, as for that of those near him. We would indeed say that a hammer gun should always be unloaded when getting over a fence, or when jumping a dyke.

A loaded gun *may* explode, an unloaded one *cannot*, and after all this movement of absolute safety is but a matter of seconds. A source of danger in cocking and uncocking a hammer gun is thus done away with, especially in guns with low hammers with the combs much turned back and the hammers out of the line of sight. We may here remark that in the matter of safety the hammerless has the advantage of the hammer gun. In the former there is *no* excuse for not putting its safety bolt to 'safe.' If game suddenly rises the safety slide can be pushed forward as the gun is put to the shoulder ; but with a hammer gun, however careful *some* men may be, there will always be *others* who are over-keen, and who will keep their guns at full cock if game is known to be close to a hedge or ditch over which the sportsman has to pass. Though a young sportsman be careful not to point his gun towards a man, woman, child, or dog, or anything that is not game, he must also be equally careful not to fire in the direction of shelter, such as a hedge or wood, behind or in which someone or something might for the moment be concealed from his view. It is no use exclaiming afterwards, ' I did not see you ! I really did not know you were there !' He should never on any account have fired towards the place where a person or dog *might* have been. He will also have to learn what is, and what is not considered—and usually for a very good reason—sporting behaviour when he is out shooting ; that to wound by firing very long shots is almost a crime, and that to destroy game for the table by shooting too near is a serious error. That to endeavour to jockey another shooter by getting in front of him is unpardonable. That on no account should he be ever inclined to boast of or enter into self-laudatory accounts of his own feats when shooting, especially so when out with older men than himself, who, though they say but little on such a subject in regard to themselves, are doubtless, and long have been, infinitely superior to our young shooter in all he does or thinks he does with his gun.

The Young Sportsman.

The practised sportsman does his work so quietly and with so much self-possession that for a time it may not be remarked by the novice. To hear a young shooter exclaim to a good shot after or during the day, ' Did you see the bird I killed which *you* missed ?' is not uncommon. Perchance the former does not realise that it was missed because it was a very difficult shot, and killed by him because of its extreme simplicity.

A young shooter (especially if an ardent one) should always go out and shoot alone when first taking the field, so long as he has an experienced sportsman at his side. He should of course have been previously taught to handle his gun, to load it with empty cartridges, raise it and pull the trigger with confidence.

At first a small charge of powder only may be used, and he may be taught to fire this off at small birds, every attention being paid to his handling his gun with safety as if it were loaded. He may next be encouraged to shoot at small birds with a half-ounce of shot. If he succeed pretty well, and is above all things careful in the way he manages his gun, he can next be permitted to fire at pigeons (with their wings slightly clipped, so as not to fly too fast) from under a flower-pot or out of a trap, at a distance of fifteen yards or so. Should he progress satisfactorily, as regards safety and steadiness apart from the question of accuracy of aim which will come by practice only, he may be taken after partridges with a steady pointer, if such an assistant be forthcoming. His tutor, still at his side, can now lead him up to the point, and teach him to fire at the birds as they spring. Great pains must be taken to overcome any sign of flurry or excitement, both of which are most detrimental afterwards to good and safe shooting. He must at first be taught to select the bird that is the best and easiest mark out of a number rising, and on no account to blaze off at several together ; secondly, so to choose his first bird that he will be enabled the more easily to kill one near it with his second barrel, and to endeavour by degrees to think of killing two birds out of several, without wounding the others ; in short, to pick out and fire at a brace as much apart as possible. He should also learn to take the farther and less easy of the brace he selects for his first barrel, so that with his second barrel he may be offered a pretty sure shot.

Having become so far proficient, the young shooter may be taken out with one or two friends to walk birds up. He should now have it carefully explained to him what birds he ought to fire at and what he ought to leave alone, and why he should do as directed ; that he is only at liberty to fire at birds which rise in front of him, and nearer to him than to any other shooter ; that he should on no account fire across the front of his neighbour's gun, or at birds that belong to the latter through having

How to carry a Gun.

risen nearer to his companion than himself. Every bird or animal that gets up, out shooting, is for him or for his neighbours, and it is fitting that every man should consider whether it is proper for him to fire at it, or to leave it for another gun.

A young shooter when expecting game should not carry his gun at half-cock ; notwithstanding that some old and practised sportsmen—notably the present Marquess of Normanby—habitually do so, as a rule it is a dangerous habit to cock a gun when game is rising, and has caused many an accident.

A gun is perfectly safe when carried full-cock if it is not pointed dangerously, and there is no chance of a slip or fall ; a careful shooter *never* points a gun loaded, or unloaded, so that it can injure, or even risk injury to, anything but the game he seeks.

For if a shooter carries his gun carelessly when it is not loaded, he will do just the same when it is at full-cock, in which case he will not follow these instructions, and should not be allowed to associate with other sportsmen, whose regard for his safety he does not reciprocate.

It is often said that in choosing a gun the shooter need not trouble his head about length of stock, slope of butt, weight of barrels, and so forth ; that all he need do is to fix on one that, when he points it at a mark (say the face of a clock) level with the eye and at a few yards' distance, brings the muzzle fair and true on the centre of the object, so that he has not to correct the aim on bringing the weapon to his shoulder. Though the broad principle of this is correct, still we do not agree with the doctrine *in toto*, for our experience is that few practical sportsmen can judge as well as a successful gunmaker who has skill and aptitude in suiting his customers, what really does fit them, and we are certain that very few beginners can tell at all. As an example, we may say we have known many instances of men who have shot for years, and who, having been recommended to a first-class gunmaker to fit them with a new gun, have found that they had actually been shooting with their left eyes without knowing it. Anyone can discover if the left eye is the more powerful by taking up a gun, and sighting it at a mark a few yards distant with both eyes open, then keeping it in that position, shutting the left eye.

If the aim is correct, if the sighting, that is to say, remains the same, one eye is as good as the other. But if the sight moves to the left on closing the left eye, that eye is the stronger. When the sight of both eyes is equally good, shooting with both open is a great advantage, but if the left eye has the better sight, then, in the majority of cases, the readiest cure is to close the left eye momentarily as the gun touches the shoulder in the act of aiming, and to open it again instantly, or otherwise the shooter will not see any game approaching from the left for another shot. A curious instance of inability in this respect was furnished by a surgeon of high standing, who would scarcely credit that when aiming he used his left eye and not his right ; but the truth was brought home to him, as in having a new gun made, adapted to his sight, he was suddenly transformed from a very bad shot to a very good one. Though it may not be suspected, there are many men in whom the left is the master eye, either from the right one being weaker than the left, or from a curvature or some other cause. In such case the sportsman must either use a 'cross-eyed' stock, learn to shoot from the left shoulder, or else close the left eye on firing. Shooting with the left eye means aiming about 8 feet to the left of a cross shot at 40 yards, supposing a direct aim to be taken. The shooter will, however, if the gun comes up properly to his shoulder, and is suited to his sighting, place the centre of the shot circle on the game aimed at instead of the outside pellets, the latter being the only ones which strike when a gun does not come up properly to the eye, and much wounded game is the inevitable result. He must learn to hold the gun well forward along the barrel with the left hand ; this is more important than may at first appear. All our best shots do so. The effect is that the barrel is well supported and kept up in firing, and the aim does not fall under the mark, as is sure to be the case if the left hand is cramped up near the trigger guard, and the elbow much crooked, the latter then having little sustaining power in consequence. In this place some observations on aiming may be conveniently introduced.

A well-known sporting writer ('Nimrod') once complained, and the sentence has since become a proverb among hunting men, that there are some horsemen who follow the fox but will not 'gallop.' So in shooting there are some men who shoot day by day and year by year, but whom nothing will ever induce to shoot 'forward;' some men we verily believe would shoot behind the sea-serpent. Aiming forward is the great secret of successful shooting, knowing how much to shoot forward is another secret which is only learnt by instinct as well as by practice. To aim forward is, however, the golden rule of shooting. Every shot, save at something going away from the gun in a perfectly straight line in easy range, requires a forward aim. It is, however, no use *aiming* forward and *pulling trigger* when the bird is opposite the line of the barrels ; *that* means shooting *behind* the mark. The trigger must be pulled at the *time* the gun is aimed in front of the object, and the aiming and trigger pulling must be instantaneous.

It is better to fire a yard too far ahead of a bird flying, or of ground game running, than to shoot an inch too far in its rear. In the former case the shot *may* meet the mark, in the latter it never can. In the former if it does count a hit it means one in a vital part, the head ; in the latter it means a wound in the extremities. Shot far more frequently passes behind game when it is missed than before it. The fault of aiming too great a distance ahead of a moving object is easy to correct in comparison to the fault of shooting too much astern. How much to aim in front is a question of how fast the mark is travelling, as well as whether it is crossing at right angles or nearly so, or whether it is going partly away from the shooter. In both cases, and especially in the latter, the aim should be a little above the object; for it must be borne in mind that the game is often rising as well as crossing, and that the shot is falling by the natural law of gravity. To tell a young shooter to aim one foot, two feet, or two feet and a half, in front of the mark is nonsense ; he may as well be directed to aim fifteen or seventeen inches. It is utterly impossible to measure distances in the air in front of a flying bird or running game ; instinct, aided by practical experience, will alone teach the hand and eye to obey the brain in this respect, and so give the correct distance to aim in front.

The endeavour of every shooter should be to strike his game chiefly in the head and neck. This is to be easily done with winged game by practice, as well as with hares and rabbits.

A good shot when low-flying pheasants are passing him will pick off bird after bird in the head and neck so as not to damage their bodies for the table; and this is really good aiming, as well as sporting behaviour in its true sense. Many a man would not think of the head and neck only as a mark should

'Too near.'

low or easy birds chance to be crossing him; he might scarcely fail to *kill* a shot, but the cook or game dealer would comment freely and very unfavourably on him as a sportsman. It is very disgusting to see the inside of game on its outside, the result of bad or wanton shooting. So it will be perceived that aiming comes under two separate heads, one of which consists in *killing* the object, and the other in killing it *properly*. Too many gunners think only of the first meaning of the word 'aiming.'

Whether to aim with one or two eyes is a subject frequently discussed. Many shooters do not know how they aim, whether with one eye or both ; but they can easily find out by asking a friend to watch if they close the left eye or not when firing.

Very few of our first-class shots aim only with the right or left eye ; a man who does so may be a safe and steady shot, but he can scarcely be a quick, that is, a brilliant marksman.

It *must*, under every circumstance, take longer for the shooter to draw a sight on his game when using one eye. He is also at a further disadvantage for a second shot, as he has to open and shut his left eye before firing again, and cannot instantly take in the position of the second object at which he is desirous of discharging his remaining barrel. In fact, by closing the left eye a shooter shuts off a considerable portion of the sky and ground, and whatever may be in or on it to his left side.

Now, with both eyes open, everything moving can be seen all round the gun, and on both sides of the gunner ; and, a matter of the greatest importance, he can instantly direct and fire his gun without having to align the barrels with one eye only, the latter naturally a slow process in comparison to the former.

Some may say, 'I have always shot with one eye only, and when I try to aim with both eyes open, I find I cannot shoot nearly so well.' We would answer, 'Never mind. Do not fret if at first an accurate aim is lost by suddenly reverting from one eye to the use of two. In a few days you will be amazed by the quick way in which, with both eyes open, you bring your gun up and drop the bird, and this too while scarcely perceiving the barrels at all. Gun, game, and yourself all seem to get together in one line, just as the ball, billiard cue, and striker do at billiards. Having reached more or less proficiency at two-eyed shooting, and come to like it, return for a few shots to the use of one eye again, and it will at once strike you very forcibly how slow your aim is in comparison, how much less plainly the game is seen, and how very prominently the barrels of your gun appear, and interfere with *quick* aiming. One of the greatest recommendations of keeping both eyes open is that, at driven game approaching the shooter, he can aim well in front of it and yet *see* the mark. With one eye shut, the barrels completely cover an object flying toward the shooter when he aims in front of it, as in nearly every instance, we repeat, he should do. In shooting, however, with two eyes open, we can, under certain conditions, see two images of the gun barrels, and it is maintained by some theorists 'that each eye then aims at its own separate image, and that in consequence the eyes get confused, and do not know which of these images is the right one to point at the game,' or 'that sometimes the wrong one and sometimes the right one is used, a hit or miss being the result respectively.' Now two-eyed shooting gives rise to a most interesting and complicated argument, if it be considered deeply in regard to these double images of the gun. It is altogether a very curious question, and to anyone who has one eye stronger than the other, or sees in actual shooting two gun-barrels before his face, as some folk most undoubtedly do if they aim very slowly, or keep their guns pointed for some time in one position, we would recommend the employment of the 'shooting corrector,' invented by Mr. Gilbert, as a possible cure in certain cases.

Still our crack shooters, who never miss a fairly easy shot, and make three and sometimes even four out of five difficult ones, do not seem to require it, and have brought marksmanship to what may be called perfection without its aid.

Few men, who have not shot in company with the very best of our game shots, know what really good aiming is. These men are as superior to what may be locally known as tiptop performers as is Roberts or Peall at billiards to firstclass amateurs, or as Grace in his prime at cricket to the ordinary player who is good enough to represent his county. As a specimen of what *can* be done with the gun by crack shots, we give the following couple of incidents, the accuracy of which we personally vouch for. The sportsmen on both occasions were the same, and notably the two best marksmen in England.

These two noblemen were standing side by side in a deep hollow between wooded hills at Studley, in Yorkshire, and close to the well-known Abbey of Fountains. The pheasants were crossing high over their heads as they were driven from a distance by the beaters. Each gun took by mutual agreement alternate birds, or to their right and left as they chanced to come. They killed and picked up 98 between them, two birds alone escaping, one to either gun, each shooter having fired exactly 50 shots. The second occurrence was even a finer example of quick, certain aim, and of knowing which bird to fire at and which not, a difficulty, when two guns are shooting in company, that often requires instantaneous decision.

The sportsmen were waiting at the end of a covert in Norfolk, when suddenly, instead of the expected pheasants, a covey of eight partridges swept overhead, and seeing the shooters, scattered in all directions. The one shooter laid a brace low, and with his second gun another brace. His companion succeeded in performing the same feat, and so the *entire* covey was brought down, and, what is more, picked up on the spot.

In concluding the subject of aiming, we annex the following interesting tables of shooting by the late Lord Malmesbury, of Heron Court, a manor elsewhere alluded to as being so famous for the number and variety of its game and wildfowl. The present Lord Malmesbury informs us that these extracts are perfectly trustworthy.

The late Lord Malmesbury kept a journal of his sporting life, even to the quantity of powder and shot he used, the game he killed each day, the time he was out, the distance he walked, and the weather.

[FROM LORD MALMESBURY'S JOURNAL.]

Grand summary of game and fowl shot on Heron Court manors and shooting beats in thirty-nine seasons, from 1801 *to* 1840 *inclusive.*

Black Game	184
Partridges	9,331
Quails	8
Landrails	118
Pheasants	10,292
Woodcocks	1,387
Snipes	5,375
Wild Swans	11
Wild Geese	22
Ducks	2,885
Widgeon	122
Teal	1,371
Other fowl	389
Bitterns	22
Hares	9,494
Rabbits	14,990
Total .	56,001

Grand total killed by Lord Malmesbury, in forty seasons, to his own gun, from 1798–1840.

Black Game	81
Partridges	10,744
Quails	50
Landrails	95
Pheasants	6,320
Woodcocks	1,080
Snipes	4,694
Wild Swans	3
Wild Geese	8
Other fowl	2,756
Bitterns	10
Golden Plover	6
Hares	5,211
Rabbits	7,417
Total .	38,475

Summary of shots, killed and missed in forty seasons, ending **1840.**

Shots .	.	.	.	.	.	54,987
Killed .	.	.	.	.	.	38,221
Missed	.	.	.	.	.	16,766
Days out	.	.	.	.	.	3,645

Allowing the distance walked at two miles and a half per hour, according to the noble journalist's account, he would have covered a distance of 36,200 miles, or very nearly once and a half of the circumference of the globe ; and during that time he was never confined to his bed one day by sickness or accident—firing away about seven hundred and fifty pounds' weight of powder, and four tons of shot.

SHOOTING SCHOOLS.

Since the importance of small things has been admitted in connection with shooting, the leading gunmakers started trial grounds whereat their customers could try their guns for pattern and penetration, and ascertain whether the guns fitted them. In course of time this idea became developed, and 'shooting schools' resulted, institutions which must be regarded as most useful to those who, whatever their age, are without much experience in the handling and management of a gun, and the proper method of aiming, or perhaps, to speak more correctly, in the knack of getting hand and eye to act together.

In previous pages stress has been laid on the importance of carrying a gun in a safe position, and observing various precautions so as not to endanger the life of any fellow sportsman, and at the shooting school the instructor will from time to time correct any laxness on the part of the pupil.

Clay 'pigeons' are of course chiefly the game to be shot at ; but live birds and rabbits can be had, and, by a careful arrangement of traps, the gunner can have presented to him every variety of shot he is likely to meet with during a season's shooting. The tyro can practise at birds going away from him, as though he had walked up grouse or partridges ; opportunity will be afforded him of making a right and left, birds will cross from left to right, and from right to left ; the pupil can encounter birds coming towards him, while a multiplicity of traps will serve to give a mimic drive. Nor is covert shooting neglected, for he who desires to get his hand in for this kind of work can be stationed outside a plantation, and shoot at clay birds released from traps placed on a lofty stage, thus affording shots which are as like as may be to the flight of the pheasant put up by the beaters. Of course even a beginner will not need to be told that the flight of a clay saucer differs materially from that of a bird, for one thing because the further it goes the slower it goes, whereas the pace of a live bird increases with the length of its flight. There are also arrangements by which the pupil can practise shooting at ground game, a metal imitation of a rabbit being made to run along a line. Then, again, a bird can be made to pass along quickly in front of a white iron target, and the shooter can see for himself in an instant whether he shoots in front, behind, over or below the mark, and as the bird is visible for a moment or two only, quickness in throwing up the gun is indispensable. In short, these shooting schools afford an excellent opportunity for novices to receive more individual instruction than is generally possible in the field, while the middle-aged can be coached up in all those little points which, in the case of sons of residents in the country, are picked up by degrees (and best learned) under the tuition of parent or keeper. At the same time the gunner who does not shoot regularly, or who may be out of form, may with advantage spend a day or two at a shooting school to get his hand in again or overcome some bad habit. Indeed, the instructions given to beginners in the foregoing pages can well be observed by attendance at one or other of the shooting schools.

Those within easy reach of London are :—

The London Sporting Park, Hendon ; Messrs. Holland and Holland's (The Badminton Shooting School), Kensal Rise, N.W. ; Messrs. Lancaster's, Stonebridge Park ; and Messrs. Cogswell and Harrison's (Blagdon Shooting School), Willesden.

R. P. G.

'The Old and the New.'

CHAPTER IV.[1]

A SHORT HISTORY OF GUN-MAKING.

GUN-MAKING proper, as applied to sport, may be said to have originated in the last years of the seventeenth century; though the flint lock is reported to have come into use early in the same century as a weapon of war, there are few records of its use as a sporting arm till many years later. Previously to the flint-lock, guns were fired either by means of a slow match, or else by a notched wheel which was fixed near the touchhole; this wheel was acted on by a spring which rapidly revolved it against a flint, so that on the gunner disengaging it by freeing a stop or rough trigger it struck sparks, and so caused his weapon to explode. Flint-locks were brought into England in the reign of William III., and from that time grew gradually more and more popular, till they came into general use in the country, both as sporting and military weapons.

As late as 1842 flint locks were served out to British soldiers, but were generally discontinued in the army in 1840.[2] At

[1] Revised by W. C. A. Blew.

[2] We believe, however, that in the Sutlej campaign, 1844, the whole army had detonating muzzle-loaders. —ED.

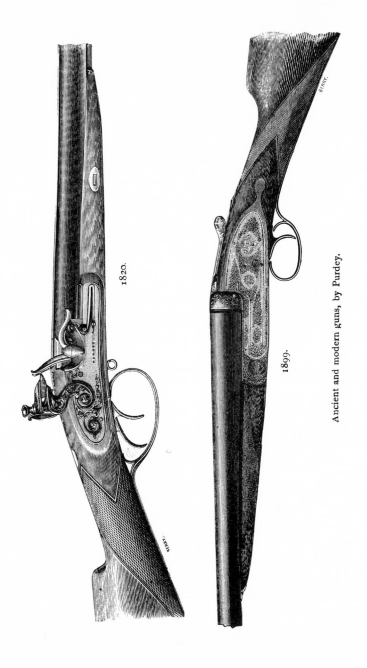

1820.

1899.

Ancient and modern guns, by Purdey.

the beginning of the present century nearly every sportsman used a single-barrelled gun, and it was not till about 1800 that double guns became popular. Their introduction was largely brought about by one of the most famous gunmakers that ever lived—Joe Manton; and it was he who also, about 1815, perfected the flint lock as a sporting weapon to a far greater degree than it had attained before his time. Even now Joe Manton's guns are perfect models of workmanship in every part. He was the first great English gunmaker, and by excellent work was the means of turning to London the eyes of all sportsmen who required a *good* gun. Before his time Continental makers, especially the Belgians, were as much in favour as our own.

We give on the previous page an illustration of a gun by Purdey of 1820, and one of the present day (1899) by the same firm; one that succeeded Manton in reputation and whose celebrity is now world-wide for turning out weapons of first-class shooting and lasting powers, which are also models of balance, symmetry, and finish, to an extent unequalled, in our opinion, by any other gunmakers in existence, though Manton's flint locks were quite as excellent in their day.

But flint locks, even when made by Manton, had serious drawbacks. They were slow in their ignition. To put it plainly, a man firing at a moving object with a gun ignited by flint was obliged to *follow* his mark till his gun exploded, as there was often a considerable interval between the pulling of the trigger and the discharge of the shot from the muzzle. The priming of a flint lock was also liable to get damp and even wet from exposure. Hence gunmakers and sportsmen began to look round for some quicker and more trustworthy method of exploding the powder in a gun.

At first, and as soon as the idea was started, all manner of patents were taken out for firing the charge with detonating powder, the latter being used in small tubes, between discs of paper, as pellets, and in various other ways. These were laid opposite, or over, the touchhole; and on the hammer falling, and firing them by concussion, the flame caused ignited the powder inside the barrel.

But all these plans, though for several years in demand, proved unsatisfactory, and finally the copper cap, and gun to suit it, almost as now known, was devised. This came into general request about 1830 for sporting, and in 1840 for military weapons, to be in time superseded by the breechloading system. Since the introduction of the perfected double flint gun as made by Manton, it has been one constant dispute among sportsmen in England as to which is and which is not the best kind of weapon to use on game. The flint gun after a long fight gave way before the detonator, the latter was superseded by the breechloader hammer gun, and now the hammerless breechloader has been for some time to the front. Formerly the shooting powers of each of the older systems of guns were excelled by its newer rival. Now, that attribute of a gun seems as near perfection as can be, and it is rather its mechanism that is a subject of attention.

When breechloaders were first introduced, the advocates of the muzzle-loader called them by every hard name they could think of; and lastly, being beaten at all points, took as their standpoint that muzzle-loaders were far superior to breech-loaders in their powers of shooting. So they undoubtedly were in the very early days of the latter, but the first weaknesses in the breechloader were speedily amended, and it at once became popular in the hands of shooters, though there were still a few men, well-known shots, who in Norfolk and Suffolk adhered to their favourite old muzzle-loaders till about the year 1870.

The first breechloader brought before the sporting public in England was the Lefaucheux gun (pin-fire), already patented in France, which was introduced to British shooters by Lang, of Cockspur Street, about 1853. This gun, though but a crude forerunner of the modern breechloader, immediately attracted the favourable notice of sportsmen ; but though it was admitted to be extremely convenient to use and load, its strength of shooting was pronounced far inferior to that of the muzzle-loader. The result was that some of the leading sportsmen and gunmakers of the day arranged a public trial between the two systems of loading, and this was held in 1858.

It was then proved that, though the muzzle-loader undoubtedly was superior to its rival, it was only slightly so. The scale has since then been completely turned the other way, and a good gun as now made will shoot so much stronger and better than the very best muzzle-loader ever constructed, that comparison is well-nigh impossible. The original breechloader (or practically the original, for many previous attempts had been made to perfect the system without success), invented by Lefaucheux, was, as we have said, a pin-fire gun—that is, the cartridge was ignited by a projecting pin. This being struck by the hammer ignited a cap placed on a small metal anvil in the charge of powder at the base of the cartridge, the cap being of course on the opposite end of the pin to that struck by the hammer.

Though a few pin-fire guns are still now and then to be seen, since about 1867 they have been practically out of use ; from that date nearly every breechloader sold has been a central-fire gun, with its own automatic cartridge extractor—an immense improvement on the pin-fire system, which not only necessitated the empty case being drawn out of the barrel by the small projecting pin, but also required the cartridge to be inserted in the gun in exactly the right position for the pin to fit into its proper place, or else the breech action could not be closed—the latter an inconvenience entirely obviated by the use of central-fire cartridges.

The first breechloaders were almost invariably made with a lever placed under the forepart that had to be pulled sideways to open the gun, and forced back again to shut it, a plan that in these days would be reckoned clumsy in the extreme, as indeed it was. It was also a slow method, as the lever required to be pushed well home and in line with the barrels before the action of the gun was securely closed. This lever has long been discontinued in expensive guns of ordinary weight and charge, and the snap-action lever used in them in preference, one that completely closes the gun itself without the use of the hands to assist it in doing so, and a much greater rapidity of loading is the result. The lever over the guard is, however, generally used for heavy guns and rifles, as well as for cheap guns for rough use abroad, in consequence of its strength and great binding power, and on account of its simplicity and little likelihood of getting out of order. The Lefaucheux, or, as we may now say, the breechloader (for all the celebrated gunmakers within a few years of its introduction brought out breechloaders of their own) was next further strengthened, and improved in various ways, principally by the addition of two lumps under the barrel instead of one, as was at first the case, both lumps being gripped by the action of the opening lever. In 1862, Mr. Westley Richards, the well-known Bond Street gunmaker of former days, exhibited the first snap-action breech loader—that is to say, one that the action snapped to of itself like a spring lock, on shutting up the breech. This gave a lead to the gunmakers in a new direction, and ever since the choice of snap-action breechloaders by the dozen, and of various patterns, has been offered to the sportsman.

The gunmakers having, it may be said, perfected the shooting and easy working of breechloaders about 1865, now began to strengthen the new gun as regarded its connection between stock and barrels, on account of the frequent complaints of guns, under constant firing, giving way between the false breech and the barrels. First came Messrs. Purdey & Sons, with their famous action, which has been borrowed, copied, and used by every gunmaker of note in the kingdom, and which consisted of a bolt that kept the lumps under the barrel in the very strongest manner possible in their proper place when the gun was closed. About the same time (1862–63) what is termed the 'top extension' was devised.

This consists of a hole in the centre of the surface of the false breech at its top, in which hole the slightly projecting end of the rib that connects the barrels is made to drop. It was first made in the form of a wedge known as a 'doll's head,' so that it was a source of strength in keeping the barrels from pulling away from the stock. It was then found, however, that, as it only acted laterally and forward, it did not prevent the barrels from inclining upwards, and in that manner shaking loose from frequent strain and wear. In consequence of this, the projection of the rib was improved, for while it resisted as before a lateral strain, it had a hole or step cut in it, through or in which a cross-bolt fitted when the gun was closed, and it then took the upward strain as well, and assisted in securing the action from damage.

This is one of the strongest actions in some respects that has yet been, or perhaps ever will be, devised. It was patented with some subsequent improvements by Mr. W. Greener in 1873, and it is Mr. Greener's boast, and a very pardonable one, that out of all the thousands of guns with this action which he has sent out both abroad and at home, rarely has one been returned in which the action has given way, whether it be black or chemical powder that has been used by the owner. How annoying it is when one's gun goes wrong in the course of a quiet and comfortable day's shooting at home need not be said, but it is infinitely more serious abroad, hundreds or thousands of miles from the maker; and the value of a really trustworthy weapon is incalculable.

The chief disadvantage of the top extension besides its clumsy appearance is that the cartridges are not, owing to its presence, readily extracted when the fingers are cold, as the projection of the rib is in the way at all times. Another objection is, that should a gun, especially if fitted with a doll's-head top extension, require 'closing up' (owing to the bearing surfaces wearing, as must eventually be the case under hard use), it is difficult to refit the extended rib into its place again as well as was originally the case. Though the extended rib enables a gun to withstand any sudden or violent strain, it has no actual binding power, nor does it in any way prevent a gun from shaking

loose, in whatever form it is applied.   That these are not very
important faults we admit, but yet they are defects, though
such as may be overlooked when weighed in the balance
against the absolute safety from accident that, as far as human
probability can insure, the 'top extension' confers on the man
who handles the gun fitted with it, especially if the gun is not
of first-class construction.   Indeed, we do not believe that a

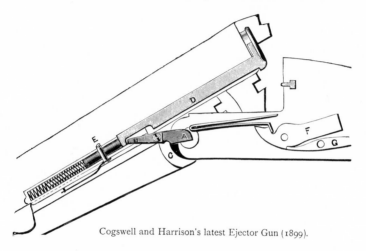

Cogswell and Harrison's latest Ejector Gun (1899).

cheap gun could be made to stand really hard work without
the assistance of the top extension.   But in more expensive
weapons (such for example as those made by Purdey, Holland,
Grant, Woodward, Rigby, &c.) it is well known that the top
extension is not required, as a first-class gun will stand year
after year the hardest of work without its assistance.

For this reason our best gunmakers do away with the·un-
sightliness of the projecting rib, by omitting it as unnecessary
in a really good gun of the usual weight and shape.

The top extension is in great favour with the Birmingham
gunmakers, who do not seem able to guarantee the safety of
their guns without it, and who apply it in various grotesque

forms such as 'Giant' and other grips, none of which at all equal Mr. Greener's patent in strength and simplicity.

We have tried one of Messrs. Cogswell and Harrison's ejector guns lately (see page 55), and as it has stood a good deal of rough work, and acted very well, it certainly deserves our praise. It is very simple in construction. There is not a single extra limb or alteration in the lockwork of this gun that is caused by its ejecting mechanism. Two scears are hinged on the fore part, the one end controlling the propelling rods, which are placed in a metal box on the under rib. After firing, the engagement takes place, and the rods are held back until the gun is opened to the extracting position, when by an ingenious movement of the scear the rods are released and spring forward, thereby jerking out the exploded cases. In the newest pattern gun there is a more powerful ejector spring than was formerly in use. (For an extended notice of ejector see p. 59 *et seq.*) The box containing the ejector spring is made in one piece with the fore part loop, so that the latter having four or five times its original length it is practically impossible to have a loose fore part, a great consideration for sportsmen abroad.

Hammer breechloaders having been brought to as near perfection as might be as long ago as 1870, or what was considered at that date to be perfection, the gunmakers, an enterprising race, set their wits to work to design something new in guns that would catch the fancy of their customers, make their own particular name or firm famous amongst their fellows, and hence draw the custom and support of sportsmen —a tribe, by the way, ever on the look out for the best and most recent inventions connected with their amusements. They turned then to the subject of so-called hammerless guns—we say 'so-called,' for hammers these guns all possess, though they be inside the lock instead of outside, and so hidden from view.

It is true that when breechloaders first came into fashion Mr. Needham brought out a hammerless gun, but owing to its complicated construction it was not a success. The subject was after that left untouched till 1871, when Messrs. Murcott of the Haymarket patented their invention of a hammerless gun, the first of its kind that was at all successful, though it has since been superseded. The next hammerless gun deserving of notice was invented by Messrs. Gibbs and Pitt of Bristol, and was a considerable improvement on the ' Murcott' principle, which, however, it resembled. Messrs. Westley Richards next combined both 'Gibbs and Pitt' and 'Murcott' in a hammerless gun put forward by them in 1876 ; but the first gun of this kind at all approaching perfection was also introduced to the shooting public by Messrs. Westley Richards. Anson and Deeley were the inventors, and this gun, being afterwards slightly improved, was much recommended by Mr. Greener in 1877. Since then the market has been flooded with hammerless guns by all the well-known makers. Having inspected most if not all of them, we give illustrations of those weapons which we consider the best in every respect, both as regards safety and mechanism ; and we will add our opinion that, for choice, a sportsman could not have safer or better guns than the two examples we now give, by Messrs. Purdey and Holland respectively, both of which are beautifully constructed for hard work and absolute safety, and are besides of extreme simplicity in design ; in fact, these may be considered perfect specimens of hammerless guns as now made. We can from long personal experience praise the regularity and strength of shooting of the guns turned out by the firms here mentioned.

Messrs. Purdey & Son's hammerless gun possesses externally the neatness of shape which is characteristic of their weapons, while the construction of the lock is very ingenious. Its especial feature consists in the application to a hammerless gun of the well-tried and universally approved principle of the rebounding lock, one effect of which is that the weapon can be opened and cocked with remarkable ease, while the mainsprings are so strong that all risk of misfires is avoided.

Fig. 1, p. 58, shows the position of the working parts when the gun is open and ready for loading. The hammers are at full cock, but the mainsprings free and uncompressed. In shutting down the barrels the cam A drives the rod B and through this the cam C backwards. The latter, passing over a small roller in the mainspring, depresses the topside D of the mainspring, making the spring effective, the hammer being held in bent by the scear G.

The gun is now ready for firing as shown in fig. 2, p. 59.

Fig. 3 on the same page shows the lock after firing.

The scear being drawn out of the bent by the trigger, the underside E of the mainspring impels the hammer forward to strike the plunger and so discharge the cartridge.

FIG. 1.

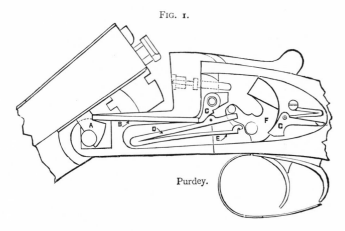

Purdey.

On opening the gun the parts return to the position shown in fig. 1.

The rebound of the mainspring is made to act strongly, so that on opening the gun the hammer cannot fail to be driven fully back and the scear lodged securely in the bent. The scear and the bent are of great strength, and continuous hard use has convinced the makers that only a simple automatic 'safety' on the triggers is really necessary, although other (patent) intercepting safeties are fitted in addition for still greater security.

The gun has an efficient vent to insure the lockwork remaining clean even under considerable escape from a faulty cartridge.

To this gun has been added by Messrs. Purdey since the earlier editions of this book appeared a strong and simple ejector mechanism, which has proved a success during the ten years in which it has been in use. When it is remembered

FIG. 2.

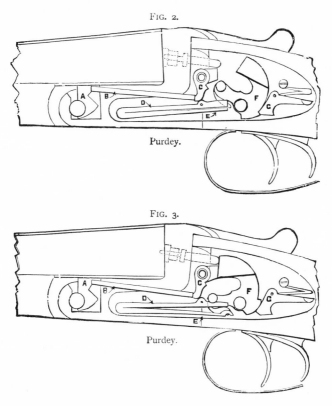

Purdey.

FIG. 3.

Purdey.

that some men shoot from 15,000 to 20,000 shots in a season from one pair of guns, it need hardly be said that the test speaks well for sound workmanship and correctness of principle.

Nearly all guns are now made with what are known as 'ejectors,' that is, they eject the empty case after firing,

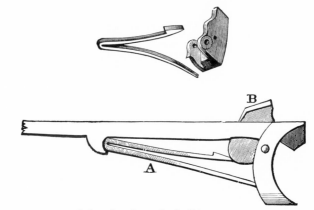

A is the main spring, and B the kicker or hammer.

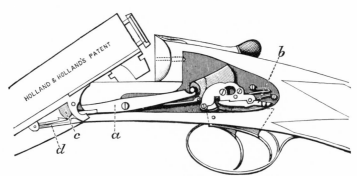

a is the cocking lever ; *b*, the intercepting safety bolt ; *c*, the ejector kicker ; *d*, the ejecting spring.

examples of which we give. To some extent there is truth in the claim put forward on their behalf, that in a grouse butt or at a warm corner one gun will do the duty of a pair, so quickly can guns with ejectors be reloaded. They are especially useful to a sportsman using one gun, as he can thereby fire a few shots very rapidly, should occasion require, putting himself for the time being on a par with the shooter who is using a pair of guns.

We give a description and illustration of an admirably designed ejector brought out by Messrs. Holland, of 98 New Bond Street, and known as the 'A B' ejector model. It is fitted with what to our mind is a *sine quâ non* in all modern guns, i.e. an absolutely trustworthy safety bolt, which in this case is an intercepting one.

It is claimed for this new gun that it combines all the latest improvements, and has the simplest and most effective ejector mechanism of the day. In the early days of ejectors they were very complicated and liable to get out of order; they consisted of eight or nine parts. In the new 'A B' model Messrs. Holland have been enabled to dispense with all but two parts—a mainspring and a kicker or hammer.

In Messrs. Holland's new mechanism there is no scear or scear spring in the ejector lock; the hammer, or kicker, being held in by the action of the short arm of the spring itself. As the gun is opened the barrels are depressed; the tumbler until the short arm of the spring (A) acts upon it forcing it against the end of the extractor, which then ejects the cartridge with considerable strength. No more force is required to open the gun and eject the used cartridge than in the case of a non-ejector gun; the extractor comes out sufficiently far to enable the shooter to easily withdraw unfired cases—a great point in ejectors, as they sometimes lack this advantage; while the weapon can in a short time be made into a non-ejector by taking out the springs, an advantage which sportsmen proceeding abroad, where gunmakers are not to be found in every street, will not be slow to appreciate.

Four-barrelled guns have long been offered for sale by Mr. Charles Lancaster, of New Bond Street, and very perfect weapons they are, too, of their kind. They are now made without a draw-pull, similar to a revolver, as formerly was the case, but pull off just like an ordinary gun.

In the year 1874 a great stir was occasioned among shooters and gunmakers by the report that a new system of boring gun-barrels had been discovered, by which their range and power were vastly increased—it was said as much as fifty per cent. One of the strongest advocates of the new system, and one who carried his opinions to practical proof, was Mr. Greener of Birmingham, for besides his own private experiments in the matter, several of his customers, well-known game or pigeon shots, spoke very highly of his guns when bored on the new 'choke' plan ; and these were also seen by others, well able to judge of the performances of a gun in the field, to make shots far exceeding in distance, as well as in certainty, the best execution of guns bored on the old principle.[1]

This 'choke' boring, though modified and slightly different as practised by various gunmakers (such as 'recess' boring, in which case the barrel is bored out egg-shape an inch or two under the nose), always has its basis on the same system, which is the contraction at the muzzle of the barrel a half inch to an inch from its end by five to forty thousandths of an inch, according as the gun is intended for a full or a modified choke.

The result of choke boring is that when the charge reaches or nears the muzzle it is suddenly constricted, and the pellets are in consequence shot out of the barrel in a closer group than would have been the case had the barrel not been choked. The pellets being kept together and diverging less

---

[1] There is no doubt that, though 'choke boring' was first generally applied to our guns in England by Mr. Greener, this system had previously been experimented on by Mr. Pape, of Newcastle, and had also for some time been practised in America.

than they do when fired from a cylinder barrel, naturally reach the game in a closer cluster and put more shot into it. The consequence is that with choke bores game is killed more effectually at an ordinary range, and with greater certainty at a long range, than it is with a non-choked gun. These points being naturally of great interest to sportsmen, at the first appearance of 'choke bores' in the market it was decided that a fair and open trial should take place to test the supposed superiority of the 'new boring' over the 'old.'

This trial was held in 1875, and it proved indisputably that for close shooting and long range, the 'choke' was very superior to the 'cylinder' gun. The former averaged from 180 to 200 pellets on 30-inch target at 40 yards ; the best of the latter only from 130 to 140. The new gun was next tried at pigeons by some of the best shots of the day, and was found regularly to drop birds dead at a distance of several yards beyond the range of the best cylinder guns. This settled the question ; but though there was a rush for the new guns at first they are not now so popular as they were, as it has been found that they are not so well adapted for an ordinary marksman as is a gun which makes a larger killing circle—that is to say, spreads the shot more, and so does not necessitate such accurate aim. It was also proved that the penetration of a choke bore was but a trifle above that of a cylinder, its success consisting in the number of pellets it put into the game (some of which were sure to disable or kill), rather than in any extra power of shooting. It is not now therefore incorrect to say that full chokes are comparatively seldom seen, while perhaps the greater majority of shooting men who use chokes at all content themselves with having the left barrel slightly choked.

BARRELS, ACTIONING, ETC.

The bore or size of a gun-barrel is ascertained by placing in the barrel a perfectly round bullet which exactly fits it. The number of these bullets which go to the pound is then ascertained, and if twelve go to the pound the gun is 12-bore; if sixteen bullets make up the pound the gun is of 16-bore; and so on. The length of gun-barrels is adapted to their bore and the amount of powder they are required and able to burn. In 20- and 16-bores the length of barrel varies from 28 to 30 inches; in 12-bores from 28 to 33 inches, the usual length being 30 inches, though for the sake of lightness the barrels are sometimes made as short as 26 inches; but if this be the case, not only is their penetrative power decreased, but unless the barrel be choked the pattern becomes very open for anything but a near shot.

At most but an ounce is saved for every inch the barrels of a gun are shortened, and no practical man will for a moment admit that a gun with 28-inch barrels can compete with one which has 30-inch barrels.

30-inch barrels have been proved to suit a 12-bore better than any other length, nor is the least advantage gained by guns of this bore having longer barrels, though they are sometimes made 32 inches long under the mistaken impression that the extra length enables the gun to consume the powder more thoroughly. Instead of this, the increased friction caused by the extra surface of metal only diminishes the velocity of the shot, besides adding weight to the gun and hindering the shooter from taking aim as quickly as he does with a gun of the usual length. There are now two materials for gun-barrels, viz. Damascus and steel. The latter came into fashion about fifteen or twenty years ago, but has the disadvantage of being of plain appearance ; moreover, it does not at sight bear evidence of its quality as does a Damascus barrel. In regard to steel barrels, there is, indeed, no method by which the purchaser can decide whether his gun has best steel barrels or those only of second-rate or even bad quality ; he has to trust entirely to the integrity of the seller in this respect.

Still, if the manufacturer can be relied on, and the purchaser can therefore make sure of securing a gun with 'best steel barrels,' he may rest assured that the weapon, if otherwise sound and well turned out, will practically last him for his life. Steel thus treated is of marvellous tenacity, and gives way only under an enormous strain—a strain considerably in excess of what would damage a Damascus barrel. Such a severe test to a gun is not with common care likely to happen, it is true ; but steel has another advantage, and that is that the barrels so constructed, being stronger than Damascus, can be made proportionately thinner, and a lighter gun is the result therefrom, though perfectly safe nevertheless. In our experience steel-barrelled guns are slightly more effective in regard to their shooting than are those made of Damascus, but several of our best gunmakers go further, asserting that they are much superior, and, ignoring their plain appearance, strongly recommend them. The price of a gun with best steel barrels is now only slightly in excess of a gun with Damascus barrels.

Damascus barrels are of various degrees of excellence, from the single Damascus or skelp twist, formed of one ribbon of twisted iron and steel, to the fine Damascus material, composed of four to six bars twisted and welded together, and so differing materially from the old plain barrels, that were long ago constructed of the flat slip of metal of one kind only which was then used in welding a barrel.

The boring and straightening of a gun-barrel is an art in itself, and the more carefully this is done the higher is the price charged therefor.   In this, as well as in other parts of the construction of a first-class gun, none but the very best and most highly paid workmen are employed—men who will not touch a cheap gun, and who, having gradually, and by their skill, worked themselves up to the top of the tree in gun-making, consider it *infra dig.* to have anything to do with the manufacture of a second-rate weapon.   The latter is left to new or less skilful hands, and is sold as inferior in consequence, as indeed it is; for no manufacturer would care to trust his most valuable materials, such as are put into a really good gun, to hands unfit for high-class work; less expert and lower paid men are therefore relegated to the construction of less valuable weapons which they are not likely to spoil, and these are as a result cheaper in comparison.

We are not aware of a single gunmaker in London who forges his own barrels, 'Fullerd' having been the last to do so.   These are made in Sheffield, Birmingham, at the works of the Henry Rifle Company at Hoxton, while in some cases the barrels are imported from Belgium.   They are delivered as required in a more or less rough state, for the gunmaker to put together, bore, and finish off ready for use.

A barrel before it is ready for shooting undergoes three distinct stages, viz. : rough-boring ; fine-boring ; and polishing or lapping.

On the barrel being received from the maker of the tubes as they are invoiced the tube is rough-bored inside, first with small bits and then with larger, the largest one representing the bore of the barrel.   If a choked barrel, the choke is introduced as the tube is rough-bored.   The next process is to 'set' or straighten the barrel inside.   No instrument has yet been found so perfect for the purpose as the eye of a practised workman accustomed to 'setting,' who, looking through the tube, tells whether it is true by observing the outline of the shadows that fall on its inside when held to the light. If not correct the 'setter' revolves the barrel on its axis and taps it here and there with a considerable number of small indentations at short intervals till he obtains a perfectly even and straight tube—a performance which, though quickly done, necessitates a large amount of skill and practice on the part of the workman. Till the beginning of this century this system of judging the accuracy of a barrel by the outline of a shadow thrown along its interior to prove its correctness, according as the outline of the shade was straight or uneven, was not known, and hence up to about 1800 there was practically no such thing as a perfectly true barrel in existence. The tubes having been bored and set, they are planed and lathed, and rings are turned at intervals of about six inches to reduce the outside here and there to the proper gauge. The raised parts between these sunk rings are then ground down or struck off till all is level together. The steel lump is next fitted and brazed in, and the ribs and loops attached, the barrel maker adjusting the inclination of the barrels in doing so, so that both will strike the same mark at forty yards.

The barrels being now rough-bored and set true, they are next fine-bored. This is done by means of a bit that revolves at much less speed than that used for rough-boring, and has only one cutting edge. The boring is now done very carefully indeed ; the sides of the bit are packed with a spill of wood and packing of paper to press its cutting edge against the barrel. The tubes are next polished inside. The polisher, or 'lap,' as it is called, consists of an iron rod round which is secured a leaden plug the exact size of the tube. As the lap revolves at a high speed inside the barrel, it is kept covered with a mixture of oil and emery, and the barrel is moved backwards and forwards, so that the lap acts on all parts of the inside it is wished to polish or finish off with a shade more boring. This latter process leaves the barrels inside as smooth as glass and bright as silver, and ready for use as far as their boring is concerned.

The barrels are now chambered—that is, enlarged at their breech ends to take the cartridges. Being so far advanced the gun is next 'actioned.' This is one of the most expensive parts of the building of a gun. It consists in the fitting up of the action to take the steel lump which is attached to the barrels. It is in the square and accurate fitting of the lump, and the soundness of the bite which the fastenings of the action have upon the lump, that a very considerable portion of the expense of a well-made gun is incurred. The fitting of the ejecting apparatus and of the single-trigger mechanism, when they are required, also takes place at this stage.

The soundness and wear of a breechloading gun depend chiefly upon this portion of its manufacture. In a hammerless gun there are additional arrangements necessary for placing the locks at full cock as the barrels are dropped on opening. The gun is now stocked and screwed, and then in the rough state is sent to the ground to be shot and regulated. When this is done to the satisfaction of its maker it is chequered and finished off. It is then placed in the hands of experienced men called strippers, and by their assistance a very important duty is performed, especially in the case of hammerless guns. The stripper takes the gun to pieces down to the minutest detail, and carefully examines and regulates it in every way. It takes an experienced stripper from two to three days to do this thoroughly. The ironwork of the gun is next polished, engraved and hardened, the latter operation giving strength and preventing wear. The finisher then gathers all the parts and fixes them together (the hardening process having caused the delicate adjustments of the action and fittings to shrink and twist a little out of shape) and by great skill readjusts them, making all parts work smoothly, and yet keep a perfect fit.

Finally, he regulates the pull of the locks and other minor details, and the gun is ready for use, and probably sold to a sportsman who, oftener than not, has no idea of the care and outlay bestowed upon it and merely grumbles at its price. The pull of the locks of a gun should be on the average : right, 4 lbs., left, $4\frac{3}{4}$ lbs. ; but shooters vary greatly in these requirements owing to accidents to the fingers or other causes, some requiring their guns to pull off at a very slight pressure. For instance, the late Lord Eversleigh, a first-rate shot and sportsman, had the locks of his guns to pull off at : right, 9 oz. ; left, 1 lb. Again, the late Duke of Rutland required a pull off of : right, 5 oz. ; left, 12 oz. A light pull off for a nervous heavy-fingered man who feels his triggers some time before firing is of course dangerous : but to a quick delicate touch, and yet a safe shot, a light pull off is a great advantage.

It is worthy of note that a shot and ball gun has at last been perfected, a weapon that will be invaluable for the use of sportsmen in wild countries who may, as not unfrequently has occurred to us, require at one moment to kill a duck or snipe, and shortly after a deer or other large animal, such as a bear or a wild boar.

The first gun of this kind was the invention of Colonel Fosbery, V.C., and we can say from experience that it shoots shot as well as a high-class game gun, and a conical bullet up to 100 yards with the accuracy of an express rifle. The gun is externally an ordinary 12-bore of usual weight and balance, and, being such, can be sighted, when used with a bullet, easier and quicker than could any rifle, and owing to its high velocity and large bullet would deal as deadly a wound. The gun, which is known as the 'Paradox,' is manufactured for its inventor by Messrs. Holland, of Bond Street ; but since this gun was brought out other makers have placed similar weapons in the market. In order that the gun shall carry a bullet, it is necessary that the barrel shall have a slight twist ; but the rifling is so slight that the action of the shot does not injure it.

R. P. G.

The Gun-room.

CHAPTER V.[1]

PRICES OF GUNS.

THE PRICE OF A GUN is a frequent theme of discussion
among a certain class of shooters. It is sometimes asked
why a shooter should pay forty guineas for a gun when he
could get one as good (as he says) for fifteen. The theorist
then proceeds to ask why the gunmaker should charge his

---

[1] Revised by W. C. A. Blew.

customers forty guineas, when a gun can be made quite as good for about a third of the money?

Now we will first remark that the finish of a gun, though derided by the users and sellers of cheap firearms, is, if excellent, a pretty sure sign that the weapon is a valuable one as regards its general workmanship, the quality of its material, and its shooting powers. No first-class gunmaker will ever really finish off well a common gun to hide defects, as it is often said he will do. If the gun be cheap, and so a more or less common weapon, he will leave it unadorned, and merely proclaim it as a sound workmanlike gun of good shooting quality; he cannot truthfully assert that it will stand as much wear and tear as a gun twice or three times its price, and so much more carefully turned out, even down to the smallest screw or pin. The sellers also know that the purchasers of cheap guns give their guns an amount of wear and tear, in the matter of shots fired, that is trifling compared with what a gun has to undergo when used by a hard shooter; [1] for the man who buys the latter, being able to afford forty to fifty guineas for his gun, is probably as well able to afford himself constant shooting with it throughout the season, and the strain of firing a couple of hundred shots a day out of a gun pretty frequently is a very different affair from firing thirty or forty, which is perhaps the average number of shots, a little more or less, that the cheap gun is taxed with in a day's sport. Those purchasers of cheap guns who so often assure us that a 15*l.* gun is as good as a 45*l.* weapon usually make this assertion to 'soothe their pride of purse,' fearing that they may be suspected of not being able to purchase a more expensive article. That there are many exceptions to this rule we admit, for numerous shooters candidly own that they cannot give more than a low price for a gun, adding 'they would do so if they could.'

Still, many of our best gunmakers make cheap guns for those who require them. They are obliged to do so, but if

[1] Besides which there is a much larger percentage of profit made by the seller out of cheap guns than out of those which are costly.

asked, they honestly admit the inferiority of these weapons, as regards lasting capabilities.

There are gunmakers and gunmakers as there are sportsmen and sportsmen. One gunmaker turns out guns for one class of sportsman, another for another class. The shooter who is satisfied with a fifteen-guinea gun is so usually because this price suits his pocket ; he is also most likely a man, as pointed out, who fires a small proportion of shots in the season, perhaps not more than 500 at most, often only half that number. The man who requires a first-class gun is one who fires, perchance, 3,000 to 4,000 shots a season from it. To do this, and to stand such hard wear and tear season after season, a gun must be made absolutely perfect in every detail, even down to the smallest spring or screw, and each detail has to be tested by means of a severer ordeal than is ever required for a cheap gun. Then, too, these highly finished guns are beautifully turned out, light, and handsome in outline. A cheap gun is invariably clumsy and rough in comparison with a high-priced one. It is the only way by which it can be made to stand average hard use.

The dealer in cheap guns guarantees that each gun shoots well ; that is enough for him, and enough, as he believes, for his customers, who rarely know what vast effect good force and a regular pattern have on game-shooting when a gun is continually used.

A high-class gunmaker will spend days in shooting a gun in order to get its pattern and force up to the mark he considers requisite to make it a perfect weapon, and one that he is justly proud to place in the hands of a sportsman who knows ' what is what ' in guns, as well as in shooting.

We will give two comparisons as between cheap and high-class guns : we could give many others. It is not contended that a cheap gun is a thing to be despised : some such weapons —Messrs. Bland's, for instance—are excellent *as far as they go.* We are only endeavouring to show that the difference in value between the two is no imaginary one.

Twenty years ago we purchased a new cheap gun, price 16*l.*, and a second-hand high-class gun, price originally 40*l.*, for wildfowl shooting of the roughest description, i.e. punting. Both came under equal use in all kinds of weather, ashore and afloat. The cheap gun utterly broke down—in fact, *shook* to pieces in the second year. We purchased another, which lasted a year and then collapsed—stock, lock, and barrels—under the effect of salt-water and hard usage. Since then we had three similar guns, all of which broke down except one, and that was made extra strong, and was such a lump of a thing in consequence that we avoided using it as much as possible. The more costly gun (we will give the makers' name, Holland & Holland) never failed us.

Another example. There are many guns now in the hands of game-shooters and owners of shooting made by Purdey, Holland, Grant, and other so-called expensive gunmakers, that have during the past dozen years had 70,000 to 80,000 shots apiece fired out of them with heavy charges. For instance, some seasons ago *one* shooter to our knowledge fired 18,000 shots from a pair of Messrs. Purdey's guns, several shooters as many as 15,000, and many from 10,000 to 12,000. In our opinion, no gunmaker could sell a gun for fifteen guineas—or, for that matter, under forty—that could stand without repairing the same amount of wear and tear as is represented by so many shots. A best London gun is somewhat superior to a best Birmingham one as regards its strength and excellence of shooting, but it is immensely superior in finish and general appearance, as well as in its balance. The very best workmen find their way to London, as in the metropolis they receive higher wages than in the country ; they are, in fact, picked men. It is nonsense to maintain, as many do, that the finish of a gun is nothing and of no importance. A sportsman will always be more satisfied and do better with a high-class than with an inferior article, whether the article in question be a gun, a rod, a horse, or a dog. It is a common remark amongst a certain class of shooters, ' I do not care to pay for the engraving of a gun,' in the belief that the said engraving is put on by the gunmaker to add greatly to the cost, ignorant of the fact that a gun can be smothered with the best and most extravagant engraving for 4*l*. An expensive gun, if honest value for money is given, must necessarily, therefore, have a great deal of money and a great deal of time and thought bestowed on it and on its *shooting*. A cheap gun has little money, and, as a rule, no time or thought, bestowed on its performances.

The following remarks, extracted from Mr. Greener's admirable book, 'The Gun and its Development,' so completely bear out our own experience and ideas on the subject that they are given here.[1]   He says :—

Sportsmen often remark that they are unable to understand why there is so great a difference in the prices of guns, and also that they cannot distinguish between a gun at forty guineas and one at twenty guineas. Some makers advertise their best guns at twenty-five guineas, others at fifty guineas, or even sixty guineas (Purdey, for instance). The barrels of best guns are made from the *best* iron and steel, and welded by superior welders. The cheaper grades are made from inferior metal and made into barrels by inferior workmen, who, from receiving a lower price for their work, have to weld a larger number of barrels per week. In the boring and grinding the common barrels have to be done at half the cost of the best ; this is managed by grinding them without turning and trueing them in a lathe, and by not being so particular about the setting, and if a few rings are left inside from the rough boring it is counted of no consequence.

In the filing of the barrels the difference is more marked ; the common barrels are soldered together with sal-ammoniac and soft solder instead of with rosin, which is far superior, as it prevents the barrels from rusting underneath the ribs. The lumps also are plainly let in, not dovetailed, and the barrels are not struck up or planed round to remove the hills and hollows. Commoner ribs are also used—that is, either scelp, twist, or plain iron, and there is not so much care used to insure the rib being tapered, levelled, straightened, and equally placed on both barrels. The locks also

---

[1] After very thoroughly going into the whole question of gun-making as to wages, material, and care, we are of opinion that no really first-class hammerless gun can be *honestly* made at prime cost under 35*l*. to 36*l*.

greatly vary ; they may be purchased from two shillings to three guineas a pair. In common locks the tumblers, scears, and swivels are of iron, and only the springs of steel. In medium grades the tumblers and scears are of steel, but the breaks are not so well shaped or the bents so well cut and squared. We believe there are quite ten classes of workmen in the gun-lock trade who file the locks at various prices according to their abilities. The furniture is also different in common guns ; the triggers and bows are frequently filed from malleable iron castings, instead of from best forged gun-iron. The stocks also vary greatly in quality. In best guns great care is taken in choosing a handsome, sound piece of wood, but in the cheaper grades a few small shakes, galls, and want of figure are not accounted faults.

Breech-actions also vary greatly in quality. Common actions may be fitted complete at nine or ten shillings each, whereas some of the best quality hammerless actions cost as much as 12*l*. or 15*l*. to get up ! In breech-action fitting, as well as in lock filing, various classes of men are employed, each working at his own quality of work. . . . In the stocking the prices also vary, being chiefly governed by the shape of the lock bridles and the breech-action and the size of the gun. The screwing and finishing vary in price from 3*s*. 6*d*. to 5*l*. The polishing, browning, &c., all vary considerably in the same manner. The engraving is a branch of the trade supposed by many sportsmen to add greatly to the cost of a gun, but it is inconsiderable compared with other branches. It is now possible to completely smother a gun with cheap common engraving for a few shillings. The very best clean-cut fine scroll engraving may cost as much as four or five guineas, according to the quality placed upon the work. . . . The chief item in the cost of good guns is the regulation of the shooting and alterations of the choking and boring. In addition to the expense of fine-boring, occasionally large numbers of cartridges are required and a deal of time occupied in the shooting and regulating of first-class guns. Most of the leading gunmakers try each of them in the rough as well as in the finished state. Next to safety this is certainly the most important point in a gun, and great care should always be bestowed by the maker in testing his guns, so as to insure good results when in actual work ; this is a point that the makers of cheap guns never trouble about. . . . The difference between a best gun and an inferior one by the same maker is that the one has bestowed upon it every care throughout, and is as near perfection as the ability of that particular maker will allow of its being

made, whilst his inferior guns are very possibly those which, originally intended for best, have been found to possess some slight
fault that has thrown them to a lower grade. . . . None but the
most skilled, intelligent, careful, and willing of workmen are
capable each of working out harmoniously a preconcerted design.
. . . By such a corps, and by no other means whatsoever, can fine
guns be produced. . . . Gunmakers who can command over 50*l.*
for one of their best guns are few, and it is a mistake to suppose
they receive such prices because they are fashionable makers.
The truth is they produce an article worth the money.

We conclude this chapter with illustrations of hammerless
guns by the celebrated makers, 'Grant and Lancaster' :—

A is the pivot pin which connects the barrels to the stock.
On the pivot pin is mounted a tumbler or lifter *a*, which, as the

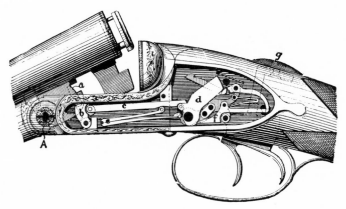

Grant's Hammerless Gun.

barrels are opened, rocks a second tumbler *b*, and pushes forward a
cocking bar or rod *c* pivotted thereto. This bar *c* presses against
the hammer *d* to cock it. As the barrels are closed, this bar *c* is
drawn back, leaving the hammer *d* free for firing when the trigger
is pulled. *e* is the mainspring, which is partly cramped as the
barrels are opened, and completely cramped as the barrels are
closed, thus the opening and closing of the gun is effected more
easily than heretofore. *f* is the scear which holds the hammer in

the cocked position until released by the action of the trigger. The gun is provided with the usual safety bolt *g*, to prevent the movement of the triggers and to release the hammers before the gun is required for use.

To guard against the firing of the gun through the accidental release of the hammer, independently of the movement of the

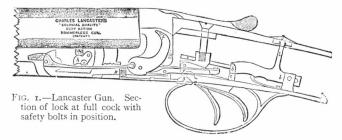

FIG. 1.—Lancaster Gun. Section of lock at full cock with safety bolts in position.

triggers, a safety catch *h* is provided, which catch, so long as it is not lowered by the triggers, will remain in the path of a projection at the back of the hammer, and thus prevent the contact of the hammer with the firing pin.

We highly approve of Mr. Grant's system of cocking the locks of his gun. We may point out that by the plan he adopts he divides the force requisite for cocking between the motions of opening and closing the action, so that no inconvenient strength has to be exerted by the shooter in loading.

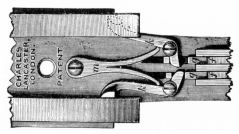

FIG. 2.—Lancaster Gun.   Blocking safety bolts.

Description of the Lancaster Gun.—The top lever is moved to the right, which withdraws the holding-down bolt of the barrels, whereby the barrels are released and made ready to be opened, allowing the cartridges to be inserted in the chambers in the ordinary manner. As the barrels are depressed, they bear upon the front end of the long flat mainspring, which projects in front of the knuckle-joint of the action and through the fore-end; as the pressure is given, the rear ends press on the top side of a notch cut in the tumbler, which movement throws the tumbler to full cock; the scear then engages in the bent and holds it there. As the gun is closed, the bar *e* attached to the under side of the barrels pressing upon the rocking or falling cam *h* (which is provided with a friction roller), in its turn presses on the mainspring, whereby the set or tension is given to it, so that, when the scear is removed from the bent by the trigger, the mainspring, pressing on the lower side of the notch cut in the tumbler, carries it forward, whereby the blow is given to discharge the cartridge. The mainspring, as will be seen from fig. 1, being of a simple and novel construction, the safety for the triggers is very strong and reliable. As the top lever is moved to open the gun, it withdraws the holding-down bolt or slide *a*, the rear end of which pushes against the front end of the connecting-rod and safety slide *b b b b*, the middle of which is carried over the triggers at point *c*. At the same time, the upper portion of the safety-slide *b*, engaging with the cover *d* at the top of the strap or tang of the action, uncovers the word 'safe,' by which the position of the locks is clearly shown to the sportsman handling the gun. This prevents any accidental movement of the triggers, and, as shown, is automatic in its action. When the safety cover *d* is pushed forward, it carries the safety *b b b b* with it, so that it disengages with the triggers at point *c*, and the gun may be discharged at the will of the shooter; the front end bears against the holding-down slide *a*, ready to be returned to 'safe' when next the gun is opened for loading either one or both barrels.

To prevent any possibility of an accidental discharge, a trustworthy automatic blocking safety is provided (figs. 1 and 2, *k*), and as the gun is opened the interposing blocking safety *k* is carried under the mainspring by its spring *m*, thereby effectually blocking the action of the mainspring (see fig. 2, which shows the blocking safety *k* under one side and withdrawn clear by the trigger on the other side, showing that the mainspring has fallen).

As the trigger is pulled, the front end *f* engages a connecting piece *g*, the front of which engages with the short arm of the blocking safety *k* (see figs. 1 and 2), so that, as the trigger is pulled it withdraws the blocking safety clear of the mainspring, thereby allowing it to fall and carry the tumbler down to give the blow on to the cap, and, as the gun is opened, the mainspring being raised, the blocking safety *k* is carried under the mainspring again by the aid of its spring *m*, ready to interpose or block the spring in case of an accidental jarring off of the lock.

This efficient and trustworthy safety combination is applicable to other plans, especially the Anson and Deeley action. The main-

FIG. 1 illustrates the gun closed with the ejecting mechanism cocked, ready for action, with slide *c* forward in position to release ejector after the gun has been fired.

FIG. 2 illustrates the gun opened, the ejecting mechanism released, and the fired cartridge-case ejected, slide *c* withdrawn, having performed its office.

a is the ejecting hammer and tumbler combined. *b* is the ejecting mainspring, scear and scear tang. all in one piece. *c* is the independent slide for releasing the ejector work. *d* is the point where the scear *b* engages with the notch or bent of ejecting hammer *a*.

N.B.—The ejector is neither worked from the tumbler of lock, nor by a sliding mainspring.

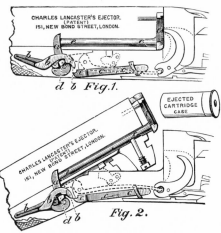

Charles Lancaster's Ejector (Patent).

spring being straight (that is, not V-shaped), and never under compression when the barrels are taken out of the action, can be easily removed and replaced without the assistance of a lock-vice or cramp ; also the gun cannot be put away in its case with the mainsprings under compression—herein differing advantageously from many other systems, for continual tension causes them to lose their power, and thereby induces misfire. This we consider a decided recommendation. The admirably devised blocking safety arrangement is also a very valuable feature in this gun.

Mr. Lancaster also makes this well-tried gun with an ejecting mechanism fitted on the fore-end. He retains the lock, as before shown in his hammerless gun, together with its very safe blocking safety bolts. The ejecting mechanism is certainly simplicity itself, as there is a tumbler, swivel, mainspring and scear in one fitting—only three pieces in all, neatly secured inside the fore-end, and apparently very strong and trustworthy in their movements.

R. P. G.

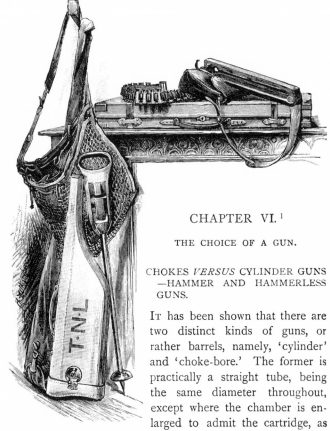

CHAPTER VI. [1]

THE CHOICE OF A GUN.

CHOKES *VERSUS* CYLINDER GUNS
—HAMMER AND HAMMERLESS
GUNS.

It has been shown that there are
two distinct kinds of guns, or
rather barrels, namely, 'cylinder'
and 'choke-bore.' The former is
practically a straight tube, being
the same diameter throughout,
except where the chamber is enlarged to admit the cartridge, as
of course its diameter is larger than the wads it contains,
which latter exactly fit the barrel. Though called 'cylinder,'
few barrels are precisely what the term implies, as it has long
been the custom of gunmakers to deviate from an absolutely
perfect cylinder. Sometimes the barrels are enlarged at both
breech and muzzle, the narrowest part being in the centre
of the length; they may be enlarged for some ten inches

[1] Revised by W. C. A. Blew.

from the breech end, or again slightly tapered the whole length from breech to muzzle. These systems of boring cylinders were well known and practised in the days of muzzle-loaders, and though not in reality cylinder barrels were always called so. Choke-boring, as before said, consists in contracting the muzzle of a barrel. A barrel contracted five-thousandths of an inch is termed a slight choke, twelve to eighteen thousandths a moderate choke, a full choke being narrowed at the muzzle to the extent of thirty to forty-thousandths of an inch. This narrowing of the diameter of the bore must finish from a half-inch to an inch from the muzzle, to make the gun shoot well as a choke.

The relative performances of choke-bores and cylinder guns have been compared on page 63, but it may be added that the charge used was 3 drs. of powder and $1\frac{1}{8}$ oz. of No. 6 shot, 270 pellets to the ounce.[1] It has been seen what an immense advantage a choke-bored gun has over a cylinder, *provided the aim be true.* In the one case a partridge might receive but two or three pellets in the body, in the other maybe six or seven. In fact, the pattern or number of pellets a choke will put into, say, a partridge at forty to forty-five yards is as many as a cylinder will be capable of at thirty to thirty-five yards.

Now, as to using a choked or cylinder gun, it is evident that the former requires straighter aiming than the latter, because it keeps the shot grouped together longer in its flight ; hence the size of the diameter of its shot-circle is less than that of a cylinder all through its flight after leaving the gun.

In regard to the cylinder gun, the diameter of its shot-circle enlarges, that is, spreads much more from the moment it leaves the muzzle, than is the case with the same charge fired from the choke-bore. The result is that at forty yards the pellets fired from the cylinder are comparatively wide apart, whilst

[1] A round target 30 in. in diameter, placed at 40 yds. from the muzzle of the gun, is the recognised test as regards proving the pattern of a gun.

those fired from the choke are close together. In one instance a bird might fly through the shot-circle at forty yards and be scarcely touched, in the other it could not escape being hit.

From this it will be readily seen that it is not so easy, however true be the aim, to stop game at forty yards with a cylinder as it would be with a choke-bored gun. On the other hand, it is not so easy to hit game (especially a crossing shot) with a choke at twenty-five yards, on account of the smallness of its shot-circle at that distance, and the close group in which it must travel to strike a 30-inch target at forty yards as thickly as we know is the case. With a cylinder it is the reverse, as at twenty-five yards the pattern is as close as is that of the choke at forty, and the object being nearer, it is much easier to aim at, besides which less allowance of distance has to be made.

To the ordinary game-shot a good cylinder gun is to be strongly recommended. We emphasise the word *good*, as no guns vary more than do cylinders. It is far more difficult to make a cylinder gun put 130 pellets with evenness, regularity and penetration on to a 30-inch target at 40 yards, than it is to make a full-choke average 200 or more. Many a badly bored cylinder will not average 110, with variations from 85 to 120. Everyone should know how he shoots, as he should know his powers of walking, running, playing billiards or tennis. A fair marksman is one who kills, say, once for three cartridges fired, taking one species of game with another, throughout the season. To him a cylinder will be by far the most effective gun, for with it he will account for all ordinary shots, always provided the gun is a *good* cylinder. It is true that with a choke he would now and then make a brilliant shot, but he would miss very many easy ones, and shooting is like billiards—it is the easy shots that add up the total in the end.

Many and many a shooter lessens his bag very considerably by using a choke-bored gun when a cylinder is better adapted to his powers of aim ; he may even suspect this in his heart, though loth to admit it.   Let him try rabbits dodging about in covert with a cylinder, after missing them time after time with a choke, he will doubtless learn a lesson, and a useful one too ; or let him experiment on driven game with a cylinder after failing to bring birds down with a choke, and he will be surprised at his success.   Let it be understood that an ordinary shot is here referred to, and not a good one, or even one above the average.   As a matter of fact, however, a full choke gun is seldom seen now-a-days, and the majority of even the best shots content themselves with a slight choke in the left barrel only.

FITTING A GUN.

When choosing a gun it is necessary to put it several times quickly to the shoulder at an object level with the eye, and if the sight taken comes fair on the mark aimed at, the gun (provided the gunmaker is practised in fitting a gun, and the question of sight is considered) will probably suit.   We will add that should the aim require correction—that is, the sight come up under or over the mark pointed at—then the gun will never be a suitable or quick aiming gun to the purchaser. If, when out shooting, a sportsman has to correct his aim, through his gun pitching up to his shoulder either too high, too low, or to one side, he is certainly handicapped in comparison with the man whose gun suits him, and comes instantly in line with the game he aims at, though the former may be no more skilful a shot.   Many shooters' guns, as before pointed out, do not suit them, though their owners may not know it, and this causes them to aim at a different point from that which they intended, and imagine they do aim at, when putting the gun to the shoulder.   The aim has then to be corrected, and time is lost in consequence, for the game does not wait whilst errors are being rectified.   It is therefore of great importance that the form of a gunstock should fit the eyes and shoulder, and be adjustable to the height and length of arm of a shooter ; the gun that will suit a man with a long neck will never do for one with a short neck, any more than will the same collar do for both. When a shooter boasts of the excellent killing power of his gun and of the long shots he makes with it, it is oftener because of his putting the centre of the charge well on the object aimed at through the weapon coming fair to his eye and shoulder, than by reason of any great superiority of his gun over guns in general.

The lay of a gun to the shoulder when aimed depends as much upon the 'cast off' and slope of the heel-plate as upon anything else. A tall man with good length of arms and neck will generally require a gun that has its stock long and well bent, a short man just the reverse. If when trying a gun the muzzle tends downwards, then the stock is too much bent or too short ; if the muzzle points upwards, then the stock has not bend enough. In fact, the gun should come up to the shoulder fair on the mark aimed at, easily and naturally, and so comfortably; there will then be no straining of neck or arms, or twisting of the body to take a shot a little to the right or to the left. Fitting a gun to a customer is indeed, we may say, one of the most important parts of a gunmaker's business. A good gunmaker not only prides himself upon his success in doing this, but considers (and quite rightly) that such a qualification is one of his strongest recommendations to sportsmen who understand shooting. This attribute is, indeed, the speciality of a good London gunmaker, and one for which Mr. Purdey is so justly famed. A sportsman who writes, say to Birmingham, for a new gun, without sending a pattern one that suits him in every respect, may just as well expect a tailor to make him a suit of clothes without measurements.

A gun requires to be very well balanced—an art carried to perfection by London gunmakers, but one hard to describe. It chiefly consists in making the muzzle and stock of the gun divide their weight, neither one nor the other being a half ounce too heavy. A well-balanced gun and one badly balanced,

though both be of the same weight, are easily told apart; it is
a pleasure to use one, an annoyance to use the other.

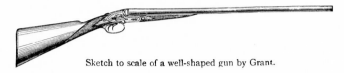

Sketch to scale of a well-shaped gun by Grant.

We here give a cut of a favourite gun by Holland (fig. 1),
showing what a well-shaped stock for a man of about 5 ft. 10 in.
to 5 ft. 11 in. should be like. We also give a cut of what a

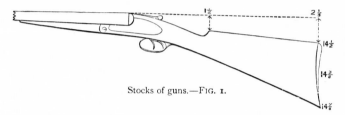

Stocks of guns.—FIG. 1.

stock for such a man should not be like (fig. 2), the latter also
being a bad shape. In fig. 3 we show a very good shape
under certain conditions.

Fig. 1.—Bend at face, $1\frac{1}{2}$ inch ; bend at bump, $2\frac{1}{8}$ inches.
Length from front trigger to centre of heelplate, $14\frac{3}{8}$ inches.
Length from front trigger to bump, 14 inches.

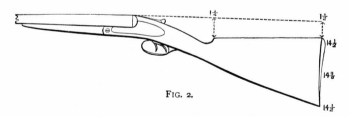

FIG. 2.

Length from front trigger to toe, $14\frac{7}{8}$ inches.
Cast off at bump, $\frac{1}{8}$ inch ; at toe, $\frac{3}{16}$ inch.

Of course the length required depends as much upon the length of a man's arms, thickness of chest, &c., as upon his height.

The fault of fig. 2 is that, although the stock is well bent at the face, it is straight at the bump, with a short toe. The tendency with this gun is to get the butt too high on the shoulder.

It will be noticed that fig. 3 is straight at the face, only $1\frac{1}{4}$ in.,

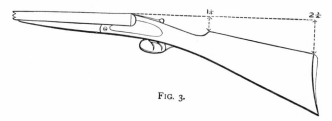

FIG. 3.

and decidedly bent at the bump, i.e. $2\frac{3}{4}$ in., with a long toe to keep the muzzle up. This shape mounts very comfortably, and is suitable to sportsmen with long necks or sloping shoulders. The only drawback is a tendency to kick the face. Guns on these lines should therefore not be made too light.

TRY GUNS.

In order to ensure as far as possible that the customer shall have a gun which is in every way suited to him, most

Holland and Holland's Try Gun.

makers now experimentalise with a try gun. Different forms of dummy try guns were used by gunmakers before Jones's pattern came into the market. The merits of this invention, however, were quickly seen, and Messrs. Holland and Holland bought the patent rights, and afterwards improved upon the original design. We give an illustration of it. There is a double joint just in front of the trigger guard which has both a lateral and vertical action, while the screw seen underneath the stock acts upon the movable top with a double action by which the cast-off and bend are regulated. Appended also is an illustration of the try gun used by Messrs. Cogswell and Harrison, of Bond Street and the Strand.

The object of the employment of the try gun is to ascertain the cast off, bend, length of stock, and slope and depth of heel plate with which the customer can best shoot, and this appliance enables the gunmaker or his fitter to decide upon the required pattern of gun. In the latter model there are two hinges in the stock, and some elongating screws by which every detail of the

Cogswell and Harrison's Try Gun.

gun can be altered to suit individual requirements. The intending customer can fire at a moving target as often as he pleases, and after each shot the fitter can change the measurements until he hits upon the build which he deems most suitable. Some makers do not use a try gun, but trust to their general knowledge in fitting a buyer ; but many of those who have used the try gun are greatly in favour of it, and declare that by its use they have been enabled to obtain a gun which has considerably improved their shooting, by reason of its being adapted to their individual peculiarities.

HAMMERLESS *v.* HAMMER GUNS.

It may be well at this point to say something on the question of hammerless *versus* hammer guns. When the former
were first brought into the market they were asserted to be
a great improvement on the hammer gun, inasmuch as the
hammer was said to interfere with aiming. Whether this was
the case or not is a matter for individual opinion. It was
stated too that they were quicker and easier to load than
hammer guns, but this is hardly borne out in practice.
Originally the hammerless gun was more difficult to open, inasmuch as when the barrels were depressed the gun was cocked,
and this necessitated more exertion on the part of the shooter.
Now, however, gunmakers have overcome this, and there is no
more trouble as a rule in opening a hammerless gun than one
which has a hammer.

It must be remembered, however, that hammerless guns
are always at full cock when in use, and indeed always, unless
the shooter extracts the cartridges and snaps off the lock ; but
this danger of being always at full cock is obviated to a great
extent by the use of an intercepting safety bolt. With regard,
however, to the danger of carrying a gun always at full cock, the
holder may again be reminded that in the case of a breechloader
there should be no danger of an accidental discharge, inasmuch
as the cartridges can be extracted in a moment when crossing a
foot bridge or going through a gap. The hammer gun was
not invariably safe, even at half cock, for if some obstacle
struck the hammer the gun was liable to be instantaneously
discharged. Improvements have, however, gradually taken place,
and at the present time it is safe to say that ninety per cent. of
the men who go in for high-class guns use those of the hammerless
pattern, though at the same time there are a few, and some of
them well-known sportsmen, who remain faithful to the hammer
gun, just as there are a few who use a non-ejector.

SINGLE-TRIGGER GUNS.

When the writing of the first edition of this work was undertaken, ejector mechanism was the question of the day ; but now the single trigger for a double-barrelled gun is the subject for discussion and competition. The single trigger, however, is not an idea of yesterday : gunmakers and mechanicians turned their attention to it quite a century ago, if not more, and at the time when the firm of Egg had premises close to where the London Pavilion now stands— Egg's shop will be within the recollection of middle-aged men —there were in the place certainly drawings, if not models, of incomplete single-trigger apparatus.

When, however, ejectors and hammerless guns had been virtually perfected, the inventor looked around for some other scope for his ingenuity and selected the single trigger as his subject. As long as double-barrelled guns have been in use, shooting men have complained of bruised finger, while a few of the highest class shots have thought that a certain amount of time is wasted in passing the finger from one trigger to the other, an operation which has been said to alter the direction of the gun, and therefore to tend to missing. Be the reason what it may, single-trigger guns are at the present time a good deal sought after, though at the same time a fair number of well-known shots decline to use either hammerless or single-trigger weapons. It must of course be a matter of individual taste ; but for those who like the single-trigger, gunmakers have certainly done their best.

We believe that we are correct in stating that Messrs. Boss & Co., of St. James's Street, were the first to attempt to solve the problem of the single trigger, and no one is more willing to confess than they to the failure which for some time attended their efforts. Just when success seemed assured something or other broke down, and fresh investigations had to be made. One of the difficulties, and it may be said the chief difficulty, was the virtually ensuring that the discharge of one barrel should not cause the other to go off as well. In early times shock had no doubt a good deal to do with unintentional discharge, but later on it was found that the accidental discharge of the second barrel was not so much owing to faulty mechanism as to the unintentional pull on the part of the shooter, and now this difficulty appears to have been, humanly speaking, overcome.

Then arose another difficulty, and that is what is now known as selective mechanism ; in other words, that the shooter should be enabled to fire either the right or left barrel first. The demand for this became marked when it was pointed out that if a man were indulging in what is commonly known as rough shooting he might meet with either a snipe, a partridge, or a wild duck, and if he had small shot in one barrel and large in another, he might either discharge the large shot at the snipe or the small shot at the duck. It was, therefore, of importance that he should be able without loss of time or without any difficulty to fire first whichever barrel he chose. This defect has now been solved by Messrs. Boss and by other makers. On the right-hand side of the gun and just above the trigger is a small sliding lever ; at the end nearest to the stock is the letter 'R,' at the end farthest away is the letter 'L.' If the lever be slipped forward the letter 'R' is exposed, and so long as that be so the gun will fire its right barrel first. If, however, the lever be drawn backward, the letter 'L' is exposed, and then the left barrel is first discharged ; and so long as either letter is left uncovered, the barrel it represents will be discharged first for an indefinite number of times.

More perhaps by way of showing what can be done in mechanism than in the hope of having a large sale of the weapon, Messrs. Boss have also made a three-barrelled gun, the three barrels all being abreast and working by a single trigger.

When in certain cases a single-trigger gun is required by their customers, Messrs. Purdey have a very simple one-trigger system, which in connection with their hammerless ejector has worked successfully in the hands of some of the hardest shooters.

We give illustrations of a very effective single-trigger gun, patented by Mr. Beesley, of St. James's Street, which has just the same number of parts as a gun with two triggers, but is a 'straight-pull' gun ; that is to say, the shooter pulls to discharge the first barrel, and then continuing to pull at the trigger the

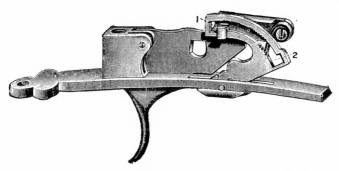

This represents the 'straight-pull' single trigger complete, and ready for firing. When the finger pulls the trigger backward, the small key ⊏⊐ is lifted upward out of the recess 1 and fires the first barrel. The fan-shaped piece then revolves until the recess 2 is over the key ⊏⊐, when the second barrel may be fired.

second barrel is fired, so a quick right and left is ensured. In other guns it is necessary to relax the finger for a moment between the two pulls. Mr. Beesley's gun is so sensitive on the pull that the slight kick of the gun is just sufficient to give that slight but imperceptible relaxation of the finger touch which is all that is necessary for the discharge of the second barrel. To the shooter the feeling is that of two consecutive pulls without relaxation.

Among other makers Messrs. Cogswell & Harrison have a single-trigger gun the mechanism of which is as simple in its construction as may be, and has stood the test of time.

In the trigger is situate the fulcrum A upon which the inner trigger C works. On raising the trigger the front part of C on the right side with the right lock is released. The releasing motion of the trigger permits C to be urged forward; a left projection on the limb comes under the left lock, which is fired

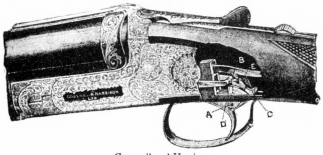

Cogswell and Harrison.

on a second pull. An intermediate catch, in C, engages in a hook of the ordinary safety slide, B, and so retards the second discharge, thereby eliminating the involuntary pull. The gun shown above is not fitted with selective mechanism; but it can be made in selective form if required.

Mr. Charles Lancaster's single-trigger gun is also represented, and appended is a description.

A is the ordinary trigger plate; B is the trigger with its pivot at b^2; C the switching trigger, free to act either on the right or left hand lock; D, the safety slide, mounted on the trigger plate A, and connected with the vertical lever E, which is in union with the 'safe' slide cover at the top of the gun. The front, or rod, portion of D is carried forward so as to be almost in contact with the ordinary holding-down bolt of the breech action. An inclined plane at d^2 actuates the switching trigger C, whereby the usual means of acting upon it by the tumbler of the right-hand lock is not necessary ; it is not therefore requisite to cut out so much wood, so that the stock is strengthened, and there is greater ease in 'putting together.'

The gun being opened for loading, the bolt of the breech action forces back the safety slide D, and the vertical lever E acts upon the slide cover F, which then shows the word 'safe' upon the top of the gun. As the safety slide moves, its inclined plane at d^2 causes the switching trigger C to be carried under the scears of the right-hand lock. A recess therein

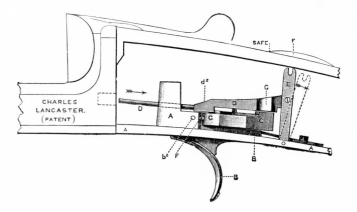

ensures its retention by a hook on the scear, so that when the safety slide D is pushed forward, ready for firing, it is retained. The right barrel being fired, the switching trigger C is free to be carried over to the left lock by its spring H, but a 'timer' at G on the safety slide D is so arranged that the switching trigger cannot pass from the right-hand lock to the left until the trigger has been released from the pressure of the finger.

A portion of the safety slide has a device at G which prevents the switching trigger C from being raised by a pull on the trigger until it has been returned to its normal position by the downward pressure of its spring H, and assumed its extreme position under the second or left-hand scear.

WEIGHT, BORE, AND CHARGES OF GUNS.

The weight and bore of our guns is a very important point with shooters, and one much discussed. Hot disputes often rage in the sporting papers among the advocates of 16-bores, 12-bores, and 20-bores, even 28-bores being strongly recommended by some. It is the old story that 'what is one man's meat is another man's poison ;' the same gun, or rod, or horse, or something else, whatever it may be, will not and cannot be made to suit everybody and every style of employment.

Many sportsmen advise 20-bore guns—28-bores need not be discussed, as anyone who has experimented with them knows they are foolish toys when used on anything except a young partridge at short range, and that it is ridiculous to maintain that they will hold their own with a larger bore. Certainly a 20-bore is a nice, pretty little weapon, but for good marksmanship it is too small. Let anyone aim at long or cross shots with a 20-bore, and he will find the muzzle of his gun very unsteady compared with what a larger weapon would be. A 20-bore is undoubtedly a convenient gun for an elderly gentleman, or a weak one, to walk partridges up with under a hot sun and to kill easy shots. But it is impossible that so small a bore and charge can nearly equal in its execution a 12-bore, as the 20-bore fanciers maintain it does. The recoil, too, of a 20-bore is excessive on account of the lightness of its barrels, unless it be loaded so lightly as to make killing a hare with it at thirty yards an uncertainty.

As very few shooters ever experiment at a target with their guns (the only sure test of the capabilities of a gun), they are quite ready to believe almost anything that may be told them. There are even shooters as well as gunmakers who, though numerous and most accurately carried out trials completely negative the idea, maintain that 20-bores kill as well as 12-bores, and that there is no difference in power between the two sizes, utterly ignoring the very obvious fact that the charge of a 20-bore is smaller, lighter, and has a less killing circle than has a 12-bore.

If a shooter be not strong by all means let him carry a 20-bore as a matter of ease and comfort, but it is nonsense to say one gun will *kill* as well as the other. A light gun is a comfort to a weak man, as he can take aim with it at the end, as well as he did at the beginning, of a day; whereas a too heavy gun will tire him, and cause him, by its excessive weight, to fail in bringing it quickly on his game when he is a little fagged. For this reason, when walking and carrying a gun the shooter should never feel it a burden to his arms, and must, in fact, suit the weight of his gun to his strength, remembering always that the heavier the gun he can carry, the less it will recoil and the harder it will shoot. Recoil causes headaches, and a headache utterly destroys all pleasure and comfort in shooting. Many years ago we purchased the best pair of 20-bores we could obtain. We first used them walking up partridges in September, and were delighted with them ; later in the year we began to try them on rocketing pheasants and hares, but our delight soon vanished when we found them, time after time, failing to drop *dead* fairly long shots—shots that to a 12-bore were wellnigh certainties. At strong driven grouse, too, the guns were disheartening in the extreme ; at wildfowl practically useless.

This is our experience of 20-bores, and, we find, of most of our friends also. For young birds or easy shots flying straight away, as when walking up partridges early in the season, they are all very well ; a 28-bore would kill such birds ; but for game when it gets wild and strong, or for driving, or for ground game—save rabbits in covert underfoot—a 20-bore heavily handicaps a man for successful shooting, and it must be remembered that there is more recoil with a 20-bore charged with say 32 or 33 grains of Schultze, or its equivalent in other powders, than with a 12-bore pretty heavily loaded.

A 16-bore is much praised by shooters who happen to possess a gun of that size; but now that a 12-bore can be constructed almost of the weight of a 16-bore, the latter weapon is not in the same demand as it once was. A 12-bore lightly made and lightly loaded will, by reason of its larger killing circle, act better on game than a gun of smaller bore loaded with the same charge; and therefore, if a light gun be a necessity to a shooter, a light 12-bore is more effectual than one of smaller calibre. It may also be mentioned that a 16- or 20-bore will not shoot so well as a cylinder of 12-bore, by reason of the shot being placed in longitudinal form in the cartridge. Hence choking is more required in the case of guns of small bore than in the case of a 12-bore, to ensure regularity of pattern. A 16-bore, though it has some of the disadvantages of a 20-bore, approaches more nearly in its performances to a 12-bore, though it cannot equal them, whatever the advocates of the 16-bore may say. By using a 16-bore the shooter slightly reduces the weight and bulk he has to carry; but he loses more than this weight in value by reason of having in his hands a gun which is not the equal in its charge and force to a 12-bore. A 16-bore gun should not weigh less than 6 lbs. to $6\frac{1}{4}$ lbs.

There is no doubt whatever that the ordinary 12-bore is the most effective gun the game shooter can use. A weapon weighing about $6\frac{3}{4}$ lbs. is surely all that can be desired, as it can carry a fair charge and gives the minimum of recoil as a rule. In short, the shooter should remember that with extreme lightness and usual loads we have excessive recoil and diminished killing power.

The capabilities of a gun are of course in a ratio with its strength, weight, and bore. A 12-bore good cylinder gun, for

example, with any kind of powder, should, if held straight, kill
to a certainty at 40 yards, if the feather or fur be in the centre
of the pattern. This does not seem very far; but comparatively few shooting men are aware how near the game
really is when they kill it : a high rocketing pheasant is rarely
30 yards above ground, often less. A choke bore should
account for anything up to 50 yards, if properly aimed. Both
kinds of guns often during a day's shooting bring down game
at distances far beyond those quoted; but the above are
given as examples of what the gun will do with regularity if the
shooter hold it straight; the blazing away at birds or ground
game at 60 or 70 yards has already been condemned because
of the obvious chance of inflicting a wound without killing.

POWDER

The old black powder which for so many years stood
sportsmen in such good stead has now joined the flint-lock gun
in museums of antiquities, and one or other of the nitro-
powders is now invariably used by game shots.

The first chemical mixture manufactured for charging a
gun with was what was known as 'Schultze' or 'sawdust'
powder. It was partially discovered in 1846 by a German
chemist named Schönbein, who proved the explosive properties
of cotton steeped in nitric acid. The discovery was subsequently perfected by Captain Schultze, of the German service,
who substituted sawdust for cotton. This powder came into
immediate use among sportsmen, for there was no doubt it
had great advantages over the old powder in its absence of
recoil and smoke, as well as in its cleanliness. It, however,
fell off in popularity on account of its uncertainty, as it sometimes shot hard and true, at other times very indifferently ; on
occasions, too, so very violent was its combustion that it
deafened the shooter, or damaged his gun ; at other times it
exploded so feebly that the charge of shot almost rolled out
of the barrel. One thing was nevertheless made certain—

that the Schultze powder, when it did behave well, was equal to the black in penetrative power. But a point soon presented itself which had not hitherto been discussed, and this was the method of loading the new mixture. It was found that it had been treated in just the same fashion as black—that is to say, the powder was rammed firmly in the cartridge case. It was discovered that when so treated Schultze acted very much less satisfactorily than when it was not subject to such pressure. Experiments endorsed this opinion, and consequently its regularity of shooting was greatly inproved by its being carefully loaded by hand. But loading by hand proved a slow and more or less uncertain method, as the pressure exerted on the powder was often unequal, and it was demonstrated beyond question that the pressure used in placing the new powder in the cartridges had everything to do with its success. The cleverly devised loading contrivances which have since been invented bring out the best qualities of nitros. It should be borne in mind by those shooters who use chemical powders and who load their own cartridges, that 'a light charge of shot, by reason of its offering less resistance, does not produce as much explosive power in a charge of these powders as a full load of shot will do.' Hence we found that with usual and similar charges of powder (E.C. or Schultze) an ounce of shot is not driven with as much penetrative force as is $1\frac{1}{8}$ oz.

Some years ago the Explosive Company of the Stowmarket Powder Works further improved their powder known as E.C., and it is in every way excellent. Since that time, however, other nitro-powders have been invented and have been placed on the market. It is unnecessary to discuss in detail the characteristics of each powder; but shooting men may be warned that, speaking generally, to keep nitro-powders either in bulk, or in the form of cartridges, in a hot room is to increase their explosive strength, as moisture is thereby absorbed; and, conversely, to keep these powders in a damp place is as a rule to diminish their strength: they should be kept in a dry but not a hot place. Some of the accidents, too, which have happened through the use of nitro-powders have been attributed to the increased force acquired by the charge when the cartridge has been held in a gun-barrel heated by rapid firing.

We give on pages 102–3 a list, in alphabetical order, of the nitro-powders now on the market ; but it must be understood that we do not give one preference over the other. In his selection each shooter must please himself. We also give the loads for guns of 12, 16, and 20 bore.

On looking over the following table, it will be seen that the number of grains of the different nitro-powders for the charge of a gun of any specified bore varies considerably. The explanation is that in the early days of nitro-powders the intention was to make the bulk of the new explosives about the same as that of black powder, so that there should be no material change in the length of the cartridges. In several of the above varieties it will be seen that 42 grains correspond as nearly as possible to three drams of black powder by measure. In order to make the bulk the same, or nearly so, a certain amount of inoperative matter was introduced into the powder, and then others were brought out from which the inoperative matter was wholly or partially omitted, consequently fewer grains are needed for a charge. Several gunmakers have taken advantage of this fact to manufacture short cartridges, and among them is the firm of Lancaster, which sends out 'Pygmy' cartridges, two inches in length, loaded with 28 grains of Walsrode powder and an ounce of No. 6 shot. There are also the 'Parvo' cartridges, of about the same size, loaded with ballistite. For these cartridges of reduced size it is claimed that there is a saving in weight and bulk, and that the pocket or cartridge bag will accommodate more than of the $2\frac{1}{2}$-inch cartridges ; while these short cartridges can be used in a gun chambered for ordinary cartridges. An extra charge for a 12-bore gun weighing not less than $7\frac{1}{2}$ lbs., and used for wild fowl, pigeons, long shots at grouse, hares &c., may be 47 grains of Schultze (or its equivalent) and $1\frac{1}{4}$ oz. of Nos. 4 or 5 shot.

SHOOTING.

Name of Powder	Bore	Grains	Shot oz.	Special Instructions
Amberite	12	47	$1\frac{1}{4}$	Special cases not essential. An extra grain of powder is recommended for 'ejector' and 'grouse' cases.
	12	42	$1\frac{1}{8}$	
	12	40	1	
	16	36	1	
	20	33	$\frac{7}{8}$	
Ballistite (sporting)	12	24	1	Special cone cases are necessary, and special caps must be employed.
	12	26	$1\frac{1}{8}$	
	12	28	$1\frac{3}{16}$	
	12	28	$1\frac{3}{16}$	
	12	29	$1\frac{1}{4}$	
	12	31	$1\frac{1}{4}$	
	16	22	1	
	20	20	$\frac{3}{4}$	
	20	20	$\frac{7}{8}$	
Cannonite. No. 1. Fine grain	12	35	$1\frac{1}{8}$	Special cases must be used, and special caps also.
	12	40	$1\frac{1}{4}$	
	16	32	1	
	20	30	$\frac{3}{4}$	
Cannonite. No. 2. Coarse grain	12	42	$1\frac{1}{8}$	The bulk is the same as that of black powder, and neither special cases nor caps are required.
	12	46	$1\frac{1}{4}$	
	16	36	1	
	20	32	$\frac{7}{8}$	
Cooppal (smokeless)	12	46 to 49	$1\frac{1}{4}$ to $1\frac{3}{4}$	—
	12	45	$1\frac{1}{8}$ to $1\frac{1}{4}$	
	12	42	1 to $1\frac{1}{8}$	
	16	42	$1\frac{1}{8}$	
	16	38	$\frac{7}{8}$ to 1	
	20	38	$\frac{3}{4}$ to 1	
	20	35	$\frac{3}{4}$ to $\frac{7}{8}$	
E.C. No. 2	12	42	$1\frac{1}{8}$	—
	16	37	1	
	20	32	$\frac{7}{8}$	
E.C. No. 3 (Improved E.C.)	12	33	$1\frac{1}{8}$	—
	12	36, 38, 40	$1\frac{1}{4}$	
	16	28	$\frac{7}{8}$	
	20	26	$\frac{3}{4}$	

Name of Powder	Bore	Grains	Shot oz.	Special Instructions
Kynoch (smokeless sporting)	12	42	$1\frac{1}{2}$	—
	12	46	$1\frac{1}{4}$	
	16	38	1	
	20	32	$\frac{7}{8}$	
Normal	12	34	$1\frac{1}{16}$	Any cases may be used, but if they have no cones the charge should be slightly reduced.
	16	27	1	
Schultze	12	49	$1\frac{1}{4}$	—
	12	45	$1\frac{1}{8}$	
	12	42	1, $1\frac{1}{16}$ or $1\frac{1}{8}$	
	16	37	1	
	20	32	$\frac{7}{8}$ or 1	
(SS) New issue, 1898	12	41	$1\frac{1}{4}$	—
	12	38	$1\frac{1}{8}$	
	16	35	$\frac{15}{16}$	
	20	32	$\frac{13}{16}$	
Shot-gun rifleite	12	41	$1\frac{1}{4}$	—
	12	37	$1\frac{1}{8}$	
	16	32	$\frac{15}{16}$	
	20	29	$\frac{13}{16}$	
Walsrode	12	$\frac{26}{28}$	1	Special caps and short cases.
	12	31	$1\frac{1}{8}$	Special cone cases and special caps required.
	16	29	1	
	20	28	$\frac{3}{4}$ to $\frac{7}{8}$	
Anglo-Walsrode	12	31	$1\frac{1}{4}$	These loads are for the special Walsrode cases.
	12	29	$1\frac{1}{8}$	
	16	27	1	
	20	25	$\frac{3}{4}$ to $\frac{7}{8}$	

SHOT.

The shot pellets we use in our guns vary considerably both in size and roundness as well as in hardness. Before the introduction of choke bores soft shot was in demand; but it was found that when a charge of soft shot was fired from a choke-bored gun it suffered not a little by reason of its being suddenly jammed up together at the narrowest part of the barrel—the part, that is to say, that formed the choke. It is a well-known principle that any body travelling through the air which by reason of its smoothness offers the least resistance in its flight, flies faster, and usually strikes harder, than is the case with a rough and irregular missile. To meet this difficulty, hardened, or, as it is improperly termed, chilled shot came into request. This latter was proved to be less liable to damage when fired from a choke-bored gun than was the case with the more susceptive soft shot.

The most perfect shot would be such as could not be bruised or flattened in being propelled from the barrel of a gun. Iron or steel shot would, for instance, have this quality, but, being much lighter than lead, would have less striking force.

'Chilled' shot was originally so called because when first made it was hardened by means of a current or blast of cold air being played upon it as it solidified; and though formed of pure lead, this method caused it, or was supposed to cause it, to harden more than was the case with lead not so treated. However, 'chilled' shot is now made by hardening it with an alloy of antimony, so that the word 'chilled' does not really apply to its manufacture.

This latter treatment, however, causes the hard shot to be a trifle lighter as well as of somewhat larger bulk than the soft (the latter being made of pure lead), so that though the supposed number of pellets per ounce of both kinds is the same, their sizes vary, the hard or lighter shot really numbering a few more pellets to the ounce than its rival. Thus, in making target trials, it is necessary when counting the number of pellets on the plate to know exactly how many the charge contained, and to adhere, in consequence, to either hard or soft shot throughout experiments of the kind.

Soft shot is said to be most suitable in a cylinder, and hard in a choke-bored gun. The soft shot does not become irregular by a sudden contracted pressure in the former, as it invariably does in the latter. It is also slightly heavier, and, in our opinion, flies truer and strikes harder (especially in wind) than does the hard shot, if used in a cylinder gun. On the other hand, hard shot retains its shape when fired from a choke, and thus penetrates deeper into the game, a quality which may be said to counterbalance its slight want in specific gravity. Every description of shot is made by dropping lead, in a melted state, from a height into water. In its transit through the air it assumes a globular shape, and on reaching the water is at once chilled into this form. The use of hard shot appears to be more the fashion than the use of soft, but no real advantage can be claimed for it over soft or patent shot for a cylinder gun. The use of hard shot, many gunmakers assert, is the reason why the wear and tear of barrels is now generally found to be greater than before its introduction.

When the shot is made it is passed through sieves, each size corresponding to the holes in its particular sieve. It is nevertheless very difficult to get the ounces of any sized shot exactly the same one with another, as regards the number of pellets each contains, the reason being that the holes in the sieves, besides wearing larger with use, are sure to vary slightly in size. Thus the contents of one charge of shot in a cartridge may be even a score pellets larger or smaller in number than is the case in another. This inaccuracy will not only affect the shooting of a gun, but will cause all target experiments, unless this point be considered, to end with uncertain results. The fault is completely obviated if the pellets in each charge be precisely similar in number—a result which is perfectly obtained by some of our best cartridge-makers, as, for example, by Mr. Greener, of Birmingham, who uses a kind of flat iron spoon with shallow holes in it, corresponding in number to the correct charge required. This is plunged into the basin of shot by the cartridge-loader, and as the spoon has holes in it, in each of which a pellet rests, the exact number is transferred by a funnel to the cartridge, neither one more nor less. Taking a half-dozen cartridges at random out of several thousand obtained from Mr. Greener, a difference of two pellets between one and another will rarely be found. Such perfection of loading is of great value to a shooter, far more so than is generally considered to be the case.

Very few people agree as to what is the best size of shot to use, and many forget that the charge which will suit one gun and one description of game will not do as well for another. Usually, one gun will shoot better one size of shot than will another, and we may safely say that large bores shoot large shot better than do smaller bores.

The smaller the bore, the smaller should be the shot used ; for, as the bore decreases, so does the charge, and, as a consequence, the number of pellets in it. For a 20-bore No. 5 shot is not suitable ; No. 6 would be better.

The usual sizes of shot, subject to slight deviations, are as follows :—

HARD SHOT.				SOFT SHOT.			
No.	Pellets to the oz.	No.	Pellets to the oz.	No.	Pellets to the oz.	No.	Pellets to the oz.
1	104	5	218	1	80	5	218–225
2	122	6	270 [1]	2	112–120	6	270
3	140	6	300 [2]	3	135	7	340
4	172	7	340	4	175–180		

For partridges, early in the season, No. 7 is, probably, the best size. Later, No. 6. For grouse, pheasants, wildfowl, and ground game No. 5 is unequalled at all times ; this is of course for 12-bore guns.

[1] London size.   [2] Northern size.

If a shooter be a good shot he may use No. 6 early in the season, and only for partridges; afterwards nothing but No. 5. For the average shot No. 6 is best throughout the season.

Of course the more pellets in a charge the easier can young game be killed at short distances; but, after September, when the birds are strong in feather and in full plumage, no shot smaller than No. 6 should ever be fired at game by a sportsman out of a 12-bore. As No. 6 is of less weight than No. 5, it cannot kill as cleanly or drop game as dead, when not a near shot, as does the larger size; but then No. 6 has more pellets to the ounce, and with an average shot more are thus likely to strike the object than if he used No. 5. Still No. 5 (save for early partridge shooting, in which case No. 5 is liable to spoil the flesh) is far the most satisfactory size for a *good* shot to use—a man, for instance, who does not require the aid of an increased number of pellets in his charge to enable him to hit, and who likes to feel that he is using shot that will kill, and kill clean, often some dozen yards farther than any smaller size.

It is often said that the user of small shot (No. 6 or 7) is on a par with a man who uses No. 5, and that the killing power of both large and small is equalised by the fact that four or five pellets of No. 6 or 7 deal as serious a wound, in fact, disable the game as much, as two or three pellets of No. 5. In practice it will not be found that this is the case, as repeated experiments have shown. The shooter who uses No. 5 and No. 6 on alternate days throughout the season will undoubtedly kill his game much cleaner and farther with the former than with the latter, provided he be a good shot. On the other hand, an average shot would certainly find he succeeded much better with No. 6 than with No. 5.

As to quantity, not less than $1\frac{1}{8}$ oz. of No. 5 should be used in a 12-bore, of ordinary weight; an ounce, as before remarked, gives rather too open a pattern with this sized shot, though one ounce only of No. 6 may be used if desired on account of the number of pellets this shot contains to the ounce. Again: $1\frac{1}{8}$ oz. No. 5 will not, from its larger size, and so its less amount of friction, cause more recoil than will an ounce of No. 6. An ounce and an eighth of No. 6 may be fired to advantage from a fairly heavy gun—one, for instance, weighing 7 lbs.; if under 7 lbs., this charge will be found excessive, should heavy shooting be indulged in. In concluding the above remarks, the shooter may be advised to bear in mind that shot increases in penetration with the larger sizes, and also becomes of course more open in its pattern—that is, the pellets, being fewer, diverge more and more, and leave a greater space between them for game to escape through without being struck. With the smaller the reverse is the case; each lessening size strikes with diminished force whilst its pattern increases—that is, the pellets strike closer together, as they become more numerous to the ounce. The smaller the shot the larger must be the proportion of powder, as small shot, in consequence of its excess of density and friction over large shot, requires more propelling power to drive it properly. The larger the shot, the less the recoil experienced. For this reason, we have found that $1\frac{1}{4}$ oz. of No. 4 shot in a full-sized 12-bore gun of 7 lbs. with the equivalent of $3\frac{1}{8}$ drs. of black powder does not give a recoil perceptibly heavier than $1\frac{1}{8}$ oz. of No. 6, and certainly the former is a deadly charge to use on strong wild game.

CARTRIDGES.

It has already been said that when breechloaders were first introduced nothing in the shape of a central-fire case or gun was thought of; pin-fires alone were offered to shooters. At first, too, the cases for the breechloader were troublesome in the extreme—they split, they stuck, and had other serious faults, not the least of which was a frequent miss-fire, and a cartridge extractor was a necessary item in the shooter's equipment. They were much too weak, and it was a constant and most annoying occurrence to pull off the base of a cartridge when endeavouring to extract it from the gun. These defects were, however, gradually remedied, and when the central-fire gun came into use the cartridges for it may be said to have been well-nigh perfected. The latter were at length made capable of being loaded several times ; a percentage of but one miss-fire, or even less, was obtained in a thousand shots; and they were constructed of such uniform size and of such damp-resisting material that there was very rarely any difficulty about extracting them. In fact, from the early days of breechloaders down to the advent of hammerless guns, little fault has ever been found by shooters with their cartridges. Hammerless guns, however, gave a fresh impetus to the inventive powers of the cartridge-makers, for they had to overcome a defect in their manufacture previously considered of no moment, and scarcely even recognised as existing. This default was the slight escape of the gas, generated by the explosion of the powder round the cap placed in the base of all central-fire cartridges. Now it was found that this escape, slight as it was, and though it did not regularly occur, was quite enough to rust the delicate mechanism inside a hammerless gun, which mechanism it reached by passing round the strikers and so directly into the locks of the gun. This disadvantage could not, of course, occur with a hammer gun, as there is in such a weapon no connection between its locks and the base of the cartridge, however much the gas escaped from the latter. This little trouble it was necessary to overcome, as the locks of a hammerless gun, besides being liable to accident from the rust caused by the action of the gas forced into them, could not easily be taken to pieces and cleaned.

The retention in the cartridge and barrel before the shot was expelled of all the gas developed by the combustion of the powder was in consequence insisted upon in the interests of the new guns. The cartridge-makers had for some years previously warranted their cases gas-tight, and used various elastic solutions, such as indiarubber or varnish, to make them so ; but the most perfect cases frequently proved faulty in this respect when fired from hammerless guns, as the interiors of the latter, when examined, too plainly demonstrated, and especially so when used with quick-burning powders.

The first cartridge maker to remedy this state of affairs was the well-known manufacturer, Mr. Joyce, who in 1882 patented a perfectly gas-tight cartridge case. This he achieved by making his cases slightly smaller than usual at the base, and for a short distance up their length; this space he filled up with the sides of a capsule of very thin brass, the crown or head of which fitted over the base of the case, and so entirely covered the cap. The capsule was of such thin material that the strikers were able to ignite the detonating cap through it, and the former being strong enough not to give way under pressure, it confined the gas inside the cartridge at the moment of explosion and prevented any escape at its base, such as had formerly been liable to occur. This case answered all its requirements admirably, but fearing lest the monopoly of the sale of gas-tight cartridges should go to one firm, the gun-makers did what they could to improve hammerless guns, so that they might be used without damage to their locks with any other cartridges in the market. The result is that nearly all hammerless guns are now made with small channels cut into the face of the false breech from the strikers to the outside of the gun, this being supposed to conduct the gas that escapes from the cap of the cartridge into the outer air. Though this plan is fairly successful, and in part succeeds in keeping the locks from rusting, it does not do so entirely, as does Mr. Joyce's absolutely gas-tight cartridge case.

Formerly there were but four descriptions of cartridges, green, buff, blue, and brown; but now several other colours have been added by different makers, so that it is not possible to classify them. The all-brass cartridges are not as a matter of fact largely used at present, but the best, and those in most favour, have a thin brass case covered with paper. Messrs. Eley have for some time made brass cartridges, as have also various American firms—indeed, in the States an inferior kind has been in use for a long time. But it rested with Messrs.

Kynoch, of Witton, near Birmingham, to produce a better style of brass cartridge case than had been previously known, and this they did in 1882. This case is drawn out of solid brass without a joint, except, of course, at its base; is perfectly watertight; weighs exactly the same as a paper case, to which it is, for certain purposes, such as, for instance, wildfowl shooting, superior. It is, however, necessary to explain why it has not come into general use.

The brass case, though of precisely the same outside diameter, being very much thinner in substance than the paper case, has necessarily a larger interior diameter; consequently the wads that fit it are of larger size than those that fit a paper case. Thus it stands to reason that if a brass case be used in an ordinary gun bored for a paper case, the wads in the former, being somewhat too large for the bore of the barrel, offer more obstruction to the powder than is the case with the paper cartridge, the wads of which just fit the gun. Hence increased recoil and loss of penetrative power are the result. On the other hand, if the gun be bored to take brass cases, then the wads of the brass cartridges are, of course, of suitable size, as in this instance the barrels are bored to fit them, just as in another gun they are bored to fit the wads fired from a paper case. The brass cases, when used in guns bored expressly to suit them, outrival in a slight degree in their performances the paper cases, as used in guns bored for the latter.

The chief reason for the supposed excellence of brass cases in shooting lies in the fact that their sides are so very thin that the wads pass from them down the barrel without meeting any obstruction, such as the cone between the end of the chamber and the barrel, which is necessitated by the paper case, and without which the latter would not fit the gun. To sportsmen shooting in wild, out-of-the-way places these brass cases are invaluable, provided they fit their guns, as they can be reloaded fifty times or more if necessary. Nevertheless, from the above remarks it will be readily seen that, unless brass cases can be made to suit ordinary guns, as bored for paper cases, they will not for many years, if indeed ever, come into general use by our game-shooters at home ; for it cannot be expected that the thousands of new guns now in use will be put aside by their owners, and other guns ordered purposely for brass cases. Besides, there is great difficulty in turning out these metal cases of accurate size, their rims now and then varying in this respect, and so causing great annoyance to a shooter by permitting the cartridge to slip behind the extractor. Another reason why they do not meet with approval is the unpleasantness of their sharp pointed ends (both in carrying and packing them), which cannot be turned down in brass as in ordinary paper cases ; while, as ejector guns are in all but universal use, men do not buy cartridge cases with the idea of reloading them ; and, after all, the magnitude of the cartridge trade is proof positive that only a small percentage of game shots in England ever load their own cartridges at all.

CAPS.

In the days of the old black powder, the cap, so long as it would explode with certainty, did not need very much selection. To-day, however, with so many nitro-powders in use, the cap is a very important item in the sportsman's ammunition. Experiments have conclusively shown that the strength of virtually all the powders is much affected by the kind of cap used, and, as will be seen by the remarks in the table of loads, special caps are required for some of the powders, a point which those who load their own cartridges should be careful not to overlook, as it is only by conforming strictly to the instructions of the different makers that the best results can be obtained. It may be noticed, however, that in no case should a strong cap be used ; the makers of all nitro-powders not requiring special caps giving their preference to those of medium degree.

WADS.

The subject of wads is not always taken into consideration by a shooter ; still, it is one of no little consequence as regards the shooting of a gun. In the days of muzzle-loaders, and even when breech-loaders were first used, it was the custom to place thin felt wads over the powder as well as the shot. Over the shot of the charge a wad is only necessary to keep it in place, and if this could be dispensed with is no more required than one would be on the bullet in a rifle. When experimenting we have made a gun shoot harder without any wad on the shot, by merely keeping the latter from dislodging through coating the surface pellets of the charge with varnish. But of course a wad over the shot is a necessity to retain the latter in position when the cartridge is moved about, or placed in the guns.

As, however, the scientific side of shooting came to attract attention, and both shooting men and makers grew to believe more and more in the importance of small things, it became apparent, even in the days of black powder, and of course much more so since the general use of the nitro-powders, that the wads in the cartridge exercised no little influence on the shooting of the gun.

The makers of all the varieties of powder have now, after making experiments, decided upon what they think is the best arrangement of wads for each. The shooter, therefore, who desires to load his own cartridges, will be well advised to communicate with the makers of the powder of his selection and obtain from them the most minute instructions, even to the amount of turnover. At the cost of sixpence the sportsman can obtain from the Sporting Goods Review Newspaper Company, 69 Aldersgate Street, E.C., a card on which are given full instructions for loading cartridges with the different powders.

Speaking generally, a card wad is placed on the powder, and then comes a felt wad, while a card only is needed over the shot. There are, however, sundry variations, some of the powder companies recommending a 'Field' card; a thick card; a thin card, or grey cloth over the powder. Others, again, leave an alternative between thick and thin felts on a second card. Various felts are suggested, but in all but one

I. I

case (Schultze) a thin card is recommended over the shot; but if an open pattern be desired with Schultze a thick card or grey cloth wad should be used over the shot, a thin card being employed when a close pattern is desired.

PROOF OF GUNS WITH NITRO-POWDERS.

So long ago as the year 1883, a well-known shooting man wrote : 'A Government proof mark on every gun was to some extent a guarantee against its bursting, as almost any charge that could be crammed into a well-made weapon would not harm it. Now, however, a very trifling overcharge of these new explosives—nitro-powders—seems sufficient to damage if not to burst even the strongest gun.' The last Proof Act was passed in 1868 ; but the new rules and regulations for the proof of guns, which appeared in the ' London Gazette ' for January 3, 1888, were for all practical purposes a sort of schedule to the old statute, though for many purposes they were virtually a new Act. The tenth rule, however, was noteworthy, inasmuch as it for the first time made the proof of guns with nitro-powders possible and attainable, though, as will be readily understood, not compulsory. The rule in question deals with barrels of weapons of any description, which, at the request in writing of any person or persons sending the same for definitive proof, may be proved with Schultze, or E.C. powder, or with any particular description of gunpowder which might be specified by the sender, after and in addition to the ordinary proofs. The service charges of these explosives were to be determined by the London and Birmingham Proof Companies from time to time, and it was provided that the quantity of the powders to be used in proof should be such as the Companies decided would give a strain as much in excess of the service charge as was the proof charge of the black powder in excess of the service charge of that explosive. This was certainly a step in advance, for in the early days of nitro-powders it cannot be denied, as already pointed out, that they varied greatly in their power according to circumstances, though that shortcoming has now to a certain extent been remedied. Still, shooting men have availed themselves to a comparatively small extent of the opportunity thus afforded them for having their guns tested by nitro-powders. It is well, however, to inform sportsmen that at a very small fee their guns can be proved with any nitro-powders they choose to select.

GUN-CASES.

A word about these. It is never safe to take valuable guns about in any kind of case whatever, except a solid one in the form of a box—one that will protect the guns from injury even though the case fall off a carriage to the ground, or be otherwise maltreated. We often see guns taken out with linen or woollen covers, and so shoved under the seat of a dog-cart, where they are liable to be knocked about. A soft cover is no protection to a gun except from what can be removed with a cloth on reaching home—a matter of no importance as regards the weapon. The parts of a gun that chiefly require protection are the barrels, as the slightest knock of these against any metal will probably injure their shooting.

If guns cannot be taken about in a solid leather box, they should, though it is not nearly so safe a plan, be fitted in stout stiff leather covers of the shape of the cloth pattern. For this purpose a very good case is now made that takes gun and stock in separate partitions. This is a good makeshift, but a shooter would be unwise to move about with a good gun even in this contrivance. The best gun-case, though, strange to say, it is seldom seen, is one that will take a gun, or two, at full length. This case is no heavier than any other; it takes up little more space—and space in this respect is not often of any consequence. On opening the case the gun is presented ready for immediate use, and the risk of letting the stock or barrels fall to the ground when putting them together out of doors is obviated. It may be imagined that there is no risk of such an accident, yet we have seen fully a dozen guns at different times sent to be repaired in consequence of keepers, when putting them together, allowing the barrels or stock, as the case might be, to slip from the fingers on the flags of a stone courtyard or else on a hard road—an accident that happens to guns oftener than their owners are aware of, the result being, perhaps, a tiny bulge in the barrels that destroys their good shooting. Besides which, a gun fitted in a case that allows it to be kept together as when in actual use saves no little wear and tear of putting together, and prevents grit or sand settling on the false breech, or breech of the barrels, where such particles do much to wear away and so loosen the air-tight grip that should exist between barrels and stock.

The best oak and leather cases for two guns cost six guineas ; for one gun, four pounds ten shillings. Solid leather cases for two guns are sold for five pounds, or for one gun at half a sovereign less ; while the Hurlingham pattern with outside pocket can be had for fifty-five shillings, and five shillings more will buy a Hurlingham case to take one stock and two pairs of barrels.

CLEANING GUNS.

Cleaning guns is a subject which must not be omitted. At the end of the day the barrels should be rubbed through with turpentine, which removes the 'leading ;' afterwards they can be oiled by means of a piece of saturated tow pushed through them with a stick ; this is a better plan than wrapping it round a brass-ended rod. There are, however, a hundred recipes that might be given for this purpose. To keep a gun clean when laid by and not daily inspected : cover the barrels, outside, with an equal mixture of best paraffin and refined neatsfoot oils ; stop up the barrels with corks or wads, and place inside each barrel a quarter of a pint of the same mixture, shaking it well up and down the interior ; then pour it back again into a bottle for further use. Another way is to coat the metal, outside, with mercurial ointment, well-strained goose-grease (a capital preparation), or, perhaps best of all, vaseline with a little paraffin added to it ; inside, draw a rag soaked in one of these mixtures backwards and forwards a few times by means of a string.

When a gun that has previously been cleaned has to be preserved from rust for a week or two of disuse, tie one end of a string to a peg in the wall (not a nail, for fear of scratches), and secure a bullet on its other end, which will pass easily through the barrel. Several pieces of rag soaked in oil can be attached to the string at intervals. For the locks and furniture of a gun a soft tooth-brush will be found very useful. To send guns home from abroad by a sea voyage with no one to look after their interests *en route* : take off the locks, fittings, and barrels ; put all these latter in a tin box with some wadding between them ; fill with oil, and solder up tight. Remember that the only method of keeping a gun clean and so preserving it consists in shutting out the air, and consequently the damp. Anything that will do this by remaining on the metal without evaporation will answer.

When a gun is put by for the season, tight-fitting rods covered with green baize are the best things for the purpose, as far as the barrels are concerned, provided both barrels and rods are absolutely free from damp.

If barrels become much leaded, some quicksilver rolled up and down inside them will amalgamate with the lead and remove it, and the mercury can be put back in a bottle and used as often as wished. Gun-locks, whether in or out of use, should never be touched with thick oil, as this will collect dirt and become sticky, and is indeed a frequent cause of 'clogging' in the action of a lock, an occurrence that is full of danger, especially in a hammerless gun. Paraffin, when left wet on a gun and exposed to the air, evaporates rapidly when by itself— in fact, creates rust. On a lock, and protected from the atmosphere, it answers well if refined, and with it a lock will 'speak' with that pleasant 'snick' that tells it is in good working order. But better than paraffin for a lock is chronometer oil,[1] as sold by the clock-makers, or else carefully refined neatsfoot. It takes some time to prepare the latter, but almost enough for a lifetime can then be refined. The following is the best method :—

Purified Neatsfoot Oil.—Procure half a pint of the best fresh neatsfoot oil ; let.it stand till all the thick has sunk to the bottom ; pour off only the clear or bright part into a bottle ; to this add a quarter of an ounce of powdered animal charcoal, shake up well and let it stand for twenty-four to thirty-six hours ; strain off into a bottle half filled with bright lead shavings ; place it in a light place, a sunny spot if possible, when all the thick and fatty particles of the oil will sink and adhere to the bright lead. It is generally necessary to pour the oil carefully, avoiding all sediment, on to a second set of lead shavings. After that it may be transferred to small bottles for use, which must be kept well corked. The whole process will take some three weeks to complete.

To keep a gun in nice order when in constant use, provided the smell is not objected to, nothing is better, cheaper, or more simple than refined paraffin to take rust off, or to use for every part of a gun ; but it must be well rubbed from all exposed parts soon after putting on. When applying oil to the action and lock of the gun it cannot be put on too thin ; the working parts of the lock especially should be very lightly touched (having been carefully rubbed dry and clean) and very seldom —twice in a season at most.

When a gun is cleaned and will not be wanted for a week or so, put in each barrel a stick covered with thin flannel or baize wrapped round several times, and then neatly stitched

[1] Chronometer oil is an admirable solution with which to touch the locks and working parts of a gun *inside* by means of a feather, these parts having been previously made *quite* clean and dry.

to prevent it from loosening, till it fits the barrel fairly tight, the flannel to be slightly coated with neatsfoot oil or vaseline : a twist of either stick, if the gun is not used as soon as expected, will keep all in order inside. These rods can be washed when necessary. To clean the insides of gun-barrels quickly use a single rod, also covered with flannel ; bind collars of string tightly round it an inch apart. This will cause little ridges to rise if the stick is thin and the covering thick. The stick may have a handle-knob at one end. Though the flannel get quite black from dirt and oil, it will polish a gun well nevertheless, and can be washed when necessary.

If a gun is in a very bad state of rust, pour boiling water over the affected parts, and afterwards rub in paraffin, taking care, however, to wipe off the oil. Paraffin will in time remove the browning from the barrels of a gun, it is true ; but that will come off, sooner or later, whatever method of cleaning is adopted, though perhaps not so soon with other oils as with paraffin.

To remove the bulk of the dirt in foul barrels, the scratch and wool brushes, screw-rods, &c., that gunmakers sell are of little use, as they do not fit the barrel tightly enough to drive the accumulation quickly out ; they merely smear it down flat and pass over it, thus giving a great deal more trouble than is necessary, and the amount of brass they are usually furnished with is detrimental to a barrel, save in most careful hands.

A keeper will find something to fit a barrel tightly soon enough, as he knows the gun will otherwise take some time to clean. But how does he often set to work ? Not unfrequently he puts in a cloth, passes it half-way through the barrel with a sharp-pointed brass-ended rod, such as are sold in gunmakers' shops. This naturally very often jams, as it wedges into the cloth more and more. Then it is a case of a sound rap of the other end of the rod against a stone floor : through come rod and cloth. The gun is polished, as the manipulator sees to his satisfaction when putting the barrel between the

light and his eye. Some day the owner of the weapon is surprised to hear from his gunmaker that the barrels of his last
new, or favourite old gun, are bulged.

A description is annexed of a very good contrivance for
cleaning out a gun-barrel; the most clumsy-fisted attendant
could not scratch or injure with it.

To make a cleaning rod for shoulder-guns as here shown :
Procure a sound straight stick of ash, six inches longer than the
barrel and a quarter of an inch smaller in diameter than the
bore. Carefully drill a hole at one end to take a thin $2\frac{3}{4}$-in.
brass screw up to its neck, leaving that part about an inch outside the wood. Procure a wad-cutter to just fit the bore of the
gun at the breech end. Stamp out of $\frac{1}{8}$-in. thick soft leather
a dozen or so wads. Through their centre work little holes with
the point of a penknife, just large enough to fit the neck of the

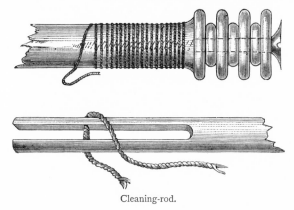

Cleaning-rod.

screw. Cut some of the wads smaller than others after the
holes are bored. Place a full-sized one and a small one
alternately on the neck of the screw, and turn the screw in
home ; bind this end of the stick with waxed thread to
strengthen against a split. The leather wads should be kept
soaked in a wineglass or small bottle of thick oil, and may be
changed on the stick about once a year if much used.

A gunmaker could, no doubt, turn out something neater with brass ferrule and washer, but it could not answer better.

At the other end of the stick, as shown in sketch, saw down a 3-in. slit with a stout saw ; bore a hole through the stick previously at right angles to the cut. Keep at hand, strung on a piece of wire, some 6-in. square bits of flannel or baize. Dip one lightly in turpentine, and, after cleaning out the rough dirt with the other end of the rod, work this end through. The flannel should be folded across and put in the slit, and a scrap of cord firmly tied through the hole to keep it fast. The bits of flannel can be washed when required, and cleaner bits kept for the final polishing.[1]

By this means the most valuable of guns cannot be damaged ; and a pet pair of Purdey's need not be cleaned on the sly rather than trusted out of hand.

SORE FINGER.—We mention this subject last, as it has no regular place in connection with the foregoing remarks. A sore finger often results from a shooter grasping his gun too loosely and too close to the trigger-guard ; the consequence being, that on firing the gun, the recoil drives the trigger-guard back against the finger with no little violence, as the gun slides through the hands of its user. The best way to obviate this troublesome and painful affliction is to grasp the gun firmly with the forefinger well free of the guard, then the latter and the former come back together and no blow results from the explosion of the gun.

If this plan fails, a pistol stock may be effectual, especially if its grip be somewhat coarsely roughed ; but the best method is to lengthen the grip of the gun, and to get the slope of the trigger-guard altered, so that by lengthening the latter it offers

[1] Do not push the rod right through *at first*, but place the muzzle ends of the barrels against a piece of soft wood or felt hung on the wall. Push the leather head up and down till all the dirt is collected at the end of each barrel, then push the rod through and finish off with the rag.

no angle to the fingers ; and in the case of a new gun, to have the triggers sloped well back in the guard, so that the shooter can pull them without bringing his second finger within risk of a blow of the guard.

A sore finger in our experience is not seldom caused by the really bad fit of the gun to the shoulder of its owner, which makes the recoil far more severely felt than would be the case with a properly fitting stock.

R. P. G.

CHAPTER VII.

SHOOTERS.

THE best kind of shooter is he who is a genuine sportsman at heart, one, for instance, who is equally happy whether he be beating a bit of marsh for the chance at the two or three snipe it may contain, waiting in the twilight for an occasional shot at a duck, or standing outside a well-stocked covert from which the pheasants are being driven over his head in scores. It is a common idea amongst men who shoot in a small way, and are pleased with, perhaps, a dozen head of game to their guns apiece in a day, that the man who, on the other hand, kills his game by hundreds, as a matter of course despises all moderate sport. This notion is an erroneous one. A real sportsman is never spoilt by the abundance of game he is fortunate enough to kill, or rather get the opportunity of killing. It is quite true that he likes his big day (so would the shooter on a smaller scale for that matter, could he get the chance), but he would be equally pleased with a healthy tramp over the country and a small bag, if a thorough sportsman—and indeed our best shots and most famous shooters are often thus satisfied with the small results gained by the exercise of woodcraft and of skill with the gun. To a true sporting shooter it is not the amount of game he kills, but the way he kills it ; and it is a certain fact that those men who get the very best shooting England can afford take more delight in dropping dead a long or difficult shot than in accounting for a hundred easy ones, which would not be the case if they cared only for the quantity of game they bagged. This feeling is so universal amongst

English shooters and owners of shootings, that their one idea is to make the game fly or run so as to afford as difficult marksmanship as possible, and hence give it as good a chance of escaping as is fair and feasible, having regard to the necessity of procuring it without wounding. There is a great deal of ill-natured, ignorant, and what may be called envious, talk about good shooting nowadays, and it is a pity that would-be critics cannot be made to realise the above statements. Of course there are exceptions to every rule, as there are shooters and shooters; now and then one hears of men who really do kill for killing's sake, and not as a means of testing their skill with the gun, who care nothing for the sporting task necessary in arranging and in carrying out a day's shooting; but such men are, fortunately, very exceptional, and are growing rarer every season.

Ignorant people imagine that a shooter who is accustomed to take a part in the killing of five hundred pheasants, grouse or partridges, as the case may be, would refuse an invitation to assist in killing a hundred. This is all nonsense; a shooter, if he be a sportsman, whoever he be, would delight in a 'small' day, provided his skill were taxed in shooting, and more especially in manœuvring, the game. He would far sooner kill his share of the hundred, if sporting and difficult shots, than join in the five-hundred-head day, if the latter were easy shooting, which is very rarely the case. As to whether a shooter account for a score or a hundred birds in the day, this in no way affects the question. A sportsman ought to be, and usually is, a man who takes a delight in using his gun *and* brains. It is a common idea that shooting on a large scale requires only the use of the former and not the latter; but never was there a greater mistake, as those who comment so unfavourably on the modern pheasant or grouse shooter would soon find out could they be put in a position to discover the truth. It has already been said that there are shooters and shooters; let us take as an example a good specimen of the race.

He is a man with a wonderful aptitude for observing the habits of wild birds and animals, combined with all the physical qualities requisite for a good marksman and a country life. He possesses great precision of judgment as to the pace and

The Right Sort.

distance of any moving object, with a wonderful command of eye, hand and nerve, and usually excels more or less in all the athletic and other amusements dear to Englishmen, such as cricket, riding, fishing, and billiards. He looks, and is, thoroughly workmanlike from top to toe, and you will find that all details of his equipment, be they his guns or the buttons of his leggings, are as perfect as may be for practical use. Like the Lincoln-shire poacher in the well-known song, he can 'run and jump,' not to say walk, as few other men can, without, of course, equalling those whose lives are devoted to special performances in such feats only. He is cool and self-possessed, never a jealous shot, and lets everybody get and keep his respective chances at birds or animals, for he is quite content to obtain his own proper share. He is kind and generous to keepers, though never familiar, is devoted to dogs, and is generally popular. When shooting, though rarely in a hurry, he never idles, nor does he move about in excitement here and there. He goes at once to his post when it is pointed out to him, and is always therefore on the watch for the first bird or animal that comes his way. With him it is never a case of 'There go some birds, I must go to my stand and finish my story another time.' No! he is always *in* his place in good time, is ever on the watch for the stir of but a rabbit, and his gun is, by the way he grasps it, also available for instant use. His gun comes to his shoulder just at the right moment without any flurry, and down comes the object just at the right moment too ; and though he never endeavours to over-reach a fellow-shooter, or takes any evident precautions to obtain an undue proportion of shots, somehow he seems to get more shooting than anybody else, not really (as it appears) from chance, but because he by instinct knows where to look for game and what direction it will take. He never, unless directly questioned, alludes to his own skill, though others do not fail to do so, and rather gives the idea that he does not himself know how well he shoots. Last, not least, a true sportsman (this implies, as shown above, a deal more than merely a good marksman) rarely wounds ; his game is retrieved without difficulty or waste of time, is never spoilt, and so made unfit for food ; it is in fact killed clean at all reasonable distances.

On the other hand a bad, 'unsporting' shot is a man who,

to begin with, is *never* satisfied with his shooting or the behaviour of the game, while of the habits of the latter he has
little knowledge. He is constantly remarking, 'I can't shoot
a bit to-day' (as if on other days he never missed), or 'The
birds did not come well for me.'

The Gent from Town.

The effect.

This latter is a favourite excuse for
a bad shot, as he wishes to imply that
the game did not give him a chance
of killing it, however well he might have
shot, though it, was evident to the onlookers that he missed shot after shot
of the simplest description. It is also
wonderful in the case of a bad shot
what an amount of game he has down
at a distance, and how very little near
him to pick up. Most of his birds, from his account, went
away desperately hard hit, towered, and fell dead just over
some hedge or clump he points out on the horizon. He
implores the keeper (who knows him well) to go at once for
them; the latter smiles grimly and remarks, 'No time now, sir;

if they be dead they won't move, and I and the dog can easily find them at the end of the day—*if so be, sir, you arn't mistaken'* (the latter sentence being a little bit of sarcasm, for the keeper knows that seeking the bad shot's towering birds is, from experience, but labour in vain). Indeed, we have known a keeper throw down a dead bird out of his pocket to the ground, and afterwards pick it up in full view of the unsporting shot in order to satisfy him and so allow the day's sport to be proceeded with. A bad, unsporting shot is for ever explaining *why* he does not shoot better—an explanation that no one cares one jot about.

He is no judge of distance, and will as readily fire at a bird or animal eighty paces off as he will at one but fifteen. After a long shot he may be seen shading his eyes with his hands as if he expected the bird to drop, and as a suggestion that the said bird was hard hit and will not go far—anything rather than that it should be thought he made a clean miss. Such a shot is also usually a jealous one, as he is anxious to get as much shooting as he can so that his bag may not be so scanty as to cause comment, and he is very fond, when he has fired at another man's bird, of exclaiming, as the better marksman drops it and he clean misses it, 'There is plenty of shot in that bird, any way. I pity the people who have to eat it!' thus implying that the bird was equally peppered by both shooters. He will, indeed, even claim it as his if he gets the chance, or say, 'I believe that last bird we both shot at was dead before *you* fired, was it not?' The bad, unsporting shot will neither keep in line when walking up, nor remain at his post when driving, game, as he constantly disobeys orders under the impression that he is in the wrong place to get shots, and would do better a little to the right or left. This he does, of course, in his own interests as he imagines, but it usually turns out a disastrous mistake, and one that affects not only himself and the other guns as regards security from accident, but also the finding or driving of the game. Such a man, too, is usually careless with his gun, as safety is the last thing in his mind, and getting shots the first, anyhow and anywhere. His gun may be seen pointing in all directions, and now and then even sweeping in its aim every living thing near him ; besides, he has a dangerous habit of constantly putting it up to his shoulder, finger on trigger,

The Wrong Sort.

at game, and then bringing it down again, for he is fearful of risking a miss. He is incorrigible too as a loiterer; if placed at a stand to be ready for driven game, likely enough he paces about cigarette in his mouth and gun over his shoulder, looking meanwhile in an opposite direction to that from which the

game *must* come, and till several birds have perchance passed
by him, either unnoticed or before he has put himself into an
attitude of readiness.

The unsporting shot has been taken as a type, but there
are plenty of merely bad shots who are excellent fellows in
every way, who readily admit they are bad shots, who never
pretend to be anything else and never will, but who are, nevertheless, thorough sportsmen as well as pleasant and fair shooters,
and who behave just as do the good shots, save only in respect
of their want of skill in marksmanship. And, let it be added,
by the good-natured way in which they stand the friendly
banter of the more accomplished sportsmen concerning their
willingly confessed lack of precision, they make themselves
popular with everyone with whom they shoot.

As in cricket, billiards, tennis, and many other games of skill,
nine out of ten people reach just about the same point of excellence, and the tenth only gets beyond the average. It is to
be this tenth man that every young shooter should strive (as in
everything else as well as shooting). Many young sportsmen,
were they to begin directly they left school and practise hard
every day, would never succeed in being number ten as far as
marksmanship with a gun is concerned, simply because, though
they do their best, they are not gifted by nature with the
peculiar powers of hand, nerve, and eye that are essential.
Though they reach a certain point, do what they will, they
cannot get beyond it ; yet to others everything seems to
come naturally, and they finally end by becoming first-class
performers with the gun, as well as in other sports that require a perfect eye, nerve, and judgment to a greater or less
degree.

Jealous shooting is an abomination, and at once fatal to
the good-fellowship of a party. Directly anything like 'wiping
eyes' begins, or is even talked of, among young sportsmen,
the older men wish themselves at home. If you do perchance 'wipe the eye,' as it is vulgarly called, of another
shooter, take no notice of it, treat it as an accident, apologise,

say you only fired by mistake, or because you thought your friend did not see the game in question, or that he hit the bird hard, and not having, as you thought, another barrel left, you judged it better to kill it if you could, which by good luck you succeeded in doing. 'Wiping another's eye' only means retribution ; the slighted man, especially if a young shooter, will never rest till he has paid you back the compliment, and, perhaps, not content with doing it once, he may do so regularly for the rest of the day, till his wounded pride is soothed, and neither he nor you will feel certain as to what to fire at, and what not, when by chance shooting side by side. Many a bird will in consequence be loaded with shot, and so quite spoilt for food. Nothing is too 'tricky' for a really jealous shot, so long as by cunning devices he can secure to himself an undue share of sport. We once saw such a 'trickster' paid off in his own coin, and though we do not in the least approve of any 'dodges' or 'tricks' as between shooters, the incident was so good that it is here related.

A parson, a keen, jealous, and very wild shot, and a well-known lawyer, with other guns, were walking up a young plantation shooting the pheasants as they rose over the tops of the trees in front of them, and driving others forward to the one gun stationed at the end of the wood, who chanced to be a very stout, lame, red-nosed, and choleric old general. The lawyer was ambling in comfort down the open ride, at the end of which the general was standing, expecting shots and getting a few now and then. The lawyer shot several times into the trees over the general's head, the latter constantly roaring out, 'Let 'em rise, sir! let 'em rise!' At last the general was seen by the lawyer, with an evident explosion of oaths, to pull out his hand-kerchief and apply it to his nose, laying down his gun at the same time, and retiring behind a tree. The lawyer realised that he had peppered the man of war, and dreaded the con-sequence. Now it so happened that the parson had several times tried to jockey the lawyer off the ride, and was jealous of

the latter's easy position in the open, whilst *he* was struggling
and tearing through the covert close by, scarcely getting a shot,
muttering against his luck, and appealing to the lawyer to
change places. This the latter offered to do directly he
perceived something was wrong with the general, owing to
his last shot having been in that direction. Highly pleased,
the reverend shooter strode down the coveted open glade, and
on at length reaching its end came face to face with the
injured general, who with a capacious bandanna was endeavouring to stem a small rivulet of blood that flowed from a
shot pellet which had lodged in the exact centre of the tip
of his nose. We *have* heard hard swearing afloat and ashore,
but anything to equal the volley of abuse that for five minutes
the wounded sportsman 'fired' at the parson we never en-
countered. 'A disgrace to your cloth, sir!' was the mildest expression used ; and on the poor parson trying to explain that
he could not have been the culprit (as indeed he was not), he
was told not to make the matter worse by trying to put the
blame on others. 'You shot me, sir!' quoth the general,
as he mopped his nose—'shot me all over—limbs, body, and
head ; you did nothing but shoot straight into me from one
end of the ride to the other, till you saw I was wounded,
and then you would have hit me again but that I got into
shelter!'

It has already been pointed out what great pains should be
taken to teach a beginner (usually a boy just leaving school) to
shoot with safety, his lessons in aiming being quite of secondary
importance compared to the way he handles and uses his
gun. A wild and ardent overgrown schoolboy with a gun is
usually an object of terror to experienced shooters. It is a
case of *sauve qui peut*, and we feel almost inclined to write, your
only chance is to shoot the boy before he shoots you. We
once knew such a one who peppered a friend's legs in shooting
at a rabbit running by him. As our friend was 'nursing' the
more injured leg of the two, and standing like a stork on the
other as he twirled round with pain, the youth came up, and,

with every honest expression of regret, remarked, amongst other things, ' You see, Mr. ——, I thought there was *a clear yard* between you and the rabbit, or really I would never have fired ! '

There are some shooting hosts who make a business of a pleasure, who, from the moment they go out till the time the final counting up of the bag takes place in the evening, carry a worried, anxious face, such as might be seen on a minister endeavouring to avoid a useless war between his own and another country. If anything goes amiss in the arrangements, from a few birds going back to the appearance of the wrong kind of pie for luncheon, such a man looks and feels miserable, and will not recognise for the rest of the afternoon any of the little humours and excitements that tend to make a day's shooting so agreeable to his guests. His looks are reflected by his keepers, who feel they will be ' spoken to ' later on, and the latter, not to be outdone, scowl on the beaters. The difference between a day's sport directed by a cheerful host, and by one who frets as to what is going on in the field, and scolds all round if a trifling mistake occurs, is vast as regards the enjoyment of the day to every man and dog who takes part in it ; for if the master is ' crossed,' so are the keepers, so are the beaters, and even the poor dogs come in for more kicks than commendation. It was said of the late Lord ——, a man of notoriously violent temper, that on finding a scarcity of partridges in a field wherein he had expected good sport, he would in a fury throw himself on the ground and *gnaw the turnips*—a story that requires more than the usual grain of salt to swallow, and yet it is one that is often repeated.

There is also the host who ranks as a martinet, with whom a day's shooting is a military pageant. Stern and silent he stalks about, and woe betide the beater who gets out of line, the boy who talks, or the dog that chases. Home any such go at once, as an example to the rest. His guests march solemnly about—they dare not jest. We recollect a disciplinarian (a bad shot, too, besides being deaf) of this kind, who, when

walking up a wood, peppered a boy, and was thus addressed
by a keeper :—

'Beg pardon, sir.'

'Well, what is it? You will put everything up if you shout
like that.'

'Beg pardon, sir, you have wounded a boy!'

'Wounded a what?'

'A boy, sir!'

'Careless idiot! Serve him right for getting in the way!
Send him home at once, and tell him not to let me catch him
out again to-day.'

While talking of martinets in connection with shooting, we
cannot forbear quoting the following story (a perfectly accurate one, too, as we happen to know) told by that clever and
thorough sportsman, the late Mr. Bromley Davenport. It
runs :—

A noble lord, a distinguished cavalry officer, and an awful martinet, had a large shooting party, when, in spite of endless loudly-
given orders, marchings, and counter-marchings of beaters, everything seemed to go wrong, pheasants included. So at the end of
a covert in which little had been found, and that little not properly
'brought to the gun,' the head keeper was summoned, and, all re-
splendent in green and gold as he was, advanced with abject mien,
faltering some trembling excuses to his now almost rabid master,
who, cutting these sternly short, asked : 'Shall we find more in the
next covert?' 'I hope so, my lord.' 'Hope, sir!' roared the
peer, with terrific emphasis on the verb. 'Do you think I give
you 100*l.* a year to *hope*? Now, go and beat that wood this way,
and I'll post the guns.' 'Your lordship means *this* wood?' said
the terrified functionary, pointing to another. 'No, I don't.' 'But,
my lord——' expostulated the man, now more alarmed than ever.
'Not a word, sir, obey orders!' Irresolute, and evidently much
perplexed, the wretched man marched off with his army and beat
the wood, in which there was absolutely nothing. Terrible then to
see was the wrath of the baffled soldier, till the miserable keeper,
seeing he was about to be dismissed on the spot, cried out in heart-
rending accents : 'It's *not your wood*, my lord. It belongs to
Lord W.' (his neighbour), 'and he shot it last Friday!' All the

keepers and beaters knew this, yet not one had dared to gainsay Achilles in his ire.

Perhaps the shooting host who is himself a dangerous or excitable shot is the most unpleasant of all men to shoot with, as he has more opportunities of causing mischief than have any of his guests, and cannot be so readily reproved for a culpable act. We remember a well-verified story applying to a man of this sort.

Mr. —— unfortunately wounded a beater. His unfeigned regret was evident ; he bewailed his luck in loud tones, handed his gun to his attendant, vowed fervently he would never shoot, or even take a gun in his hand, again, and was starting for home with sad countenance and many self-abusive remarks on his carelessness.

At that moment, unfortunately, a cry of ' Mark rabbit ! ' sounded close by. ' My gun, quick ! ' shouted Mr. ——, who not only fired over the prostrate form of the injured man lying near him, but in his hurry severely wounded the man who so unluckily drew his attention to the scampering bunny.

On one occasion, a gentleman who had not seen Mr. —— for many years, being invited to shoot with him, and remembering his host's dangerous character in former times, enquired somewhat anxiously of the head keeper on his arrival, if Mr. —— had ever shot anybody ? 'Oh yes,' replied the keeper with befitting seriousness and in a whisper, ' Mr. —— *shoots a man every year, sir !* '

That Mr. —— as a host was otherwise pleasant, and the sport he afforded first rate, may be inferred from the fact of his inducing his friends to run risks of accident ; but ' whose turn next?' must, we imagine, have been a serious consideration at all times for those who shot with him.

A different class of host is the man who, though he is not personally a careless shot himself, invites dangerous men to shoot with him, to the annoyance and risk of careful sportsmen, this serious mistake sometimes occurring from mistaken anxiety to return a compliment or grant a favour.

An amusing incident in this connection, though certainly an exceptional one, may be here related.

Shortly after a general election, the successful candidate being anxious to return civilities to some of his parliamentary supporters who lived in a manufacturing town, at their expressed wish invited them for a day's grouse-driving on his well-stocked moor. The number of applicants increased as the day appointed drew near, till at last no less than twenty-four quasi-sportsmen had permission to shoot, most of them possessing little knowledge of how even to handle a gun. But it could not be helped, and Mr. ——, after explaining matters to a friend, persuaded the latter to form one of the party, and assist in managing the events of the day. The numerous guns appeared in due form, clad in wondrous costume, with guns, dogs, and attendants of every variety. Some of the party ensconced themselves in the grouse boxes, others had to take their chance behind rocks or tufts of heather. The firing was fast and furious, though harmless to the birds, and to say the least, somewhat wild. At length the friend being hit all over his right side vowed he would go home; the situation was too dangerous; he had a wife and children to support by his profession, &c., &c. Mr. —— begged him to remain, if only to see him safely through the day, so the friend returned once more to his shelter after much demur, only to be well peppered on his left side by his other neighbour in the line. This settled the question; home he would go; nothing should now stop him from doing so, as he saw no reason why *his* life should be taken by his host's political supporters. But alas! as he beat a retreat to the railway station further misfortune was in store for him.

He ran safely past the sportsmen till he arrived near the twenty-fourth shooter, but unluckily he put up a grouse, which flying low No. 24 fired at but missed and instead lodged a considerable portion of an ounce of No. 5 shot in the truant's back.

Let us turn to another class, namely, the old-fashioned

shooting host, one with whom it is always a pleasure to shoot, a man popular alike with old and young. The old-fashioned shooter is usually a true sportsman to the backbone. He has a contempt for anyone who kills game at too close a range, instead of allowing it a fair chance. How well we know him! The first time we made the acquaintance of such a one was in the coursing field. As the hare and dogs swept by a group of lookers-on, the latter with one exception encouraged the dogs. The exception was the old fashioned sportsman, who exclaimed, 'Run, puss! run, puss!' and every lineament of his face ex‧ pressed the wish of his heart that the poor hunted hare might escape her pursuers. The old-fashioned sportsman began shooting with flint and steel, and after a long fight at length condescended to a detonating gun by the 'Bishop, of Bond Street.'[1] Now he has his breechloaders, two of which at least are probably converted from favourite old muzzle-loaders. He is popular with the most modern of modern shooters, and if he quietly 'wipes the eye' of a youngster or brings down a woodcock, everyone is pleased, and congratulates him on shooting as well as ever he did—a great compliment, for he is known far and near as having been one of the best shots of his day. The only dissentient is his faithful old attendant, half keeper, half valet, who shakes his head as much as to imply, 'Master is as good as the best even now, but isn't what he was forty years ago.' Later on in the servants' hall the old servant will take the 'smart chaps,' as he calls them, down a peg, by relating some marvellous feats of marksmanship on the part of his master, together with stories of his endurance, deeds accomplished so long ago that even if 'improved' by time, no one can contradict, usually ending up with the sentence, 'I doubt there's not a man in England could do it now!'

The old shooter uses everything he can pertaining to his bygone days. He carefully keeps a suit of clothes that long

---

[1] Bishop was the factotum of Messrs. Westley Richards, the well-known Bond Street gunmakers of a bygone day.

ago he proved were just the thing, as far as comfort and con-venience were concerned, for shooting; these he has had copied by a local tailor, who includes the copper cap pockets, the shoulder leathers, and the strap across the breast for the large topped bamboo loading rod. These are not wanted nowadays, it is true, but they are to their wearer a reminder of bygone seasons; and if a coat has to be copied as faithfully as the old sportsman insists, nothing down to smallest detail must be omitted, even the waterproof lined hare pockets, for long ago shooters went out alone much more than they do now, and often had to carry their own game as they killed it.

Everyone who can possibly do so makes a point of accept-ing an invitation to shoot with the old sportsman, for though he may be a little slow in his movements, his shooting is good and perfectly managed, his age and want of activity are balanced by his knowledge and experience, attributes which enable him to beat a manor or place the guns for driving to perfection. No one can do this better, for has he not had half a century of practice at it?—which practice has enabled him to know precisely how the game will fly in such and such a wind, and where it is to be found according to various con-ditions of weather or time of season. He is very shrewd; his head is stored with the habits of birds and animals, and valu-able hints and facts pertaining thereto drop quite naturally from his lips if the occasion requires or suggests, not otherwise. There is one thing the old sportsman insists on, and this shows his true sporting instinct as much as anything else about him, namely, the finding of a wounded bird, and if it *is* to be found he *will* succeed. Ten minutes, yes, twenty minutes, will he spend if he is of opinion the bird *ought* to be retrieved. The shooters may get impatient, keepers may fret, the evening darken, and the best beat or drive of the day may be yet to come; but there stands the old sportsman, his coloured hand-kerchief thrown over a turnip top to mark the spot, and his own perfectly broken retriever ranging in search round him. The dog's master never moves, nor does he allow others to move near him, as he considers, and quite rightly, that so doing interferes with the dog's chance of finding.

This habit of the old sporting host causes all his guests to avoid long shots, which may be likely to wound, and also teaches them to ' mark ' fallen game with accuracy, so as to avoid waste of time in looking for it, and thus allow them to get on through the day's sport without delay. Let it be here remarked that it is the exception for young shooters to ' mark ' well what they kill, and it is an art not half enough practised generally. The old sportsman is always very fair to his guests; he never puts 'anyone' in a coveted position because he is 'some one'; he gives all an equal chance throughout the day, share and share alike, invariably taking himself the least favourable position, yet when at luncheon some one remarks, 'What a strange thing we did not see a woodcock to-day !' the old sportsman will, perchance, slowly fumble in his coat-tail pocket, and lay on the table a fine specimen of 'Scolopax,' which he had quietly bagged when standing ' back ' (as woodcocks so often are obtained), and kept secret, as a surprise—a little bit of pleasantry of his own that pleases him much.

We once knew an old sportsman of this kind, whom we will call ' Squire Brown,' who had such a 'knack,' as his friends termed it, of bagging woodcock (though chance it was not, for the old gentleman knew just the spots where the cock would break out of a covert, and it is a habit of these birds to fly out of a wood through the same openings, as elsewhere pointed out in these volumes), that he was called far and near 'Woodcock Brown,' and so general was the name that strangers and tradesmen often addressed him as 'Woodcock Brown, Esq.,' an address which greatly tickled his fancy and of which he was somewhat proud. One of his grandchildren was surnamed 'Woodcock' at his special wish, and to him he left a large and valuable collection of implements of sport and sporting books. It was a fine sight to see ' old Woodcock ' teaching ' young Woodcock,' as he called him, to handle and aim a toy gun.

The old sportsman is kind and generous to everyone— guests, keepers, and tenants, yet very knowing all the same; anything at all resembling a mean trick he never forgets, if indeed he forgives. He likes to see ground game as well as winged, but religiously meets all claims for damage done by the former. Long may such old sportsmen flourish!

R. P. G.

' Down charge.'

CHAPTER VIII.

PARTRIDGE SHOOTING.

THE majority of sportsmen, who are in health and vigour, probably prefer partridge shooting to the less active pursuit of pheasants. If popularity is to be taken into consideration when judging the merits of different kinds of sport, partridge shooting must undoubtedly take a high place in public estimation. The proportion of unenclosed or cultivated land in all parts of the United Kingdom is so much in excess of the area covered by woods and plantations, that whereas covert shooting must necessarily be always a luxury, enjoyed by the few who are fortunate enough to possess wooded estates or to number among their friends those who do, partridge shooting is a sport which comes within the range of a much larger class. All must feel that there is a charm in traversing the open

fields, and an excitement about the sudden rise and hurried
flight of a covey of partridges, to which there is nothing akin in
covert shooting, unless it be a snap shot at the much coveted
woodcock.

Many are the descriptions in different books on sport of
partridge shooting over dogs, and much sound advice connected
with it is to be found scattered through the various publications
which treat of such subjects. Walking in line for these birds
has also been often described and discussed ; but the little which
has been written about the more modern system of driving
has been for the most part comparable only to descriptions of
cricket culled from the French newspapers. Some remarks on
driving as it is now practised by experienced sportsmen may
therefore be not unwelcome.

Before attempting to arrange the plan of action for the day,
it is necessary to be well acquainted with the nature of the
ground to be shot over and of the crops or other cover growing on it. The keeper of the beat should be able to afford the
necessary information as to what number of coveys are likely to
be found and on what part of the beat they will be most plentiful, as well as to suggest the best manner of working them
towards the thickest cover so as to give the chance of bringing
to bag the largest possible proportion of them during the day's
work ; but it must be remembered that a keeper may possibly
be interested in not giving the very best advice. He may desire
to spare his birds, or, very possibly, he may attach extreme
importance to securing those especially which frequent a neighbour's boundary, or to driving such outlying birds towards the
centre of the ground. Although under certain circumstances
it may be well not to neglect one or other of these considerations, the manager of the beat should not allow the day's sport
to be sacrificed to them, always presuming he desires to realise
the best possible bag. It may be freely admitted, however,
that keepers are, for the most part, as keen or keener than
their masters, and that one who would endeavour to spare his
birds, unless he labours under the disquieting suspicion that

his master's guests are of the 'tailoring' fraternity, is an exception to the general rule.

It was rumoured that that celebrated character, Jerry Jaggard, the well-known keeper to the late General John Hall, was occasionally in the habit of trying to save his birds, and some colour is given to this report by an anecdote that was told of him by General, then Colonel, the Hon. James Macdonald. Early on the first day of a week's shooting General Hall's pony fell on slippery grass, and caused the fracture of a collar-bone. The management of the day's driving was entrusted to a younger member of the party, ably assisted by the then reigning keeper, James Tillbrook. Jerry, who had retired, was simply a spectator. When it was suggested to him that it was a 'bad job' the General having broken his collar-bone, he promptly replied, ' I'll tell yeau what's a deal wuss job, Kunnel Jim—the way they're a hussl'n these here puttriges.'

So soon as harvest is over, partridges are usually to be found in turnip fields from ten to two o'clock, but after two they soon begin to move off to the stubbles and other feeding grounds, such as meadows rich in grass seeds or old clover layers.

In working with pointers it is best to 'give the dogs the wind' at the beginning of the day—that is, to start down wind and gradually to work the ground in the direction from which it blows ; but it will be well, if possible, to take a turn over the up-wind end of the beat early enough in the day to admit of the ground gone over in the morning being worked again before the birds begin to seek their feeding grounds. In this way many scattered birds will be picked up, and a better bag will probably be made on a smaller area than if fresh ground were constantly traversed. The explanation of this well-known rule is to be found in the almost invariable habit of partridges, especially early in the season, to re-seek as rapidly as possible after being disturbed almost the exact spot in the field from which they were first flushed. This habit is the more noticeable when, on first rising, some of their number have fallen to the shots, and the remainder have been in some degree scattered.

The frequency with which this occurs might almost induce a careful observer to believe that some understanding must exist among them that the rendezvous of the survivors should be held at the spot where they separated.

Where birds are scarce, wide-ranging dogs, provided always that they are steady on the point and do not run up to their birds, are very useful ; but in thick cover and among much game the dogs should not be allowed to range too widely, and in any case they should be trained to obey the voice and hand, and should not require the use, still less the too frequent abuse, of a whistle. In this kind of shooting, birds should be as little disturbed by any noise as is consistent with the necessary movements of dogs and sportsmen.

When dogs are at the point, the shooter should advance according to the direction in which he desires to influence the flight of the birds, on the one side or the other, remembering that if the wind is blowing from his side towards the birds they will afford easier shots than if he approaches them from an opposite direction.

They will nearly always rise against the wind, to get the advantage of its force in lifting them from the ground ; but in continuing their flight up wind they will skim low over the tops of the turnips or other cover, with their backs and tails only exposed, whereas in turning to fly down wind they must necessarily exhibit their breasts and heads and be almost stationary in the air at the moment of changing their direction. This change will be made at a higher elevation, and be therefore more easily taken advantage of when a strong wind is blowing than when there is little. A bird in this position may be justifiably shot at and cleanly killed at a much greater distance than a bird skimming up wind, but naturally requires a quicker shot.

If one or more men can be spared to walk the stubbles in the neighbourhood of the best cover during the very early morning, and also after the shooting has commenced, it will probably save much time and increase the bag, and this will equally apply when that method of shooting usually described as 'walking in line' is practised. Many old sportsmen still regret the change of system which has caused pointers to be now generally dispensed with in the pursuit of partridges. The introduction of the 'red-legged,' or so called 'French' bird, is usually assigned as one of the reasons for this change. Daniel ('Rural Sports,' vol. ii., p. 410) states that the Marquess of Hertford first successfully established them in Suffolk about the middle of the eighteenth century. These birds have very often been accused of communicating to the grey birds their

'Mark over.'

habit, when alarmed, of running long distances before taking to their wings, and certainly this propensity renders them manifestly objectionable to the owner or breaker of good pointers, whose training is often impaired by it.

Although in the days of shooting over pointers the 'red-legs' were naturally unpopular birds, so much so that their eggs were habitually gathered for the table on some manors in Norfolk, their habits render them particularly valuable for driving purposes. Running as they do far from the approaching line of men, they are the first to leave the field and pass over the guns; moreover, their running habits cause them to become more scattered and to arrive singly rather than in coveys, thereby affording a larger number of shots. Their flight is also straighter than that of the grey birds, and they are less apt to lie close or to turn back in the face of the beaters.

In one respect they are inferior to the indigenous species. They have decidedly less powers of endurance. After two or more long flights they are unable to rise again from the ground, and are frequently caught by the dogs at the end of a drive.

In exceedingly cold weather they seem to become weak or lazy, and may be easily approached and shot wherever sufficient cover can be found to hide them. It is not unusual in some parts of the eastern counties to find them at this time representing one-half or even two-thirds of the total results of a day's driving. The idea that they fight or disturb the other birds during the breeding season may be regarded as a popular error. Of the two species the grey bird is decidedly the more pugnacious. The nests of both are frequently found in close proximity to each other, and their eggs have even been observed in the same nest.

It is at least probable that the true cause of the abandonment of the use of dogs is to be found in the introduction of the system of sowing turnips in rows rather than broadcast. So far as can be ascertained, this manner of sowing root crops, although practised first in Scotland by Mr. Dawson of Frogden about the year 1770, did not become generally adopted in England until some considerable time after the beginning of the nineteenth century.

Whether with dogs or in walking, a greater number of shots can generally be obtained in clover fields and among broadcast coltseed or mustard than where birds can run between the drills. Another agricultural change, which has most unfavourably affected the practice of shooting over pointers and setters, has been the substitution of the scythe, and still later of the mowing machine, for the old-fashioned sickle. In the days of

WALKING UP PARTRIDGES IN TURNIPS

reaped stubbles, which were habitually left long, uneven, and not unfrequently weedy, birds could be approached, not only during the first half of the day, but equally well at a later hour when they had retired to their feeding grounds, the stubbles affording sufficient cover to hide them and to prevent them from noticing the approach of sportsmen.

This is now no longer the case. No stubble in these days is high enough to prevent birds from seeing men and dogs the moment they enter the field, and where the birds are at all wild they will not allow themselves to be approached. Whatever may be the reason, however the blame may be apportioned between the 'Frenchmen,' the scythes, and the drills, pointers have been given up in nearly all districts where partridges are abundant, and the system of walking in line, or driving, has superseded their use. A mixed line of shooters, keepers, and beaters is usually kept as straight as possible, partly to prevent the birds from turning back or to the sides when they are being purposely directed straight ahead, partly that no sportsman should by reason of undue eagerness obtain a real or imaginary advantage over his neighbours or come in the way of their shots, and partly to avoid passing birds which lie close. The eager man who always walks ten yards in front of the line really spoils his own sport. He acts as a wedge, sending birds to his neighbours on the right and left, while preventing those which they put up from flying in his direction.

Where birds are plentiful much delay may be avoided by providing at least as many retrievers as there are 'guns,' if we may use the word in its frequently accepted sense of gunners. Those who bring their own dogs, provided always that these are well broken and under proper control, are usually the most welcome guests. Each shooter who is independent of the assistance of the keepers in 'picking up' sets one man free to search for towering or wounded birds, or to afford assistance in any direction where it may happen to be most needed at the moment.

It is at least equally certain that no one will welcome the presence of what that fine shot and manager of shooting, the late General John Hall, used to call a 'nasty marauding dog.' The dog that runs in at the shot, and, regardless of signs or orders, searches for fresh birds beyond range of his master's gun, is voted a nuisance in any company, and his owner often pays the penalty by not being again invited.

A dog should be broken to go only where sent, to obey the direction of the hand, and to return quickly when called. Old and experienced dogs acquire the habit of marking where a bird falls and going straight to the spot, where they will work close until the scent is struck; such dogs can be trusted, they may be sent forward as soon as a bird is down, and will do far more good than harm, even if they put up a bird or two, by preventing the loss of strong runners.

The writer has been fortunate enough to possess more than one dog which would mark a towering bird at a considerable distance, and if allowed to go would take a straight line to the spot and stop instantaneously to the voice, if by chance they overran the mark. One of the best of these would frequently stand up on his hind legs when watching a wounded bird at a distance.

Beaters should always be taught to watch the effect of every shot, and to mark as nearly as possible the exact spot on which each bird has fallen. Without breaking the line, the man who in the general advance comes nearest to the spot marked should go or be directed to it, and should plant his stick there until the bird is gathered. If the mark is not indicated in some such manner it is frequently lost by the marker when the search is prolonged.

No one should venture to trust his eye only in marking the spot where a bird falls. If his attention is for a moment distracted the mark may be missed, or some similar object to the one borne in mind may be mistaken for it. It should be impressed upon all keepers and beaters that in marking the fall of a bird they should first observe the most conspicuous leaf, stone, or other object contiguous to the spot where it fell. Secondly, they should observe and remember some other conspicuous object, at a distance beyond it and in the same direct line ; the second may be on the horizon, in the next fence, or nearer, so long as the two objects are in direct line with one another from the spot where the marker stands. Thirdly, he should mark with his heel, or in any convenient manner, the spot from whence he takes his line, so that in the event of one or other object being lost or in doubt, he may recover his mark by retracing his steps.

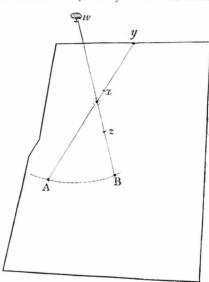

If this rule were carefully observed in all partridge and grouse shooting many thousands of birds annually left to linger or rot on the ground would be recovered for the benefit of the bag and the kitchen. The thing is easy to do when once learned, but will generally be neglected if not duly insisted upon as an established rule by the manager of shooting.

Where it is well understood and practised it is not unusual for two or more men to mark a bird which has fallen far ahead of the line, and to correct each other if at fault in regard to distance by indicating the exact spot where their two lines cross each other.

A diagram will explain.

A observes that a towering bird has fallen near a red poppy (*x*), in a line for a high whitethorn twig (*y*) in the fence at the end of the field.

B has marked the same bird, in line between a large turnip running to seed (*z*) and a tree in the next field (*w*).

A goes to the poppy, but is beyond the bird.

B goes to his assistance, and gives him the line from the big turnip top.

A retraces his steps on his own line, and finds the bird where B's line intersects his own.

In turnips, partridges are always easier to approach if the line is formed across the drills, but it is not always convenient to make use of this advantage. The drills may run exactly in the direction in which it is desired to push the birds towards other holding ground, or the field may be of such a shape that to work it across the drills will involve more wheeling or re-forming of the line than is desirable. Where it becomes necessary to walk along the drills it is well for each man in the line occasionally to change by two or three steps to the right or left the drill in which he walks. Birds which see from some distance a man advancing along the drill in which they are at rest will frequently run to the right or the left, and settle themselves again as soon as the cover hides him from their sight, and in this way, if the line is not in very close rank, they may lie until it has passed them ; by occasional changes the chance of their escape in this manner is lessened.

When there is no object to be gained by driving the birds towards any particular point, the line may wheel at the end of the field and return in the opposite direction on the next strip, taking each time as much of the ground as their number will fairly cover without incurring the risk of walking over birds by becoming too widely separated. If, on the contrary, it is desired to force the birds in a particular direction, it is usually well worth while, on reaching the end of a field, to return on the ground already traversed and to re-form the line on the next strip, taking it towards the same point as before.

Whether walking along or across the drills, it is always well, on coming near to the last corner of a field, to allow one or both ends of the line to advance, so as in some degree to concentrate the forces and encircle the birds. Many birds will run to the end but will not willingly leave the field ; others already put up and scattered will have alighted at the extreme corner, and these will often lie close until hard pressed by the closing up of the line. In this way many shots are often obtained at the corner of a field, either by the outside guns, who come within reach of birds which try to skim low over the fences to the right or left, or by the centre guns, which hang back to catch other birds returning to the field over the beaters' heads, and such as, hoping to be out of danger when the right and left wings have passed them, will almost allow themselves to be trodden upon by the men who compose the middle of the line. For the same reasons a line formed in *échelon* is sometimes found to be more effective than when quite straight, especially when it is desired to direct the birds to one or other side of the field.

Owing to the tendency of partridges to run or fly away from the men who first pass them, those guns which are placed towards the less advanced end of the line will always obtain more shots than their companions. To equalise the shooting it is well to advance each end of the line alternately, and this manœuvre has also the effect of pushing the birds always in the same direction, laterally, although approached from opposite ends of the field, thus :—

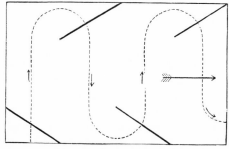

A still better plan, but one less generally adopted, is to form the line in the shape of a quarter section of a circle with one end slightly extended and flattened. This is very effective, and most useful in forcing the birds in any given direction.

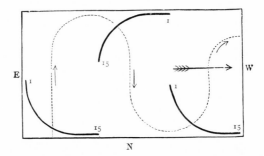

Thus, taking, for instance, a long turnip field twice or three times as long as wide, the drills running lengthways, say east and west, with another field of good holding cover, mangolds or clover, to the west of it, to which it is desired to drive the birds, whatever may be the direction of the wind, the quarter-circle line is the best that can be adopted. Starting at the north-east corner of the field, our quarter-circle stretches across the corner, the foremost gun keeping near the fence on the left, the most backward gun keeping in the same drill with the three or four men on his right and left at the prolonged straightened end of the line. The advantage which the bowed line has over the direct *échelon* is not easy to explain in words, although in practice it will generally be admitted to be a substantial one.

Anyone who has tried to approach a covey of partridges crouching in a stubble field, where the cover is insufficient to conceal them and where they can watch his movements, will probably have observed that a direct approach is almost certain to put them up out of shot; whereas, if he shapes his course to the right or left, apparently with no idea of molesting them, and only reduces the distance gradually and obliquely, he may often get near enough for a shot, even on the most open ground. It is not that the birds do not see him , it is that, so long as they think he does not see *them* and will pass by without disturbing them, they hesitate to show themselves. They are probably watching him during the whole time—so intently that, in rising at last when he more decidedly approaches them, they will often quickly direct their flight regardless of some equal danger on the other side, and a second sportsman may place himself so as to get a shot. The following diagram explains the movements of two men trying to out-manœuvre a covey of partridges on an open stubble.

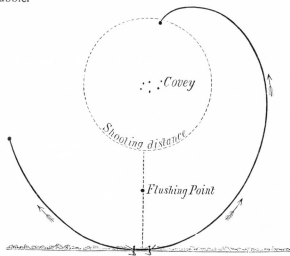

In the same manner birds which allow the forward end of the bowed line to pass them without rising will find themselves between two fires, which they could never be with the direct *échelon* line. In both formations there must be, of course, one or more men advancing directly towards the birds ; but if we take, as in the previous diagram, what may be called a shooting point and a flushing point, it will be seen that the direct advance in the bowed line will not reach the flushing point until the end of the line has passed the birds and thus

attracted their attention; whereas in the *échelon* the direct
advance must reach the flushing point before the right-
hand gun has passed the birds, and is therefore more likely to
put them up before coming within reach. The area for safe
escape is also considerably greater.

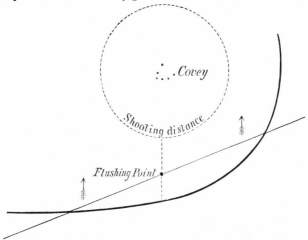

Thus the whole line advances (see diagram on p. 150) until
No. 1 reaches the south-east corner of the field, when No. 15
stops and becomes the pivot man, the others wheeling round
him and extending westwards the flattened end of their line:
No. 1, when he has taken up sufficient ground, becoming the
backward gun, and No. 15 the foremost gun in the general
advance, now in the opposite direction. No. 15 must be careful
to miss no ground, and yet must avoid going back over ground
that has already been traversed; his object should be to keep
close to his own tracks. When No. 15 reaches the north fence
No. 1 stops and becomes pivot man, and No. 15 wheels the line
and extends the flat end of it before the general advance again
towards the south, and so on until the field is finished.

The effect of this manœuvre is to give the best places
alternately to the right-hand and left-hand guns, owing to the

tendency of birds to turn away from those who are most in advance.

When working, in the first instance, down wind, the line must face the wind on returning ; thus, over half the distance traversed the birds will be driven to take the required direction or to face the guns.

It will be obvious that the adoption of the bowed line for the purpose of placing the birds as much as possible between two fires involves a necessity for great caution on the part of the sportsmen. If any one of these cannot be trusted to fire only safe shots, the danger of accidents will be much greater than in the case of a straight or oblique line, where the range over which low-flying birds may be safely killed by each gun is necessarily wider. If the flank guns fire back on the line or the centre guns fire at the flanks, the formation should be at once altered, or the offenders should be put out of action with all possible regard for their more or less injured feelings. The alternative of injured feelings or injured eyes is one in which no manager of a shooting party should hesitate to inflict the lesser inconvenience rather than to risk the greater calamity.

There is, however, no real danger in the system advocated so long as the different members of the party are up to their work, and will allow birds flying low, at an angle involving risk, to be killed rather by their neighbours than by themselves. To one or other of the line of guns such birds must necessarily afford the opportunity for a safe shot if within reasonable distance.

As also, in the case of a straight or oblique line, keepers should be distributed between the guns to regulate their distance from each other, to dress the line, and to see that the birds are picked up ; and it is desirable that they should have full authority civilly to call the attention of any sportsman to his proper position if necessary. This is frequently required, especially in the process of wheeling, when some one or more of those engaged in it are not familiar with the system.

When birds lie close and allow the advanced end of the line to pass them, they are far more apt to turn back overhead than when they rise somewhat wild. A cool and practised sportsman will not shoot too quickly in such cases. He knows there is plenty of time to let off both barrels before the covey can fly out of range, and he will prefer to take his birds at the proper distance and at the most favourable angle; his gun will not be raised to his shoulder until they have passed his head, but, mentally selecting his victim, he will throw the muzzle well forward, and the shot will reach his first bird at about eighteen yards, and his second at from twenty-five to thirty yards behind him.

Partridges, like other game birds, become wilder and less easy to approach as the season advances. When clover is cut and carried, when root crops are consumed or carted away, there is little or no cover in the absence of gorse, brakes, or heather, in which birds can be successfully brought to bag by the methods already described.

Kites are occasionally made use of in partridge shooting, for the double purpose of concentrating the birds in good holding-cover and making them lie close when they get there. In this way they undoubtedly give a great advantage over the birds for the time being; but the belief is very prevalent that where kites are too constantly employed they have the effect of driving the game to other ground, and if this is so, few people would be willing to risk the loss of their stock for the temporary advantage of killing a few more brace of birds in any one day. The opinions of experienced keepers differ on this point, but on the whole the balance of evidence does not favour the adoption of the system. Where plantations or thick hedgerows are not far distant partridges will take refuge in them to avoid a kite, and will not re-appear for several hours; and as they undoubtedly desert ground frequented by hawks, it is not unnatural that the repeated use of a kite should also banish them.

It is evident that so long ago as 1823 it was already recognised that shooting over dogs was not the most profitable method of pursuing partridges. The match between Mr. William Coke and Lord Kennedy which took place in that year has frequently been mentioned.

An extract from the *Norfolk Gazette* of that date will show the method adopted to secure Mr. Coke's remarkable bags of $80\frac{1}{2}$ brace on September 26, and 88 brace on October 4 :—

Mr. Coke was attended by several gamekeepers, and by *one dog only*, to pick up the game. Several respectable neighbouring yeomen volunteered their services to beat for game, and rendered essential service throughout the day.

The system of driving partridges appears to have been instituted about the year 1845, on Lord Huntingfield's estate at Heveningham in Suffolk. Himself a good sportsman and unerring shot, no one was more likely to understand the management of shooting or to entitle himself to the credit of effecting improvements in the accepted methods.

Driving is extremely useful and effective, not only for the purpose of affording good sport late in the season, but with the object of preventing too large a stock of birds from being left on the land. Wherever a large number of old birds are left, the quantity of young birds bred on a given acreage will be considerably less than where a proper proportion can be maintained. A pair of young birds will occupy less space than a pair of old birds, they will allow other pairs to nest within a short distance of the spot chosen by themselves, whereas old birds will drive off any others which approach them, and consequently the number of coveys produced upon a given space of ground will greatly depend upon the chance of escape of each bird during the previous shooting season. Where these chances are too much in favour of the birds, the older, and perhaps more cunning, are liable to be left in too commanding a proportion ; whereas, if the stock is fairly thinned by late shooting, a larger number of these are likely to be secured, to the advantage of their younger and less pugnacious neighbours. On one estate in Norfolk the number of birds on certain farms has been greatly increased of late by rewards having been given for every cock bird brought in by the keepers in the month of January for two successive years.

There are, of course, other causes which affect the average amount of space occupied by each pair of breeding birds, such as the abundance or scarcity of natural or artificial food, and the condition and number of the fences or other convenient nesting-places. Moreover, it must not be forgotten that by cutting down the stock too close, which, in spite of the contrary opinion, often expressed, can certainly be done by too persistent driving, the number of coveys reared, even on the most favourable ground, may be seriously diminished.

Driving has been greatly abused by the lovers of a more old-fashioned style of shooting. No one would wish to deny the pleasure of seeing a good pair of pointers at work. The greatest advocate of driving would scarcely argue that such fine old sportsmen as Sir Richard Sutton, Mr. Osbaldeston, and hundreds of others whose names are associated with the old style, were mere pot-hunters. On the contrary, all would admire and respect, not only their skill and endurance, but no less their true instincts, the *feu sacré* of sport ; and many who, for the reasons already indicated, greatly owing to changes in our system of cultivation, have been, as it were, driven to driving, would have vied with such men in their day in the keen enjoyment of 'To ho, Ponto !' and 'Down charge, Carlo !' so often depicted in old sporting prints. Admitting all that can be said in favour of shooting over dogs, and by no means desiring to decry or to despise so genuine a sport, the advocates of the 'drive' have a right to ask for equal consideration, and to claim from their opponents a certain meed of recognition for those advantages which they attach to it. In the first place, it cannot be denied that driven birds afford a far greater variety of shots than birds rising before the gun. The different heights and angles at which the shots must be fired tax the skill of the sportsman in the act of shooting far more than it is taxed in bringing down birds killed over a pointer. Many driven birds come very high overhead ; others give long crossing shots ; whilst some fly straight in the face of the shooter, and if not taken at the most favourable angle are apt to escape unscathed. The exercise of extreme quickness in bringing down as large a proportion as possible of the birds which pass is also a great test of skill. Secondly, the system of driving gives sport to a larger number of guns than walking or shooting over dogs. According to the extent of ground traversed and the length of the fences, six, eight, ten, or more may easily take part in the shooting and have an equal chance of contributing to the bag.

However keenly the possessor of good dogs may enjoy training and working them, or may appreciate the pleasure of being indebted to their good behaviour for his day's sport, such enjoyment can hardly exceed the satisfaction to be derived from the successful planning and execution of a day's driving. The amount of headwork required for this purpose, and the difficulty of properly training a number of men to carry out the system in the most effective manner under varied circumstances, must be far in excess of that which is necessary for planning a day over dogs, or even for training the dogs to do their duty according to an inherited instinct. A far larger number of birds can be brought to bag in one day by driving than by ' dogging,' and this at a time of year when the older system could scarcely be practised at all, and under circumstances the most unfavourable to it. The amount of exercise obtained by the sportsman would in nearly all cases be less in driving than in any other system of partridge shooting ; but, although this may be regarded as an objection by some young and ardent lovers of leg-work, it may be rather a recommendation than otherwise to the majority who have surpassed the *juste milieu* of age or weight.

Without further discussing its merits, it may be well to endeavour to explain, so far as this can be done on paper, the different plans of action that may be successfully adopted in driving, and to call attention to the chief points to be studied in connection with this method of partridge shooting.

In the first place, it is necessary to know where sufficient numbers of birds are likely to be found. The system can scarcely be advocated where coveys are very few and far between.

Where, as in some parts of the eastern counties, fields are of great extent ; where the hedge-rows, few and scanty, afford inadequate nesting cover, it is undoubtedly useful to plant narrow belts of trees. These serve the double purpose of sheltering the land and affording suitable breeding places for the birds. But if they are attractive to partridges, they are also attractive to wild-bred pheasants, and it will be found that pheasants are apt to interfere to some extent with a keeper's efforts to maintain a good stock of partridges. It is known that old hen pheasants, especially when they have been robbed of their eggs, will kill young hand-reared birds of their own species ; they have also been known to kill very young partridges. But they probably do more harm by laying their eggs in partridges' nests and disputing with the rightful owners their maternal privilege. Whatever may be the reason, it will be found that where the ground is occupied by any considerable number of pheasants, the coveys of partridges will be less abundant than where they can claim undisputed possession.

However large a stock may be left on the ground, or rather, however well balanced may be the proportions between old and young birds, it is impossible to count upon a good season's sport until the coveys have attained complete maturity. The weather may be wet and cold at the time of laying, which may cause the desertion or destruction of the eggs ; and even if a goodly number are hatched diseases may break out and seriously reduce the quantity available for shooting.

The most destructive disease prevalent among partridges is that which is commonly known by the name of the 'gapes.' If it were practicable to catch the birds and to treat each one separately so soon as they become affected by it, their lives

might be saved ; and with pheasants, or even partridges reared
by hand, this may be done to a considerable extent by watchful and competent keepers. When the disease attacks wild
birds it is impossible to combat it, and no method of prevention
has yet been found to supersede the too limited means of cure.
The best treatise on the subject of the entozoic parasite which
causes this disease was published in 1883 by the Entomologi-
cal Society of London.[1] The parasite in question, *Syngamus
trachealis*, is there fully described by the learned author, Mons.
P. Megnin, who recommends a solution of fifteen grains of
salicylate of soda in 1500 grains of distilled water, to be mixed
with the water given to hand-reared birds. Turpentine is undoubtedly effectual if applied by means of a feather to the wind-
pipe when the disease is not too far advanced. Although he
has ascertained that the preliminary stages of this pest are
probably passed in water, which may indicate a means of preventing it from reaching hand-reared birds, no method can be
devised for warding off the danger from those which live at
large. Old and young are alike affected by it, and it is not unusual in certain seasons to find three or four nearly full-grown
birds lying dead together where a covey has brooded for the
night. Hundreds of young partridges have been found during
harvest dead or dying from this most destructive complaint.

It is always the duty of a keeper to know what birds he has
on his beat, and what particular fields they chiefly frequent
at different times of the day. By watching the stubbles at
feeding times he will easily ascertain the number and movements of his charges, while at the same time he will be expected to know where the coveys have for the most part been
bred, and therefore where they are most likely to be found
when not feeding. If any hand-reared birds have been brought
up, it will be their habit to keep much together until very
late in the year, and the movements of such packs can

[1] *On the Gapes Disease in Gallinaceous Birds, and on the Parasite which
causes the Disease* (*Syngamus trachealis*, Siebold ; *Sclerostoma syngamus*, Dies).
the red worm of gamekeepers. West, Newman & Co.

be easily observed and noted. Moreover, if any previous shooting has taken place during the early part of the season, not only the numbers, but also the habitual direction, of the flight of different coveys should be known to those who have seen or taken part in the sport.

It has sometimes been observed that, about the month of November, more partridges are to be found upon certain portions of cultivated land than are known to have been bred there ; a corresponding decrease of stock being noticeable on other more or less adjacent beats. Although such movements of birds do take place, all evidence tends to show that they are dependent solely upon the question of food-supply. When the yield of shed grain on any stubble has been greatly reduced, or entirely consumed, those birds which frequent it will change their quarters ; but, so long as sufficient food remains to be found in the neighbourhood of their breeding places, they show no migratory tendencies whatever.

As has already been remarked, all root crops, if of fairly luxuriant growth, form favourite holding cover for partridges, and in these they will be found, except in very wet weather, at least during the middle of the day. Other cover, such as heath, gorse—if not too thick—broom, bracken, rough grass, young plantations, mustard, coltseed, and clover are much frequented ; and even freshly ploughed land is exceedingly useful for holding birds, if they can be driven on to it. But these are not perhaps so much a natural resort as are swedes, turnips, and mangolds.

Since the coveys are not easily broken and scattered except in good cover, it will be desirable to make as much use as possible of this where it exists, and to drive them from one holding ground to another without allowing them to regain the open fields, where they can more easily collect together.

Next, it is important to notice the height and position of the fences. They must be at least high enough to conceal the sportsmen, but it is convenient that these should be able to look and shoot over their hiding places, where for the purpose of

sufficient concealment they must stand close against them.
This can generally be done in the case of low-clipped thorn
fences, warren banks, or narrow borders of gorse or broom.

An old hand at the work will often be seen trimming off
with his knife or slashing down with a stick the leading shoots

' Killed as he tops the fence.'

of the fence before him, to prevent them from interfering with
the free movement of his gun or impeding a clear view of the
birds. If the fence is too high to be looked over, it will be
necessary for the guns to stand at a sufficient distance behind
it to enable them to shoot birds as they come over ; but in

M 2

this case there is always the danger, especially in driving against the wind, that the birds may see the shooters soon enough to enable them to turn back in the direction of the drivers, and thus give no chance of a shot.

For this reason a very high fence or belt of trees is more suitable and convenient for the purpose than one which is only about as high as a man's head. Birds coming over such very high fences or belts are less able to obtain a view of the guns, and have less time to change the direction of their flight before arriving within shot ; after which, if not killed, they will usually pass on in the desired direction. The distance at which guns should stand from the covering fence must depend in great measure upon its height.

There is no more deadly opportunity to the experienced shooter of driven birds than the moment at which they top the fence in front of him, especially if the wind is against them ; and it is a good test of the faith which each man feels in the quickness of his hand and eye to observe at what distance from the fence he places himself if left to his own choice. It cannot be finally left to each man's discretion, as, on the ground of safety alone, it is desirable that the line should be as nearly straight as possible, and nothing is more inconvenient or embarrassing than to be unable to fire at skimming birds—in front or behind the line—owing to guns or loaders being out of their proper position. Some men have a habit of placing a keeper or a boy in the fence to look through it and warn them of the approach of birds, forgetting that, although he is not likely to be in the way of their own shooting, his presence at an angle in front of the line may seriously interfere with their neighbour's safe range of fire.

The same objection applies strongly to placing guns round the corner of a field—that is, behind two fences more or less at right angles to each other. In this case there is often a strong temptation to fire low across the corner, and the possibility of accidents from this cause should be avoided. In exceptional instances, when it is necessary or desirable to place flanking guns where birds are likely to break out at the sides of a drive, great caution must be exercised in the direction or elevation of each shot fired.

Where guns are separated from each other by a fence running at right angles to the covering fence, great care is required that they should be in good line, and the men nearest to the dividing fence on either side of it should make known their exact positions to each other before the shooting begins.

When they are not in line there is danger that some one of them may think it safe to fire at an angle which endangers those who are hidden from his view. Thus in the following diagram it will be obvious that No. 3 by being behind the line

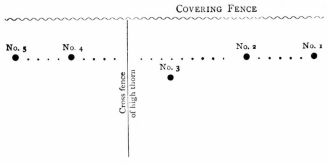

endangers both his neighbours who, knowing his position but not seeing each other, think it safe to fire in front of him. If No. 3 were in his proper place, Nos. 2 and 4 would regulate their range by his position.

Driving over a high plantation is very safe, and affords pretty rocketing shots. But such drives are not usually so deadly as those in which the birds are brought nearer to the guns.

In some parts of the Eastern Counties trimmed Scotch fir fences form excellent cover for hiding the guns, and also facilitate the act of shooting by giving them a clear sky-line over which to expect the birds. On heaths or open ground where no suitable fence is available, concealment may be extemporised by means of hurdles, with broom, gorse, or brakes drawn between the bars and projecting to a sufficient height above them. If this be done the tops of the branches may be trimmed level, and the whole should be never more than five feet high.

Two hurdles placed end to end are sufficient to hide a man and his loader, but one is scarcely enough for the purpose.

Battery made with hurdles.

In some places on open heaths shallow pits have been dug in the required positions, and the earth thrown up to form a bank in front of them to a convenient height. At Buckenham, on the late Lord Ashburton's estate, where it was customary to send some guns with the beaters when driving low belts of broom and gorse, other guns being placed ahead to catch the driven birds, high wooden shields were erected, formed of mortised boarding, sufficiently shot-proof to secure the safety of those behind them ; but these could only shoot at birds that had passed the shields, as the rattling of shot on the boards warned them that it was unsafe to look out round the corners.

Two guns were placed behind each of these shields, one to take birds to the right, the other to the left. The writer will not easily forget the lively time he passed in one of these places with a most excitable and over-anxious friend, who, not getting enough shooting to please him on his own right side, passed his time in firing with great rapidity at all superfluous birds to the left, totally disregarding his neighbour's head. Another kind of permanent battery can be easily made by planting circles or semicircles of Scotch fir or spruce, and keeping them trimmed to the proper height.

Such permanent batteries should never be less than sixty yards apart, which is about the distance that may be conveniently allowed between guns stationed for a drive, although it is sometimes necessary to command a greater length of fence by placing them at increased distances. Where a fence is thin or very low it will be useful to set up in it a few branches in each place where a gun is posted, to afford better concealment.

Old hands at this kind of sport are careful as to the colour of their hats or caps, anything approaching to white or black being far more noticeable at a distance than intermediate shades of colour, and therefore more likely to turn the birds. The nearest possible approach to the colour of a leafless thorn fence is the least conspicuous. The rule applies almost as much to loaders and keepers in attendance as to the sportsmen themselves, for although it is not equally necessary for such men to hold their heads above the fences, yet all are apt to endeavour to get a view of what is going on in front, and often fail to drop their heads at the critical moment when birds arrive near enough to take notice of what is before them.

In driving over a road it is almost invariably preferable to place the guns behind the second fence so that they may have the road in front of them. Thus, if the fence behind which they stand is not too high, they will be able to shoot approaching birds as they top the opposite hedge, and will have the additional advantage of being more perfectly concealed.

Given a sufficient choice of suitable fences, the next point for consideration is in what order and succession the different drives shall follow throughout the day. And this is not only the most important, but also frequently the most difficult, matter to decide.

A general plan should be thought out beforehand. But as the details must greatly depend upon the force and direction of the wind, it should never be finally decided until the morning of the day's shooting—or should at least be subject to such modifications as can be made known at that time to those entrusted to carry it out, without involving any complete alteration of the system proposed. The invariable propensity exhibited by all game birds to return with as little delay as possible to the places from which they have been driven when first disturbed becomes again an important factor in planning out a day's driving.

By beginning at the up-wind end of the beat and driving down wind the facilities for carrying on the birds and accumulating them in a given direction are greatly increased, and if at first more difficult shots are obtained owing to their flying faster and higher with the wind behind them, a larger number of more easy victims will be brought to bag when at last their flank is turned and they are driven back in an opposite direction. Bearing this rule in mind, we should be first disposed to collect as many birds as possible by driving the stubbles into any available cover at the up-wind end of the beat. Much ground may thus be brought in before the shooting begins, without involving loss of valuable time during the day. But this must not be done more than half or three-quarters of an hour before the guns arrive, or birds driven from a distance will have already commenced with legs and wings to re-seek their former haunts by passing or outflanking the line of drivers.

When partridges have been driven down a strong wind as far as it is intended that they should go, it may happen that, in spite of their natural inclination to return to their own ground, a little mismanagement may spoil the day's sport. In shooting on the Abbey Farm, near Thetford, several years ago, the beat had been driven with the advantage of a very strong wind for the whole of the early part of the day in the direction of the town. A large number of birds were thus collected on a single field, and it was intended to drive them back over a belt of young trees, the beaters having gone round for this purpose. A boy who was sent to get some ammunition from a cart stationed at the other end of the belt, instead of going on that side of it where the birds could not see him, went along the very field in which they were. The consequence was that they rose in large numbers, and being unable to face the wind flew far away over the town, and neither then nor at any future time found their way back again.

Had they been undisturbed until the beaters got round them, they would have skimmed low against the wind until they reached the shelter of the belt, when they would have flown singly between the tops of the young trees and passed over the guns ; but the danger which they apprehended having appeared on the wrong side of them, in turning to avoid it they were mastered by the force of the gale, and so a great day's sport was spoilt, and a stock of at least three hundred birds was lost to that beat. It was on this same Abbey Farm, the property of Lord Ashburton, that the late Sir Richard Sutton, one of the finest sportsmen of his day, killed over one hundred brace of partridges in 1854 during the early part of one day. Being near the boundary of his own estate he shot his way home afterwards, and is said to have added between twenty and thirty brace to his score.

Next in importance to securing the assistance of the wind is the adoption of the best means of breaking or scattering the birds. Very few men will be required to put birds off an open stubble, and the main strength of the force should be concentrated in the thickest cover. It will be obvious that whereas a shooter can only kill two birds out of each covey coming quickly over his head, yet if a covey of fifteen birds settle in a hedgerow and get up one or two at a time, they may all be shot at. The first time a field is driven, whole coveys, and frequently packs of several coveys, will rise together and quickly pass over, and therefore the first drive off fresh ground is never the one that adds most to the bag. But as these birds, when driven to a distance and scattered by being frequently flushed, will find their way back singly to the field from whence they came, a second or third drive from the same field is likely to be more productive. For this reason it is never well to take up too much fresh ground, supposing, of course, that there is a good show of birds.

It is rather desirable to encourage the return of birds to the beginning of the beat, and to go over the same ground two or three times during the day, always provided that a sufficient number of birds escape in the first instance. No more killing system can be devised than to drive alternately backwards and forwards in opposite directions so long as birds continue to come over the guns.

A whole day may sometimes be passed in this manner, where a sufficient extent of ground can be brought under the operation on each side. Such a plan, although in some in- stances contributing to a large bag, is devoid of the interest and variety which are essential to a good day's sport. A very telling modification of the practice is where, after each drive, the guns can face about and walk in line over more or less country to take up their positions for the return drive. Besides picking up in this way a number of scattered shots, they will secure a very large percentage of wounded or towered birds, which might otherwise be lost.

There must always be a certain number of such birds in every day's shooting, according to the skill of the performers. But whereas in walking or shooting over dogs a large proportion of shots are fired at birds going straight away, these shots are less frequent in driving ; thus the probability of wounding birds is reduced. A mixed system of driving and walking is often very effective. When it can be done without involving delay, as while drivers are on their way round to bring in fresh ground, it is useful to walk the guns across the fields of turnips or other likely places which have already been driven before leaving them for good, whenever birds have had the chance of returning to such fields.

It would be invidious to mention names, but some four or five notable instances are present to the mind of the writer, of keepers who thoroughly understand the art of driving and the manage- ment of a partridge beat. But even these would probably recognise one of the earliest masters of the profession in James Woodrow, of Buckenham, whose talents have been transmitted to at least two of his pupils. Although long since retired from active duty, in the brilliant performance of which he was one of a somewhat small minority, it may be hoped that the time is yet distant at which he will be called to join the great majority, already including so many of those who enjoyed the benefit of his skill. No one among gentlemen understood the management of driving better than the late Lord Stamford, not even excepting another master of the system, General John Hall. On the heavy clay soils at Enville, in Staffordshire, the results he achieved were really marvellous.

Lord Stamford was well aware of the use to which fresh ploughed land could be put for the purpose of breaking birds. Coveys running on such land are sure to become scattered. The soil clogs the feet of the birds, so that instead of rising all together they crouch singly in the furrows, and allow the drivers to approach before flying forward. Late in the day, especially after better cover has been thoroughly worked, a drive across fresh ploughed land is sure to be productive if it lies within the previous line of escape.

Such land, unlike an open stubble, cannot be cleared by widely scattered beaters, and is therefore much resorted to by harassed birds.

It is a great mistake in driving to form a straight line of beaters at the end of a field, who simply march across it up to the guns, leaving both sides open for escape. The flanks should always be protected, if only by one or two men on each side at considerable distances. These men will not only push in the outlying birds, but will often influence in the required direction the flight of others flushed in the centre of the line. In cases where a strong cross-wind prevails, or where ground much frequented by birds lies at the sides of a drive, the men on the flanks may be of far more importance to its success than those who walk straight towards the guns. Keepers who know their work will cause the men to deploy out on either side until the line assumes the form of a large semicircle, of which the points should be constantly advancing and contracting towards the spot to which the birds are to be directed. The distance at which drivers should walk from each other must depend entirely upon the thickness and extent of the cover or holding ground, as to the chance it may afford for birds to lie close and to be passed by. If the number of beaters in the field is not sufficient to admit of their being divided into two distinct parties without distributing them too thinly over the ground, much time will be lost in sending them round after each drive, and during these periods the guns will be kept waiting. It is there-fore always desirable, if possible, to engage a sufficient number to cover two drives at the same time. By this means, while one party is advancing, the other party can be preparing for the next beat by collecting and concentrating the birds, and forming themselves in line at a suitable distance to await the signal for advance. This can be given when the guns are in their places either by a good voice or by two barrels of a gun fired in very rapid succession. In wide open country, where the drives are necessarily long, the latter signal is often required, especially if a strong wind is blowing. We have heard of whistles and bugles being also employed for this purpose. Although in an enclosed country, where small fields prevail, much shorter drives are more frequently effective, a mile is no unusual distance to bring birds to the gun on the large open fields or heaths of Norfolk and Suffolk. Half a mile will, however, even then, be found a more convenient and manageable distance. This is a matter in which much discretion must be exercised, and the manager of driving should know pretty nearly how far birds can be forced from their own ground under different con-ditions of wind and cover. Another means of effecting some economy of time in the distribution of beaters for driving is to divide them into three parties. Thus, under certain circum-stances, if we have thirty men in the field, although it is much simpler to divide them into two parties of fifteen each, it may sometimes answer better to form them into three parties of ten.

For instance, if the fences under which the guns are to be placed for two consecutive drives happen to run at right angles to each other, while twenty men are bringing on the first drive the remaining ten can form the quarter-circle on the off side of the drive which is to follow. So soon as the first drive is over, half the men engaged in it may not have far to go to join those who are already placed, and thus complete the required half-circle, while the other half can go off in another direction to prepare one side of a third drive. By this plan thirty men can be made to do the work for which forty would be properly required, without involving any considerable delay, and the advantage gained is out of all proportion to the inconvenience caused by waiting until the manœuvre can be accomplished.

Whenever the beaters are divided into two or three parties, it is very convenient to the manager of the shooting that each party should be provided with small flags of a different colour. The order, ' red to the right, blue to the left,' is infinitely simpler than picking out by name to which men each duty is assigned, and if numbers only are mentioned some disagreement is apt to ensue as to which should take the heavier or lighter task. A leader, or as it were a commanding officer, who thoroughly understands what is required and how to deploy his men, should be appointed to take charge of each division.

Touching the subject of flags, it is extremely doubtful whether they are or are not of use in influencing the flight of birds. When partridges have once decided upon a particular line, regardless of the presence of visible danger, no flourishing of flags or other gymnastics will have the slightest effect in turning them. Shouting and holloaing are worse than useless, and this rule should be observed in all driving.

The words 'mark over ' or ' coming over ' are sufficient to indicate to the guns that birds are on the wing, without unnecessarily disturbing those which have not already risen. The only way in which flags can be, and are perhaps, of use is in rendering the men conspicuous at a greater distance than they would be without them. Thus low-flying birds, which have not determinately framed their flight in a lateral direction, may be induced to go forward where they would have preferred to slip out at the sides of a drive.

Economy of time is greatly conducive to a large bag. Shooters should not delay in the first instance to take the places assigned to them, and the signal should be given at the earliest possible moment consistent with avoiding the escape of birds before the guns are in their places.

The beaters should walk fast when the shooting is slow, and slow when the shooting is fast. Each sportsman should have his own dog, or be provided with a keeper and dog for picking up. This should be done as quickly as possible after the drive is over, and wounded or running birds should be marked and followed, but not so far as to interfere with the next drive by putting up the coveys from ground which has yet to be traversed.

Each shooter should bear in mind the number he has down, and should make it his business to see that they are all gathered. Those to whom picking up is a matter of indifference are not, in the true sense of the word, sportsmen. When guns are placed very near together it is often impossible to avoid some confusion in settling claims. This is a matter in which good-feeling and good-fellowship should never give way to jealousy, and the principle of give and take should rule the day. It frequently happens that when a jealous or too zealous neighbour has picked up and claimed two or three of your birds, you may find after his departure the same number or more, obviously his own, lying neglected much nearer to where he stood.

In driving it is almost impossible to foresee who is likely to have the best place, except in the event of strong cover, such as a belt of trees or a cross-fence running straight down in front of any one gun. The fairest way to equalise the chances of sport is to draw lots for places, but even in this case, if the places are not changed for the different drives, some guns will always be in the centre and others on the outside, and on the whole the centre places are the best throughout the day.

To avoid unequal distribution of shooting the guns should change places after each drive. Thus with seven guns, No. 1 would commence on the right, facing the beaters ; he would become No. 2 in the second drive, and so on until he resumed his first place in the eighth drive. No. 7 would become No. 1

Shooter and loader changing guns—Position No. 1.

in the second drive, and so each gun would pass in succession through the whole line.

It must be admitted that, on account of the greater number of beaters required, driving is a more expensive amusement than walking up birds with or without dogs. For this reason it is not generally suited for a small party of only two or three guns ; moreover, it is difficult to concentrate the shooting sufficiently to afford good sport except with several guns.

The number of partridges usually killed in drives cannot be compared to the number of grouse, although, where they are well broken and scattered on a large extent of good holding ground, twenty or thirty birds to a good gun is not very exceptional. The writer has once seen an instance of over a hundred birds being killed by a single shooter (Earl de Grey) in one drive, he himself having killed eighty-eight in the same drive, with fewer opportunities. This was on the estate of the Maharajah Duleep Singh, at Elveden. The advantage of breechloaders in this respect is of course enormous, but they possess also another advantage in the matter of safety, which would not generally be thought of.

A curious instance occurred at Merton in 1873, illustrating the danger of muzzle-loaders in driving. The writer having two guns was placed behind hurdles about five feet high such as have been already described. His loader was of course obliged to keep very close to him under the same limited shelter, and was kneeling down to load the gun immediately on his right hand. As the gun was fired over the loader's head against a very high wind, a spark of unburnt powder blew back from the muzzle, and ignited the charge which was at that moment being poured into the second gun, causing the explosion of a strong metal powder-flask containing nearly three-quarters of a pound of powder in the poor fellow's hand.

Although, in the special circumstances of this case, the cause of the accident has probably been rightly described, it is quite possible that it may have resulted from a grain of burning powder remaining in the barrel of the empty gun—through neglect of the proper precaution of tapping the butt with barrels inverted after firing. Fortunately the injury sustained was only of a temporary character, but the hole blown through the broom faggot, with which the hurdle was thickened, by one half of the powder-flask (afterwards picked up at a distance of about thirty yards) was sufficient to indicate the narrowness of the escape.

Here it may be desirable to mention what cannot be too

often repeated and impressed on all whom it may concern, namely, the urgent necessity of extreme caution on the part of loaders in handling guns. They should be made to learn always to point the gun clear away from everyone, in charging it to depress the muzzle while turning away from the shooter, and in shutting the gun always to raise the stock to the barrels, and not the barrels to the stock, so that if by any accident the charge explodes it can only make a hole in the ground.

Shooter and loader changing guns—Position No. 2.

Secondly, they should be warned never to bring the hammers (if there be any) to full-cock, and a sportsman who has any regard for his own safety will never place a cocked gun in the hands of his loader.

With a very careful and experienced man this rule may perhaps sometimes be infringed, but only in most exceptional cases, for the sake of greater speed in firing. But a man must

I.

indeed have great confidence in the carefulness of any person whom he would trust to handle a cocked gun immediately behind him.

Probably more serious accidents happen in the shooting-field through careless loaders carrying guns pointing towards their master's legs than in any other way. Poor Colonel Buckley was killed in this manner in Norfolk, and in that case the gun was undoubtedly cocked. At the same place where that accident occurred the writer owed his life to a cartridge which missed fire, although the cap was driven in by the plunger when the gun was pointed straight at his spine within six inches of his back. This was one of five bad cartridges during the day.

Much time is often wasted in the act of changing guns. The empty gun should be handed with the right hand to the left hand of the loader, and the ready gun should be placed by the loader's right in his master's left, in such a position that he shall not require to shift his hold in raising it to his shoulder. The position No. 2, as illustrated, where the loader stands on his master's right hand, is much more convenient than No. 3, where he is on the left. Not only loaders but sportsmen themselves have nothing to lose by a word of caution—*Never let the gun point towards yourself or towards anyone else whether it is loaded or not loaded.* This simple rule can be easily observed, and impressed upon the mind by constant habit it its infringement becomes a rare exception.

It is well worth while to go through a few days' drill with your loader if you have the opportunity, to secure rapidity of action in the process of changing guns. Those who shoot much, when their second barrel has not been fired, instinctively drop the hammer to half-cock in the action of handing the gun to the loader, and this should never be omitted. Hammerless guns, of course, do away with this necessity. But unless anyone uses them exclusively, he is in danger of losing the safe habit of half-cocking his gun, or may let off the hammerless gun in the instinctive but unnecessary attempt to do so.

A good workman will fire in front or behind the line, but will never follow a low bird across it. The butt of the gun should always be dropped from the shoulder and the muzzle raised at the instant the bird passes the heads of his neighbours (see diagram, page 179).

The alternative system of 'traversing,' by which the gun is made to point, for a moment at least, at the head or body of the

Shooter and loader changing guns—Position No. 3.

next in line, cannot be too strongly deprecated. The slightest disturbance of nerve, causing the trigger to be pulled on instant sooner or later than is intended, must cause a foul shot, and this practice more than any other has led to the loss of eyes in shooting. Many men who shoot a great deal 'traverse' habitually, and the habit once acquired is most difficult to eradicate.

A man should always try to take two birds in front of him

if possible, not only because they generally afford easier shots at the forward angle, but because it gives him the possible chance of getting hold of his second gun in time for a straggler from the covey after they have passed him. If his position with regard to the fence does not admit of his being quick enough to do this, he should at least take one in front and one immediately after they have passed the line. The rapidity with which driven birds get out of distance, when flying strong, is very great, and the smallest delay greatly improves their chance of escape. When a bird comes straight at you on a level with your gun there is no question of holding forward ; it is like shooting a stationary object. But if it is coming higher than your head, to kill it before it reaches you it is necessary to fire somewhat above and thus in front of it ; in the same way, after it has passed straight overhead, to throw the shot in front you must hold below the bird. However near a bird may be, provided always that it is flying straight towards the muzzle of the gun, it is almost impossible to blow it to pieces; a wing may be cut off, but the feathers lying back along the body seem to protect it in a great measure against the charge, and the head only is smashed.

Where birds are within shot of two guns they should properly be left to the one who is nearest to them, but both may fairly fire where there is a choice of several birds, and it will be bad luck if they chance to aim at the same.

In Gilbert White's 'Natural History of Selborne' (edition 1813, p. 16) we find the remark—'That some time after the dry summer of 1740-41, partridges swarmed to such a degree that parties of unreasonable sportsmen killed 20 and sometimes 30 brace in a day.'

The bags made by Mr. Coke at Holkham, and by Sir Richard Sutton near Thetford, have already been referred to.

A somewhat celebrated match at partridges took place in 1850 between Mr. Crawford and Mr. Osbaldeston, the former allowing the latter a start of 20 brace, being equivalent to one brace for every year that he exceeded him in age. On the first day each sportsman killed 80 brace, on the second day Mr. Crawford killed 102 brace, and Mr. Osbaldeston 30 brace. The writer has received the above particulars from Mr. Augustus Savile's keeper, Samuel Herod, who walked with the shooters, but accounts of the match are probably to be found in some of the sporting papers of that day.

The largest bags made by walking in line, so far as they are known to the writer, were on Lord Ashburton's estate at Buckenham in Norfolk, where in 1858 314 brace, and in 1859 332 brace, were killed by eight guns, of whom in the case of the larger number it is within the knowledge of the

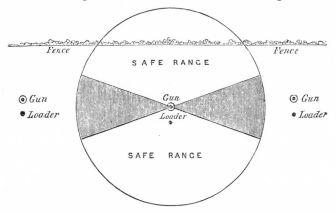

writer that four only were first-class shots. As an example of what was done upon the heavy clay soil of Staffordshire by driving and by exceptionally good management, it may be mentioned that in the middle of January 1869, 11 guns killed on Lord Stamford's estate at Enville 551 partridges in one day and 615 in another, and the game-books of that estate if referred to would probably show that these numbers have been exceeded on other occasions.

On the property of the late General Hall, at Six Mile Bottom, Cambridgeshire, the best week of partridge driving known to the writer up to that date was the last week in the shooting season of 1869, the returns showing that nine guns killed 404, 510, 600, and 426 in the four days.

The most remarkable results of careful preservation and management that have yet been recorded are to be found in the game-books of His Highness the Maharajah Duleep Singh at Elveden in Suffolk. It was here that the Maharajah killed 780 partridges to his own gun on September 8, 1876—but many of these were hand-reared birds. In the same year four guns killed from October 10 to 13, 829, 557, 662, and 483 partridges besides other game in four days. In 1878 we find another bag of 801 partridges, and in 1885 the extraordinary number of 856 partridges to three guns only ; besides three other days in the same year of over 300 brace by the same number of guns. The Elveden books also show that in the month of September 1885, the same three guns shot in 15 days no less than 6,509 partridges, giving an average of over 72 brace per day to each gun.

The latest and largest bag made by a party of guns was at Holkham in 1885 as follows :—

Date			Beat					Partridges
Dec.	8, 1885,	Branthill (8 guns) .		.	•		•	856
,,	9,	,,	Savory's Warham (8 guns)		.		•	885
,,	10,	,,	Nelson's and Blomfields (8 guns)				.	678
,,	11,	,,	Branthill and Crabb (10 guns)				.	973

Guns.—Lord Leconfield, Lord Wenlock, Lord Lyttelton, Lord Coke, Mr. Gurney Buxton, Mr. Edward Birkbeck, Mr. Pryor, Colonel Coke, Mr. Forbes, Hon. W. Coke. Mr. Gurney Buxton heading the score on each day with 172, 112, 95, and 96.

The following bag made at Lord Ashburton's, The Grange, Hants, beats the record for England up to the end of the season of 1888:—

Date			Beat					Partridges
Oct.	18, 1887,	New House (7 guns)		•	•		•	1,337
,,	19,	,,	Itchen Down	,,	•	•		.	1,093
,,	20,	,,	Totford	,,	.	•		•	716
,,	21,	,,	Swarraton	,,	,	•		•	930

Guns.—H.R.H. the Duke of Cambridge, the Duke of Roxburgh, Lord Ilchester (except the first day), Lord Walsingham, Colonel the Hon E. Digby, Captain E. St. J. Mildmay, the Hon. F. Baring, Mr. A. Wood (first day only).

There were no red-legged partridges. The cover was very scanty, some very thin mustard forming the only holding ground on the first day ; on the other days a few light crops of turnips helped to break the birds, but the success was chiefly owing to good management on the part of Marlow the head-keeper (one of the pupils of old Woodrow, alluded to on page 169), and to good high whitethorn fences, which caused the birds to rise to a convenient angle above the guns. The first shot was not fired before half-past ten, and 700 birds were bagged before luncheon at 1.45 on the first day, the writer getting 74 and 62 in the two best drives, both over the same fence. There were no hand-reared birds among the number killed.

Wonderful as this bag is, it does not come up to what has been done abroad. On Count Trautmannsdorff's estate in Austria, at the end of September 1887, seven guns killed: 1 roe deer, 1,018 hares, 205 rabbits, 209 pheasants, 1,612 partridges, 2 various, making a total of 3,047.

The system of management on this occasion was very different from anything adopted in this country. Mr. Ralph Milbank, then attaché to the English embassy at Vienna, who was one of the guns, has informed the writer that the game was all killed in a large circular covert of low undergrowth, through which the line of sportsmen and beaters walked round and round, like the spoke of a wheel. The open country around the covert was driven in by parties of men on all sides, and thus the birds were constantly rising in front of the guns—not driven over their heads, as is the case under our English system.

In Bohemia, also, 1,400 partridges were killed by three guns in four hours in 1887.

These figures serve to show that the number of partridges in those countries is greater than can be found in any part of England.

Among the criticisms that have appeared in the public press since the first edition of this book was published, one only seems to require a few supplementary sentences.

It has been urged that the system of driving is too strongly recommended, and that the writer has lost sight of the fact that in certain places partridges can be more successfully brought to bag by means of pointers, even in the present day. It is quite true that in an open fenland country devoid of fences, consisting for the most part of low rough pastures of large extent, where birds are very scarce, the use of dogs will enable a shooter to get over a far larger acreage of ground in one day, without passing the widely scattered coveys that are to be found upon it, than if he were to attempt any system of driving or walking in line; but this somewhat rare exception cannot be taken to invalidate the rule that where birds are plentiful these alternative systems are likely to yield the best results.

W.

In 1898 the following remarkable bag was made at Houghton in Norfolk, including a total of 4,316 partridges in four days to 8 guns:—

Date	Beat			Pheasants	Partridges	Hares	Rabbits	Total
Oct. 5, 1897	Bircham and Harpley (8 guns)	·	·	3	920	26	4	953
,, 6 ,,	Coxford . . . ,,	·	·	3	877	63	6	949
,, 7 ,,	Rudham Grange . ,, ·	·	·	12	1,158	50	8	1,228
,, 8 ,,	Syderstone . . ,, ·	·	·	3	1,361	19	7	1,390
				21	4,316	158	25	4,520

Guns.—H.R.H. the Duke of York, the Earl of Chesterfield, Viscount Deerhurst, Lord H. Vane-Tempest, Lord Elcho, Hon. H. Stonor, W. Low, Esq., M. T. Kennard, Esq.

The best day yielded a record for England of 1,361 partridges, but in less than one month this record was twice

surpassed at The Grange, Hants, where six guns killed 1,374
and 1,461 so late as November 2 and 4. The unavoidable
absence of some of the guns preventing shooting on the
Wednesday in this week the bag was as follows:—

Date	Beat	Partridges	Pheasants	Hares	Rabbits	Pigeons	Total
Nov. 2, 1897 (*Strong wind*)	Itchen Down .	1,374	28	109	3	1	1,515
„ 4 „ (*Fine*)	Chilton Valley .	1,461	28	63	3	—	1,552
„ 5 „ (*Very strong wind*)	Dunneridge .	701	16	30	2	—	749
		3,536	72	199	8	1	3,816

Guns.—Prince Victor Duleep Singh, the Earl of Pembroke,
Lord Newport, Lord Walsingham, Lord Ashburton, the Hon.
A. Baring (*first day only*), the Earl of Lathom (*except the first
day*).

W. *July* 1899.

CHAPTER IX.

PHEASANT SHOOTING AND WOOD-PIGEON SHOOTING

ALTHOUGH much has been published concerning the nature, habits, and specific differences of various breeds of pheasants, comparatively little has been written about the sport of shooting them, except by the use of pointers, spaniels, and setters, a system which from various causes has now been almost abandoned as ineffective or impracticable.

The modern system of covert shooting, which sprang into existence when careful preservation and artificial rearing had largely increased the quantity of game available for sport in this country, has scarcely been touched upon except by those who, with apparently a limited experience of its practice, have approached the subject for the most part in a somewhat acrimonious spirit.

Among notable exceptions the names of J. J. Manley, the author of 'Notes on Game and Game-shooting,' Henry Stevenson ('Birds of Norfolk'), and the late W. Bromley

Davenport ('Sport') should be mentioned.   Mr. Manley
counsels 'moderation in rearing pheasants,' and regards 'excessive preservation of game' as 'a mistake'; but, although he expresses some preference for 'rough pheasant shooting' where
there are 'thick hedges and broad ditches,' he by no means
falls into the popular error of supposing that a pheasant must
be always an easy shot, or that 'battue shooting should be
turned into ridicule and made a subject for sneers.'

Mr. Stevenson discusses the subject in a fair and sensible
spirit, and points out that so-called battue shooting is by no
means such easy work as is generally imagined.

Mr. Bromley Davenport criticises in amusing language the
fallacies put forward by many of those who speak and write
against the 'battue,' and describes the great amount of skill and
management required to ensure its success, drawing excellent
distinctions as to the manner in which each individual sports
man should or should not acquit himself in performing his
share of the day's work.

It was probably about the end of the fifteenth century, or
very early in the sixteenth, that firearms came to be used in
the pursuit of game.   In a book entitled 'La Chasse, son
histoire et sa législation,' par Ernest Jullien (Paris, 1868), at
p. 183 the author writes :—

L'ordonnance de Mars 1515 (Art. 2) défendait, dans le rayon de
deux lieues autour des forêts de la couronne, le port et la détention
des arbalètes, arquebuses, escopettes, filets, &c.   Un édit, 1546,
interdisait à toutes personnes, gentilshommes ou autres, de par-
courir le territoire du royaume avec des armes, et *principalement
des arquebuses* ; depuis 1554, notamment, l'usage de l'arquebuse
devenait chaque jour plus commun.

The earliest method of shooting pheasants was probably
that which now prevails only where these birds are few and far
between.   In such places they may yet be followed with
spaniels and setters and made to afford easy chances to the
sportsman, if the covert be only thick enough to prevent them
from using their legs in preference to their wings.   Arminius

Vambéry mentions in the account of his travels that in certain parts of Persia it is the habit to kill pheasants by means of sticks, in cover too thick overhead to permit them to rise. All will admit that if pheasants lie close the actual shooting of them when once on wing is made easy. There are few birds so easy to kill when rising within thirty yards of the gun as is a pheasant.

The enjoyment of such sport must therefore depend more upon the difficulty and uncertainty of finding the game than upon any great skill required to bring it to bag when found. Although this form of enjoyment is one of the first and most important elements of many different kinds of sport, and is one which no true sportsman will ever despise, there are other sources of pleasure in the pursuit of game, which, under certain circumstances, may become at least equally attractive, and may wholly or in part compensate those who rightly appreciate them for its absence.

However mechanical may be the part actually taken in a day's covert shooting by those who have no interest in the plan of action or pleasure in contributing to its success, there must of necessity be some one person upon whom the management of the beat devolves, whose duty it is in one way or another to bring the guns and the game together, and whose whole attention must be occupied, if his duties are to be properly performed, in arranging the details of the day's work. Such an one will find it difficult to dispense with proper assistance. First, he will expect the ready co-operation of his subordinates, but the more knowledge, experience, and intelligent interest displayed by those who actually take part in the shooting, the easier will be his task.

To the successful manager belongs, at least, that enjoyment which constitutes one of the chief attractions of true sport, the satisfaction of feeling that his knowledge of the habits of the game, and of the manner in which it can best be approached, has enabled him to reduce into possession, in a sportsmanlike fashion, a goodly proportion of whatever numbers may have been available within the area traversed.

To do this successfully in the case of pheasants, as of other game, it is above all necessary to observe and to study the habits of the birds under all possible conditions and circumstances, to know how these are affected by weather, by wind, by food, by covert, or by partial modification of their natural tendencies, as in the case of hand-reared birds. It is necessary to know also how to apply the results of such observation and study, that it may contribute as much as possible to the satisfaction and enjoyment of those who are invited to share the sport.

Many gamekeepers, when permitted to place the guns, make it their only object to secure the heaviest possible bag. They allot the best places throughout the day to the best shots, the worst places to the less skilful performers. This system, by whomsoever it may be adopted, must frequently produce dissatisfaction and jealousy among even the most good-natured, as exhibiting a want of consideration for the feelings of those who, by reason of their frequent failure, are often more sensitive than others who are accustomed to succeed.

A good manager should make it his business to know throughout the day who is and who is not getting a fair or an excessive share of the shooting, and should adjust the balance as nearly as he can when circumstances permit it. This may frequently be done in places where many pheasants are expected to rise at the same time, by putting those who have had less shooting in front, with those who have had more than their share behind them. By these means birds which are not shot at or are missed may be brought to bag, and those of the party who are told off to back up others in this manner are usually well compensated for having fewer chances of letting off their guns by the higher flight of the birds which pass over them, calling for the exercise of superior skill to bring them down. A man must keep his eyes open as much as possible in all directions when shooting is going on. There is no small danger of pheasants falling upon the heads of those who do not keep a good look-out.

An instance of this occurred at Riddlesworth, where a Waterloo veteran, who is still living, was heard to exclaim, in tones of supreme resignation, 'I am shot! I am shot!' when nearly three pounds of flesh and feathers descended on the side of his head from a considerable height, stopped by the unerring gun of a certain noble duke.

It will be generally admitted that all the elements of true sport are wanting when large numbers of pheasants, crowded together in low covert by surrounding beaters, rise in continuous flights over guns placed near enough to render the game unfit for food; for although there are some professors of the art who can be trusted even under such circumstances to strike only the necks and heads of the birds, almost without knocking a single feather from their bodies, to the majority of sportsmen such close proximity, if it does not prevent them altogether from attempting to add to the bag, produces a sense of disgust rather than of pleasure.

Those who have learnt to regard near shots as inseparable from the modern 'battue' have not unnaturally been disposed to raise an outcry against large bags, and to sigh for the old days of pheasant shooting over spaniels and setters, in preference to what they are accustomed to designate mere slaughter. Happily, owing to the good example set in this matter by some leading owners of well-wooded estates, among whom the present Earl of Leicester should be specially mentioned, a better system of management has of late been rapidly extending and is now largely adopted.

It no longer follows that a large increase in the number of birds brought within reach of the gun involves any corresponding diminution in the pleasures of sport, or of the wholesome and legitimate rivalry which can only be enjoyed to perfection where good nerve and real skill are required. The attainment of these satisfactory results must depend in the first place, as has been already stated, upon an accurate knowledge of the habits of the birds.

Without taking into consideration various species of the

A RISE OF PHEASANTS

(Over two lines of guns)

genera *Thaumalia, Euplocamus, Lophophorus, Nycthemerus,* &c., represented respectively by the Gold Pheasant, the Calege, the Monaul, the Silver Pheasant, and others, which have been introduced in various parts of England with more or less success (but which for the most part are birds suited rather to the aviary than to the woods), it is well known that the true pheasants, i.e. all birds of the genus *Phasianus,* Lin., when alarmed are more disposed to run than to fly. The magnificent recent introduction, *Phasianus Reevesii* (Reeves' pheasant), known in France as Faisan vénéré, is no exception to this rule, although this species rises from the ground somewhat more readily than does the common pheasant.

To the manager of covert shooting the running powers of the pheasant are scarcely of less value than its powers of flight. The secret of successfully reducing into possession any considerable numbers in a satisfactory and sportsmanlike manner is found to lie in knowing how to utilise to the greatest advantage, and at the proper times, each of these two natural propensities. Roughly speaking, their running powers should be relied upon to get the birds to the places to which it is desirable to drive them ; their flying powers should be brought into use only when they arrive there.

In determining the best direction in which to beat a covert, or series of coverts, many different points arise for consideration. Among these may be mentioned the nature of the ground, whether flat or hilly; the presence or absence of under-covert in particular places; the numbers and distribution of the game, their feeding and roosting places ; the number of guns and the space available for placing them; the proximity of ground on which game cannot be followed, and the direction of the wind.

The most usual plan adopted by gamekeepers is to begin as near as possible to a neighbour's boundary, and to drive the birds homewards, placing guns at the end of each covert in turn, and pushing the birds over them towards ground which they are accustomed to frequent; the general result of this manœuvre being that low shots and smashed game are the rule rather than the exception.

It may sometimes be advisable before beating a covert to drive the birds in from outlying woods, especially if bordering on unpreserved land ; but the danger of losing birds by driving them away from home is too frequently overrated, and many keepers

who have heard with dismay the first suggestion of such a plan have lived to learn that nothing less than a very strong, unfavourable wind or the worst of management can prevent its success. Driving homewards throughout the day seldom contributes to satisfactory sport.   As a rule, better results are obtained by forcing the birds as far as possible away from their customary

'Beaters are coming.'

resorts, in order that they may have the greater inclination to return in defiance of all obstacles. A line of beaters or of guns is an obstacle which they will face only when the disinclination to enter upon unknown ground or the desire to return to more favoured haunts induces them to incur this risk. They will then endeavour to escape the danger either by lying very close and allowing the line to pass them, or by rising as high as possible to avoid it.

The natural disposition of all birds, when driven from the spots which they are accustomed to frequent, is to return home at once, and it will be found that pheasants driven before a line of sportsmen and beaters, if they are unable to outflank the line, will try to fly back over the heads of their pursuers.

The principle upon which, subject to other favourable conditions, a covert or series of coverts should be beaten is to push the birds, chiefly by means of their running powers, as far as may be conveniently possible from their customary feeding and roosting grounds to some place where the space and undergrowth are both sufficient to hold them, and where guns can be posted between them and the ground to which they desire to return.

This may be successfully repeated at the same or in a different place, according to the nature of the ground and the amount of game remaining to be sought for.

The success of all covert shooting must in great measure depend upon proper attention being paid to the placing of stoppers. Late in the season, when pheasants become wild and unsettled, especially if they have been already disturbed, stoppers are even of more importance than beaters. They should be placed chiefly at the various angles of the coverts to be beaten, and wherever a belt of trees or a hedgerow might otherwise enable pheasants to run out of the covert unobserved. By all means let them be in position before the sound of guns or beaters can by any possibility alarm the birds.

It is impossible to establish any fixed rule as to the number of beaters required, so much must necessarily depend upon the nature and extent of the covert.

For every shooter from two to six will probably be wanted, in addition to those employed as stoppers, whose number may vary much during the day. Where wild-bred pheasants are much disturbed, a single shot fired in a plantation early in the day will, towards the end of the season, set them running to and from other woods half a mile away, but this is not the case in the beginning of the season, or where the ground has been kept very quiet. It is remarkable that towards evening, in spite of any number of shots fired by a gun stationed for wood pigeons in a fir plantation, pheasants will go up to roost as usual, and apparently without alarm, on trees within a few yards of the sportsman, whereas any movement that can be mistaken for actual pursuit will drive them from the covert.

Stoppers should be instructed to make known their presence by knocking two sticks together, or by hitting the trunk of a tree, with the double object of ensuring their own safety as guns advance and of preventing the birds from collecting in numbers in their immediate vicinity, an occurrence which is likely to lead to an ill-timed flush.

In all covert shooting it is especially important that the thickest holding places on the line of march should not be passed undisturbed. Beaters, if not properly kept up to their work, are too prone to avoid such places out of regard for their skin or their clothing. Brambles especially form a kind of covert in which pheasants, and more particularly rabbits, will remain if possible until the line of danger has passed them. Many more shots will be obtained in the course of a day if due care is taken that all patches of brambles, blackthorn, or other thick cover are well trodden through, and not merely beaten on the outside with sticks or penetrated only by the noise, which is too often relied upon by inefficient beaters in lieu of more active attack.

In many places, where there is much covert shooting in the course of the season, a picked body of men are provided with

stout gaiters and smocks to enable them to do their duty without injury to their own less durable clothing.   For this purpose
stout jean or twill is the best material, and the smocks should
be made rather on the pattern of what is called a Norfolk shirt,
with waist-belts to keep them close to the body, that they
may not encumber the action and movements of the wearer.

James Pinnock, head of the Holkham Beaters.

Such clothing is of course only required for those men who
walk in line through the brushwood; with it there can be no
excuse for any game being passed undisturbed.   It will not be
equally required in the case of stoppers or men in attendance on
the nets.

In the case of a large wood with no detached covert near

enough to be available as a flushing place, it will be necessary to
drive it to one or other of the four corners in one, two, or more
separate sections, driving always against the wind if possible,
but selecting the thickest undergrowth from which at last to
flush the birds. The shooters may stand in view of the birds
either in a broad opening cut for the purpose or in the most
open and visible positions that can be chosen in the covert
itself.

In this case the line of beaters should advance somewhat
in front of the positions taken up by the guns. This will
prevent the birds from rising too near, and will give them an
additional reason for flying high. The same plan may often
be followed with great success where a field of mustard or
turnips adjoins a covert ; birds, if not headed, can be driven
into such a field, and if the guns stand out in full sight, the
beaters advancing in a semicircular line fifty to a hundred and
fifty yards beyond them, the pheasants, turning back to the
wood, will rise high over their heads and afford very pretty
shooting. A gorse or broom covert, when available, is as
good or better for the purpose than a cropped field, provided always that a line of beaters is placed between the guns
and the birds. A row of hurdles thickened with branches
along the near side of the covert will sometimes cause birds to
rise almost as effectively as a line of men.

Having successfully brought the birds to the required spot,
the next object is to prevent them from escaping by rising all at
once or in large numbers at a time, as they will do if the covert
is too naked or if they are pressed together in too small a
space. To avoid this, the first essential condition is good
undergrowth, not hollow at the bottom—when hollow, the birds
will run and crowd themselves together—but close-growing,
such as bracken, gorse, very young spruce fir, privet, or rho-
dodendrons.

If covert is specially planted, *Hypericum calycinum*, as at
Holkham and other places, or *Gaultheria Shallon* or *Berberis*
(*Mahonia*) *aquifolia*, are admirably suited for the purpose ;

privet or lilac, throwing up many suckers in suitable soil, forms also a good stop-covert.

With the exception of stoppers left to guard the side facing the guns, where they should keep up a slight tapping with sticks to prevent the birds from running out and rising on the open ground, all the beaters should now go round, and stand as stoppers on all sides at a little distance from it. One experienced man should then advance, and, moving about within the covert, should put up as few birds at a time as possible. This will require much care, for the tendency of the game will be to run before him, and if he follow them closely too many will rise, and instead of scattering themselves over all the guns will probably all pass over the same part of the line.

To avoid this, he must advance first from one side and then from the other, often coming out of the covert and running round to head and scatter the birds. There should never be more than from ten to twenty pheasants in the air at once, but no one who has not had experience of covert shooting where game is very plentiful can have any idea of the difficulty of securing this result. A fox is a certain source of disaster, for wherever he goes the birds rise at once to avoid him, or, running together to a corner, break out in one large flight.

If the wood is large, and one man is not able to move the birds fast enough to afford general shooting, two, or even three, may go in, or the whole line may advance for some distance, so as to somewhat concentrate the birds, and then one or two men may be sent forward ; but in this case it will be found advisable not only to send on the flushers, as already explained, but to advance other men, at different parts of the line, to stand forward in such positions as will further tend to scatter running birds, and prevent them from massing together and rising when they see the beaters. As the flusher advances, birds which endeavour to avoid him by running will scatter to the right and left of these advanced sentries, and thus assist his efforts to raise them separately.

It is easy to speak or to write with satisfaction of the russet leaves, the lively spaniels, the crowing pheasant, as he rises in some wild coppice, and falls to sweep the frosted dew from a bed of rushes beneath a gnarled and knotted monarch of the forest ; but it must be remembered that in such a case he falls before he is thirty feet from the ground, nine times out of ten, an easy shot, which a sportsman cares little to make.

We find in the 'Oakley Shooting Code' (Ridgway), published in 1836 (p. 145) : ' Although shooting is a social amusement,

Shooting attitude ; high side shot.

the shooter seldom seeks for any other company than his dogs when out.' But where many birds are found many persons can meet and enjoy an equal amount of exercise and amusement ; and who shall compare the glorious delight of knocking over a really high ' rocketer ' with the pleasure of potting a pheasant rising from the ground ? Moreover, a bird flying low and straight away must almost necessarily receive a great part of the charge in the legs and hind-quarters, by which the most highly appreciated part of its flesh is bruised and injured, and the bird is rendered of infinitely less value as a delicacy for the table than if neatly shot in the head and neck as when flying overhead.

The following passage from Blaine's 'Rural Sports' (Longmans, 1858), gives a good idea of the method of pursuit adopted and advocated by some of the early opponents of the use of beaters in pheasant shooting :—

A foggy day is not unfavourable to pheasant shooting ; the birds then stray abroad and rove to a considerable distance . . . . nevertheless we have always observed that on those days pheasants are doubly alert with their ears, consequently springing spaniels are not good to quest with. We used on these occasions to go out with our steady pointer, of course unbelled, and when making our way cautiously alongside the hedgerows which skirted the covers it was amusing to see how our own mincing gait was assumed, not mimicked, by the intelligent brute, who also crept stealthily along ; and in this way, by close beating the patches of cover very quietly, we seldom failed in finding sport.

Surely this method of finding 'sport' would in these days be called pot-hunting.

In Thornhill's 'Sporting Directory' (1804, p. 114) the same system is in some degree advocated. 'If you find the birds in hedgerows you will be sure to have *sport*.'

In contrast to such a system, what can be more inspiriting than to be told, 'Here they will be as high as you ever saw them,' 'There no one has yet been able to reach them properly,' and then, if in good form, to see bird after bird collapsing to the sound of your first and second barrels, not 'slithering' down at oblique angles, with tail feathers following at a distance, but hit well forward in the necks, heads, and breasts : no runners : stunned, crumpled, dead ; and to know that good nerve, skill, and coolness have enabled you to bring down birds which, if left to less skilful hands, had at least as good a chance of getting clean away as of falling ? What a much better chance have they, in any case, than the pheasant flushed

by spaniels out of a bramble bush, with even the most moderate shot watching his dogs and pressing close up with both
barrels cocked to stop his victim !

With regard to the act of shooting, little has been written.
The subject is not specially connected with covert shooting,
except in so far as high overhead shots are more frequent in
this kind of sport than in any other.

The observation has been frequently made that shot will

Shooting attitude ; straight over.

penetrate more easily, and be therefore more likely to kill, after
a bird has passed over the gun than when it is approaching,
and this applies with special force to rocketing pheasants. The
surest angle at which to kill a pheasant is that at which the
shot is enabled to find its way under and behind the feathers,
rather than through them.

It follows that, if a pheasant is approaching high above the
head of the shooter, it is best to allow it to pass before firing,

'AS HIGH AS YOU EVER SAW THEM'

but for the sake of time and distance to pull the trigger as
soon as possible after it has done so.

The question is often asked: 'How far do you hold in
front of a bird?' but it is seldom if ever accurately answered.
In Johnson's 'Sportsman's Cyclopædia' (1831, p. 735) we
find :—

> If the bird should fly directly across or only partially so, and
> there describe the segment of a circle, the aim must be directed
> before the object—if with a common gun, 4 inches ; with a per-
> cussion gun, 2 inches ; supposing the distance to be about 30
> yards.

In fact, it is scarcely possible to calculate the exact distance
between the beak of the bird and the point to which the gun
is directed at the moment of firing. This must depend upon
a variety of circumstances, such as the distance of the bird,
rapidity of flight, power and direction of wind, quantity and
quality of powder, size of shot, &c. When a man knows the
strength of his charge and how quickly it may be trusted to
carry up the shot, he knows where the shot will be at a given
time after he pulls the trigger, and, judging the pace and distance of the bird, he regulates the advanced position or motion
of his gun accordingly.

If in putting it to his shoulder he finds it is not sufficiently
in advance, the hand must be swung forward in the direction
in which the bird is going. If, on the contrary, in putting the
gun up he places it considerably before the bird, he will fire,
without giving any swing whatever to the gun, at the moment
when he thinks the charge of shot will intersect the line of
flight.

The process is much the same as catching or fielding a
cricket ball. The fielder runs to intersect the angle at which
the ball is travelling; he regulates his pace according to the
pace and distance of the ball. If his hand is too forward it
waits for it, if scarcely forward enough he reaches out to intercept it. The best fielding and the best catching are accomplished when the hand arrives at the point of contact at the

same instant as the ball, and so in shooting: the best results are attained when, in the act of putting the gun to the shoulder, the eye, the trigger finger, and the left hand instinctively obey the brain in combining to make the due allowance for pace and distance, and bring the barrel at the instant of firing to bear upon the exact spot which the bird must reach when the charge will intersect the angle of its flight. To master this art is more essential for quick shooting among trees than for any other, inasmuch as mistakes cannot so easily be corrected. A narrow opening between branches may enable the gun to be brought to bear, but if that chance is lost the bird escapes unchallenged; in the open it would at least have to pass the ordeal of a second barrel. The habit of following birds or ground game with a gun when at the shoulder, dangerous as it is in the open, is infinitely more dangerous in covert. Those who practise it must either lose a vast number of shots or cause great risk of accidents. In covert, as indeed in the open, where there are beaters or others within range, a man should make up his mind where it is safe to shoot, and should point his gun nowhere else. When the bird or animal is approaching the spot at which he has determined that it may be safely shot, the muzzle of his gun should be pointing upwards, the point of the stock at his side level with his elbow. The stock should be raised to the shoulder and the muzzle dropped to the object only when it reaches the safe spot, and, hit or miss, it should never be allowed to follow, but may be raised and depressed again if necessary.

In some places it may be difficult, if not impossible, to carry out in all details the system of covert shooting here recommended ; but there are few, if any, coverts or series of coverts in the country in which, by proper management, pheasants cannot be made to fly within range of the gun at such a height from the ground as to have a fair chance of escape.[1] A hilly country is especially adapted for this purpose. Guns should

[1] At the end of this chapter will be found some representative cases more fully explained.

be posted always on low ground, and pheasants flushed on the sides or points of the hill above them. Few shots are more difficult than those afforded by birds flying out over open ground from a hillside to which they are bent upon returning. In this case, there are two points instead of one to be calculated in aiming the gun ; one, as in all other cases, will depend upon the

Shooting position No. 1.

rate at which the bird is moving, the other the amount of curve in its flight.

It is obvious that to strike from below an object moving along a curved line above the gun is more difficult than to strike a similar object moving in a direct course, and in addition to this difficulty there is often to be taken into the same instantaneous calculation the amount of effect exercised by the wind

in altering the position, as it were, of the curved line itself. The
diagram given on the next page may serve to illustrate this more
clearly.

The mental process required in this case to insure success may amount therefore to an instruction to the hand in
obedience to the eye to allow thirty-six inches forward for speed

Shooting position No. 2.

of flight, four inches right or left for voluntary curve in direction, and three inches for drift.

Where wooded sides of hills do not offer special facilities
for avoiding what is called 'mopping up' pheasants at close
quarters, a system objectionable to all true sportsmen, and where
the nature of the coverts entirely precludes the adoption of
the principle of getting between the birds and the ground

they are desirous of returning to even in the face of visible
and obvious danger, guns should be at least placed as far away
from the sides of the coverts as may be possible consistently
with bringing the birds within their range.

A. Position of bird at instant of deciding to fire. *x*. Point to aim at if
flight direct. B. Expected position of bird on arrival of shot. C. Actual
position of bird owing to drift. *d*. Direction of wind. A*x*. 36 inches
forward allowed for speed of flight. *x*B. 4 inches lateral deviation by
voluntary curve in direction. BC. 3 inches drift.

It has been endeavoured to show that there are few, if any,
places where it is really necessary to drive pheasants forward
(that is, in a direction in which they do not desire to go) in
the face of guns ahead of them.   Such a practice invariably
affords a majority of low, unsatisfactory shots, and constitutes the
chief cause of offence to public opinion in ' battue ' shooting.

The alternative system explained in this chapter will be
found best calculated to bring to bag the largest number of
birds in the most skilful and sportsmanlike manner.

It may be objected that this style of shooting overhead
becomes a mere game of skill.   It may be so with some who
practise it, but let it be remembered that there is more head-
work required to bring it about than is called for in any shooting over dogs.   Those who understand such head-work watch
and appreciate the plan of action, offer useful suggestions, and
by taking an intelligent, and not a mere mechanical, part in
the proceeding contribute largely to the success of the day, and
delight to feel that they have done so.   Such men, by running
to back up a weak gun when he fails to stop his birds, or by
falling back on the flank behind the line to catch those that
are breaking and would otherwise escape, or by helping to keep
the line and to prevent the covert from being headed, are far

more useful than merely mechanical good shots, who too often think it their only duty to go wherever the game is thickest, or are incapable of exercising a wise discretion as to the extent to which they may vary their appointed position. Although these matters are primarily under the control of whomsoever may be managing the beat, it is almost absolutely necessary to leave to each gun a certain limited discretion. Circumstances may arise in which his moving a few yards to the right or left, forward or back, may be of infinite service, and unless a man has shown himself utterly incapable of making a right use of such discretion it is never well to deprive him of it.

The presence of any considerable quantity of ground game will necessitate some slight changes in the manner of beating a covert. First, it will be obvious that the line must advance less quickly ; secondly, nets may be required to prevent the escape of the hares. These must be so arranged as not to interfere with the proper driving of the pheasants. Where a sufficient length of netting is available, it should be placed along the two sides of the coverts to be driven and round the outside of the stop or flushing covert. If this be done the hares can only escape by charging the line, and thus all must come to the guns. If there be not enough netting to do this, the stop covert should be netted in on the outside, the wings of the net being turned back on each side towards the coverts which are to be driven into it, but never so as to interrupt the pheasants in passing from one to the other. In this case stoppers should be placed on each side of the wood at intervals of from 100 to 300 yards, advancing as the line advances, so as to turn back as many as possible of those hares which may be inclined to face the open ground.

A substitute for nets in covert shooting, where it is desirable to stop the winged game rather than the ground game, is commonly known as 'sewin.' This consists of cord on which bunches of feathers and white or red cloth are tied at intervals of from two to four feet. The cord is then fixed by means of split sticks in the required position at a height of about three feet from the ground.

Such sticks should be light hazel or ash rods, thin enough to bend in one direction or the other when the string is pulled without entirely giving way. They may be placed at intervals of from fifteen to fifty feet, according to the weight of the cord. One man can keep 100 to 300 yards of sewin in constant motion by pulling and letting it go, and birds will not run past it so long as it is moving. It is, of course, much cheaper than netting, and for stopping pheasants from running in a wrong direction is almost equally effective.

If any portion of the covert to be driven through should be exceptionally thick, so as to interfere with the birds running forward, and to induce them to lie close or to take to their wings, it will be well to stop the line of guns, allowing the beaters to advance until this obstruction is passed. The game which escapes behind the beaters will thus come back to the guns, and the general advance can be continued when more open ground is reached.

It has been pointed out that the ready co-operation of subordinates is essential to good management. It should be the duty of every keeper to assist in keeping the beaters and guns in proper line. For this purpose as many keepers as may be available should be distributed at equal distances along the line, with special instruction to see that the beaters do not shirk their duty or too greatly vary their distances from each other. Those who have dogs under complete control should have them at heel. No wild or untrained dog should be ever allowed in a covert, for if a dog should rush forward at a critical moment, the shooting may be completely spoilt by large numbers of birds being put up together, often in a wrong direction, and escaping with scarcely a shot fired at them. It is not an unusual trick for a keeper who desires to spare his birds, with a view perhaps to compel the formation of a second shooting party and thus increase his fees, to let a wild dog follow a running bird when the pheasants are getting together in rather close quarters, and to add to the escaping flights by shouting at his dog with all his lungs. When this is obviously intentional it is well to withhold the customary fee, and if hens are being spared to drop as many as possible within full sight of the trickster, for which the confusing number of birds in the air together will be a sufficient excuse. Where the

' Standing back in covert.'

master understands and manages his own shooting this is never likely to occur, nor will the objectionable system of buying the best places by a preliminary fee to the keeper be practised, a thing not wholly unknown among jealous scorers.

It cannot be too much insisted upon that all birds should be picked up as they fall, not left to be searched for at some future time, as is the habit in many places. Each keeper should make it his duty not only to observe what game is shot, but to see that the beaters mark well the place where it has fallen, and do not fail to gather it. If a dog is required the keeper should go to the place himself, and without allowing the dog to leave him too far if the bird has run on, he should search the ground at least so far as to satisfy himself that it has moved forward and to a distance. One or two keepers with dogs following the line about one hundred yards behind it are most useful in retrieving game which does not fall absolutely dead to the shot.

At all flushing places keepers should be stationed with dogs, sufficiently far behind the guns to secure a wounded bird if one should happen to 'carry on' after being struck. To retrieve one wounded bird is more to the credit of any keeper than to pick up fifty dead ones, although this is equally a part of his duty. It should be the pride of a sportsman to give him as little cripple-chasing as possible. However carefully and satisfactorily the work of picking up is done, it is nevertheless desirable that on the day following the shooting the covert should be carefully searched with dogs, to guard against the possibility of dead or wounded birds having been overlooked.

With the best shot in the world it must happen occasionally that a bird is not killed by the shot that strike it, and the cruelty of leaving wounded birds to linger and die can and should be avoided. Keepers when searching a covert after a day's sport should be instructed to shoot any bird which shows signs of having been injured.

The practice of sparing hens having been alluded to, it may be desirable to add a few hints as to the different methods by which a sufficient stock of hens may be preserved without allowing too many cocks to escape.

On many estates it was customary, in the early part of the present century, to fine a sportsman ten shillings or half a guinea for every hen pheasant he shot. A good story is told of a young gentleman whose University allowance enabled him in the vacation to indulge in the luxury of killing ten hens at a corner of the home-wood, for which he immediately presented a 5*l*. note to his indignant father.

Some keepers are in the habit of catching before the time of shooting a sufficient number of hens to provide the eggs required for the following season, and shutting them up in mews or pheasantries. In some cases these are let out again after the sport is over, but more frequently they are kept to lay in confinement, a cock being put in each division of the pheasantry with from five to seven hens ; or, their wings being clipped, the enclosures are left open at the top that the wild cocks may have access to them. The question of breeding and rearing pheasants does not belong to the present chapter, but it is at least doubtful whether the system of rearing birds from eggs laid in confinement is as conducive to satisfactory sport, in the production of strong and high-flying birds, as is the contrary practice.

The chief advantage of catching up the required number of hens appears to be the certainty that, whatever measure of success may attend the sport of the day, a sufficient stock is secured.

In advancing along a covert it will be necessary occasionally to halt the line, to collect in convenient and accessible places game carried by the beaters. This should be counted and recorded in each case by some one entrusted with that duty ; for, however honest and trustworthy may be the men employed, it is not right to place in their way the temptation to pocket game through any carelessness or indifference in taking account of the number killed.

From this point of view, the practice of keeping individual scores may well be defended, but however interesting this may be to some sportsmen, it is not uncommonly a fruitful source of jealousy, and in any case is scarcely worth the trouble. Up to very recent days a boy was told off to each gun at many well-known shooting places, to notch on his stick the numbers of each kind of game killed and picked up. Individual scores are still recorded at Holkham and some few other places, and where shooting is well managed and consciences are not left at home the quantity of game picked up almost invariably exceeds the total amount claimed.

The pheasant must always be a favourite game bird, for reasons which are admirably expressed by Charles Waterton, who, although not unnaturally opposed to the system of 'battue' shooting, as he understood it, was fully aware of certain natural characteristics which render this bird especially valuable for purposes of sport.

In his ' Essays on Ornithology ' he writes :—

Notwithstanding the proximity of the pheasant to the nature of the barn-door fowl, still it has that within it which baffles every attempt on our part to render its domestication complete. What I allude to is a most singular innate timidity, which never fails to show itself on the sudden and abrupt appearance of an object. I spent some months in trying to overcome this timorous propensity in the pheasant, but I failed completely in the attempt. Young birds learn to feed out of the hand, but fly at the presence of an intruder, be he dog or man. This timidity is an insurmountable bar to our final triumph over the pheasant.

The experience of the writer is not altogether in accordance with this statement. He has known an instance of a cock pheasant which would invariably attack a woman employed on the place. Whenever he saw her alone on her way to the kitchen garden he would peck at her feet, and often fly up, trying to drive his spurs into her face and hands. In fact, she was uncommonly afraid of him. Similar instances are quoted by Tegetmeier, who also relates an anecdote illustrating the perfect familiarity which has in exceptional instances been acquired by pheasants.

Nevertheless, those who speak or write of pheasants as if shooting them was the same as shooting barn-door fowls will do well to turn into a covert half a dozen of the latter, and to note the difference in their behaviour when the wood is beaten for pheasants.

It may be permitted here to deprecate a habit which attaches to nearly all gamekeepers who rear pheasants by hand—the habit of whistling them at their feeding hours. Nothing tends more than this to render them tame and poultry-like. The food should be thrown down without noise on the open ground or in the glades or paths of the covert, and the man who throws it should watch at a little distance to see that the proper number of birds assemble to dispose of it. Where this rule is observed, the sportsman will be spared the dissatisfaction of seeing pheasants inclined to follow rather than to avoid a keeper, and will be more certain to have his skill severely tried by strong and quick-flying birds.

In many places it is customary to shoot cocks and hens when beating the coverts the first time in the season, and to kill only cocks on going over the same ground again. This is a good plan where it is desired to have one very good day in the coverts, but not again to take out a large party of guns ; but where it is preferred that two parties, consisting of about equal numbers, should enjoy the shooting, it will be found more satisfactory to shoot cocks only on the first occasion and cock and hen on the second. The result will be much the same in both cases as regards the stock of hens left on the ground, and as securing the proper thinning of the cocks, which cannot be too much insisted upon.

It should, however, be borne in mind that if the second day's shooting is postponed until too late in the season pheasants, and especially cocks, will become much wilder and more diffi-cult to bring to the gun than if pursued at some time before Christmas. The later they are left the more stoppers will be required, the more care will be necessary in driving and flush-ing the birds, and the more uncertain will be the chance of leaving a properly limited number of male birds to ensure a good crop of eggs in the following breeding season.

Cocks will travel long distances to seek their hens, and if

one cock is allowed for every eight or nine hens on the ground it will be found to be an amply sufficient proportion among birds left at liberty. Where there are too many cocks they drive each other as well as the hens to and fro, often to a neighbour's ground, and frequently cause the eggs to be infertile or the nests to be deserted.

This will be generally accepted as consistent with the experience of game preservers, although instances are not wanting of the expression of an opposite opinion.

In a letter published in the 'Field' of March 24, 1860, a keeper advocates leaving many cocks and shooting down the hens, on the principle that the ladies run after the gentlemen. He asserts that this enables him to get more and stronger broods. His advice has certainly not been followed on the estate from which the figures hereafter quoted are taken.

Mr. Waterton pointed out that by 'battue' shooting the 'regular supply of the market is endangered,' but the contrary effect has undoubtedly been produced by the system of careful preservation which has necessarily accompanied it. Dr. Wynter, in a paper on 'The London Commissariat' ('Curiosities of Civilisation,' p. 223), quoted by Mr. Stevenson in 'Birds of Norfolk' (vol. i., p. 364), gives 70,000 partridges and 125,000 pheasants as the approximate estimate of the number of these birds annually sent to London markets, coming 'mainly from Norfolk and Suffolk,' and these numbers have probably been exceeded during the last few years.

It is obvious that under the older system of rough pheasant shooting this luxurious supply of game birds could not have been approached. In an article in the 'St. James's Gazette' of October 23, 1884, the number of pheasants killed every season in the United Kingdom is estimated at 335,000, but this calculation is probably much below the mark.

The following figures, taken from the accounts kept on an estate of about 10,000 acres of preserved land in Norfolk, will give some idea of the rate of increase in the number of pheasants during the present century, and of the substantial advantage to the proprietor and his friends, as well as to the community in general which they represent.

Year	Pheasants killed in season	Best day	No. of guns	Year	Pheasants killed in season	Best day	No. of guns
1821	39	10	1	1854	1866	206	8
1825	89	11	1	1860	2256	219	6
1830	119	6	1	1865	2887	943	8
1835	297	28	5	1869	2697	477	8
1840	778	63	6	1875	5069	1576	9
1845	1011	73	7	1881	5363	1136	8
1850	1716	—	—				

In these accounts for 1784 the following item appears :—
' Game sent to Her Majesty : 1 pheasant, 4 partridges. Paid carriage of Queen's game, 1s. 6d.'

When we read in Mr. Tegetmeier's excellent book on pheasants (page 4) that 'one pheasant had in its crop 726 wire worms,' and another ' 440 grubs of the crane fly,' it will not be considered surprising that the estate from which these figures are taken is comparatively free from these noxious agricultural pests.

Miss Ormerod, a lady who is a high authority upon insects injurious to agriculture, might make an interesting estimate of the amount of damage which the two pheasants above mentioned would have prevented in the course of, say, three years by each daily meal.

The following figures, taken from the accounts of four distinct shooting seasons, from September to February inclusive, will give some idea of the proportion of game killed that becomes available to the general consumer, after making liberal allowance for the requirements of the owner, his friends and neighbours. The prices of the different kinds of game are taken throughout at the following average :—
Pheasants,[1] 2s. 6d. ; partridges, 1s. 4d. ; hares, 2s. 6d. ; rabbits,

[1] The price of pheasants varies greatly according to the month, or even week, of the shooting season in which they are sold.

Date		Killed	Approximate Value £ s. d.	Consumed	Approximate Value £ s. d.	Given away	Approximate Value £ s. d.	Sold	Approximate Value £ s. d.
1865–6	Pheasants	2,911	363 17 6	315	39 7 6	1,156	144 10 0	1,440	180 0 0
	Partridges	2,142	142 16 0	408	27 4 0	764	50 18 8	970	64 3 4
	Hares	4,564	570 10 0	628	78 10 0	1,907	238 7 6	2,029	255 12 6
	Rabbits	1,625	81 5 0	1,058	52 18 0	477	23 17 0	90	4 10 0
	Other game	367	12 10 0	282	10 13 2	85	1 17 4	—	—
	Totals	11,609	1,170 19 0	2,691	208 12 8	4,389	459 10 6	4,529	402 5 10
1869–70	Pheasants	2,717	339 12 6	307	38 7 6	890	111 5 0	1,520	190 0 0
	Partridges	2,002	133 9 4	520	34 13 4	732	48 16 0	750	50 0 0
	Hares	2,917	364 12 6	445	55 12 6	1,108	138 10 0	1,364	170 10 0
	Rabbits	2,055	102 15 0	1,173	58 13 0	832	41 12 0	50	2 10 0
	Other game	510	21 8 8	284	13 18 8	226	7 9 8	—	—
	Totals	10,201	961 17 8	2,729	201 5 0	3,788	347 12 8	3,684	413 0 0
1875–6	Pheasants	5,084	635 10 0	180	22 10 0	1,119	139 17 6	3,785	473 2 6
	Partridges	1,346	89 14 8	243	16 4 0	492	32 16 0	611	40 14 0
	Hares	2,246	280 15 0	267	33 7 6	699	87 7 6	1,280	160 0 0
	Rabbits	1,570	78 10 0	531	26 11 0	633	31 13 0	406	20 6 0
	Other game	185	10 1 6	137	7 15 8	48	2 0 4	—	—
	Totals	10,431	1,094 11 2	1,358	106 7 2	2,991	294 0 4	6,082	694 3 0
1881–2	Pheasants	5,344	668 0 0	177	22 2 6	957	119 12 6	4,210	526 5 0
	Partridges	2,526	168 8 0	166	11 1 0	417	27 16 0	1,943	129 10 0
	Hares	1,458	182 5 0	143	17 17 0	229	28 12 6	1,086	135 15 0
	Rabbits	1,683	84 3 0	466	23 6 0	701	35 1 0	516	25 16 0
	Other game	286	13 17 0	180	8 7 10	106	4 14 2	10	0 15 0
	Totals	11,297	1,116 13 0	1,132	82 15 2	2,410	215 16 2	7,765	818 1 8

1*s.* ; woodcocks, 2*s.* 6*d.* ; ducks, 1*s.* 6*d.* ; snipe, 1*s.* ; teal, 1*s.* ; pigeons, 4*d.*

By adding to these accounts the value of rabbits, killed by warreners employed to keep them in check, which are not included in the above figures, the total value of the game killed will be found in average seasons to cover the cost of producing and maintaining it. Roughly speaking, it may be taken throughout an average of five years, dating from 1865, that one half of the pheasants killed are hand-reared, the other half being wild-bred birds.

Any alteration of these proportions might not improbably affect in some degree the cost of preservation ; but it is certain that, with favourable soil, good coverts, fair neighbours, honest keepers, and good management, the artificial rearing of pheasants ought to prove remunerative from a pecuniary point of view, leaving out the question of sport.

On the estate from which these figures are taken the necessary conditions are present, but until the quantity of pheasants annually reared and killed was alike increased, about the year 1860, the cost of preservation was very decidedly larger in proportion to the returns than it has been of late years, nor did the value of the game killed in any season cover the expenses, whereas under the existing system it undoubtedly does so.

It will moreover be observed that the increase in the proportion of pheasants is accompanied by a corresponding decrease in that of other game, which indicates a considerable diminution in the stock of ground game on the estate up to 1882.

Some rough abstracts of the game accounts on the same estate show the following tabulated figures. These accounts, representing in each case the expenses from Michaelmas to Michaelmas, cannot be regarded as precisely coincident with the game returns in the previous table.

Any attempt to collect the record of notable bags must necessarily yield very imperfect results. But a few instances

	1865			1869			1875			1881		
	£	s.	d.	£	s.	d.	£	s.	d.	£	s.	d.
Gamekeepers' wages .	273	12	11	286	0	0	369	0	0	435	0	0
Food for game . .	290	7	0	317	1	4	472	11	6	559	16	0
Beaters . . .	55	6	9	34	17	6	64	19	4	75	18	1
Snaring to destroy hares . . .	65	10	8	15	1	6	20	6	7	0	1	9
Night watchers and extra hands . .	27	3	0	23	0	0	38	19	2	62	14	8
Presents to keepers, Christmas, &c. .	10	0	0	8	0	0	9	0	0	9	0	0
Rewards for catching poachers . .	10	15	0	14	10	0	0	15	0	4	0	0
Prosecution of poachers	1	16	0	4	19	9	0	0	0	4	4	0
Game licences and dog licences . . .	11	0	0	13	0	0	7	0	0	9	10	0
Shooting hired . .	37	0	0	35	0	0	43	8	0	43	8	0
Stakes and nets for a pheasantry . .	4	15	7	—			—			—		
Keep of horse . .	30	14	0	36	19	0	34	16	0	36	17	0
Livery . . .	15	17	4	16	10	9	11	19	0	23	8	0
Destroying vermin .	29	14	8	41	14	4	41	9	0	42	8	4
Rewards for nests preserved . . .	8	0	6	3	14	6	11	6	8	2	2	0
Bushing stubbles .	1	0	10	2	6	0	2	8	6	2	8	6
Barley meal, &c. for dogs . . .	25	4	0	23	13	6	9	0	0	12	7	6
Baskets, pails, and snares . . .	12	10	0	9	16	6	7	17	4	3	16	0
Traps and nets . .	—			10	14	6	12	10	2	—		
Harness, shoeing and repairs . . .	6	8	6	2	16	9	4	7	3	7	1	9
Faggots, &c. (Wayland Wood) . .	6	5	0	8	6	8	23	2	0	19	13	8
Rates on right of sporting . . .	—			—			8	7	7	6	8	11

may be given as possessing some interest, either as marking an epoch in the history of the sport or because of the totals being exceptional. In the game-book at Riddlesworth for 1809, six guns are stated to have shot, in January, 1 duck, 93 pheasants, 2 snipe, 19 hares, 10 rabbits—125 head ; to which is appended a note in Mr. Thornhill's handwriting : 'Have not heard so many was ever killed before.' We find in the same book, for 1810, 275 head to ten guns in November, including 110 pheasants, 96 hares, and 63 rabbits. In 1813, with eight guns, also in November, 143 pheasants formed part of a bag of 232 head.

We are not aware how far Mr. Thornhill's note can be relied upon as indicating that the numbers mentioned had not at that time been exceeded, but they must have been at least closely approached some years previously.

In Blaine's 'Rural Sports' (new edition, 1858) the Duke of Bedford and six others are mentioned as having killed, in the year 1796, on Mr. Colquhoun's manor, at Wretham, in Norfolk, 80 cock pheasants, 40 hares, and some partridges in one day.   And in October 1813, the same year as the last entry quoted from Mr. Thornhill's book, no fewer than 242 pheasants, besides other game—the whole bag amounting to 1,229 head —were killed in one day at Holkham.   In 1818 the Holkham game-book shows the best day in the season to have yielded a still larger bag, with 308 pheasants.

Some further returns from this book are not uninteresting, as showing the total number of pheasants killed on the estate in the following seasons:—[1]

1793	.	.	.	.	262	1799	.	.	.	.	347
1794	.	.	.	.	350	1800	.	.	.	.	355
1795	.	.	.	.	323	1801	.	.	.	.	480
1796	.	.	.	.	314	1802	.	.	.	.	488
1797	.	.	.	.	396	1803	.	.	.	.	261
1798	.	.	.	.	519	1804	.	.	.	.	565

That the number of these birds increased rapidly on other estates, besides the one given above as a typical example, could easily be shown.   One quotation will be sufficient upon this point.   Johnson's 'Encyclopædia' (1831, p. 609) states that 'upon some of the manors (Norfolk and Suffolk) the numbers have been so considerable as to admit the killing of 2,000 brace of cock pheasants annually.'   One of the first instances, if not the

---

[1] The writer is indebted to the present Earl of Leicester for the figures given, which will be found to differ very slightly from the returns quoted in a previous chapter.   The smaller total doubtless does not include a few birds picked up next day.

first, in which a thousand pheasants were bagged in one day, was in 1845, when something over that number were killed on the late Lord Ashburton's estate at Buckenham, in Norfolk, by a party of nine guns.

More recently, but still in the days of muzzle-loaders, the late Lord Stamford's bag at Bradgate, in December 1861, is worthy of record. The two best days at pheasants, with thirteen and fourteen guns respectively, show the following figures : First day : hares, 193 ; rabbits, 267 ; pheasants, 736 ; woodcocks, 7 ; various, 3 ; total, 1,206. Second day : hares, 173 ; rabbits, 190 ; pheasants, 1,605 ; woodcocks, 26 ; various, 3 ; total, 1,997. And on one day in the same week 3,333 rabbits, besides 26 head of other game, were killed by thirteen guns.

This number of rabbits has only lately been exceeded, in 1883 and 1885, by 3,684 and 5,086, with nine guns, on Mr. R. J. Lloyd Price's property at Rhiwlas, in North Wales. Of the latter number, no less than 920 were killed by Earl de Grey, whose skill with the gun is known to all sportsmen.

Probably the largest bag of pheasants ever made in one day in this country was at Croxteth (Lord Sefton's) in 1883. The following is the record of the week :—

CROXTETH.

Guns	Date 1883	Phea- sants	Par- tridges	Hares	Rabbits	Wood- cocks	Wild Ducks	Snipe	Vari- ous	Total
6	Nov. 20th	1444	9	310	10	5	28	2	Grouse 4	1812
6	21st	2373	20	319	123	6	—	1	—	2842
7	22nd	1415	31	175	70	5	110	—	—	1806
6	23rd	804	33	255	22	5	112	—	—	1231
		6036	93	1059	225	21	250	3	4	7691

It is not within the scope of the present volume to enter into details of shooting abroad ; but in any collection of re-cords, however small, a reference at least must be given to the marvellous bags said to have been made in France and Germany during the latter half of the last century. Some of the most important of these will be found in Daniel's 'Rural Sports' (vol. ii., pp. 404–406). The particulars of the hunting party which 'chased' in Bohemia have already been given, but the fact that no less than 47,950 head of game were brought to hand in the space of a week or two is indeed so remarkable that it may be repeated here without comment.

It has been more than once insisted on in these pages that the measure of the excellence of sport is by no means dependent solely upon the game killed. The prettiest day's shooting the writer ever saw yielded the following results :— pheasants, 508 ; partridges, 494 ; hares, 95 ; rabbits, 53 ; woodcocks, 2 (November 16, 1876. Merton. Nine guns) The guns were for the most part picked shots, and the day commenced with a flush of very high-flying wild pheasants, some coverts having been driven in the morning. Cocks only were killed at this flush, and of these about three hundred were secured. The beaters having encircled not only the flushing covert but also the adjacent fields, over sixty partridges intermixed with the pheasants fell to the guns at the same time. The remainder of the day was passed in driving partridges and pheasants, chiefly the former, through small spinneys of young trees, broom-covers, and some cultivated land, from whence there was a marching line down-wind across an open heath of considerable extent, and a very killing return drive over a low belt of trees, the heath being then walked again in the opposite direction. By these manœuvres, every variety of shooting was enjoyed ; high rocketing pheasants and partridges on a side wind in the first instance, then lower but faster pheasants and partridges down wind, then many partridges rising before the guns on the down-wind march, followed by a good drive against the wind, and ending with birds rising before the guns with the wind in front of them, the down-wind drive being probably repeated.

It is part of the duty of a keeper to be able to find his birds in the cover to which they belong. For this purpose he must, of course, give them food there. But many keepers run their masters to needless expense in the amount of food used. A few barley rakings, carted from the fields and stacked in the covert, will always give the birds something to pick at, and cause them to feed to some extent at home rather than abroad. Some additional food is generally required, but the importance of regularity in the time of day at which it is given is almost greater than that of quantity.

Pheasants find much natural food. They are especially fond of acorns and beech-mast, and in seasons when these are plentiful they will need little else to sustain them or to keep them at home.

Small galls, or 'nits' as they are sometimes called in Norfolk, although the word is not mentioned in Forby's 'East Anglian Vocabulary,' are found in considerable numbers on the under side of oak leaves. These are often called spangles and are formed by *Neuropterus lenticularis*, the parthenogenetic form of *Spathegaster baccarum*—one of the *Cynipidæ*—and are a favourite natural food of pheasants.

Thousand-head cabbage, seeds of sunflower, and many other things are regarded as useful additions to their dietary, and instances are known in which dried raisins have been distributed broadcast in a wood for the purpose of attracting a neighbour's birds.

EXPLANATORY REMARKS ON PLANS OF COVERTS.

A is the usual feeding ground of the pheasants belonging to the covert B, which forms their ranging and roosting ground. In this covert for the most part the undergrowth is not thick. C is open meadow or cultivated land. D is a clump of high but well-thinned timber with strong undergrowth. The beaters and guns advance in line along the covert B, driving the birds before them into clump D, whence they return overhead to reach the ground from which they have been driven, affording high 'rocketing' shots, owing to the sportsmen being in full view of them when they come out of or over the trees on the homeward flight. E, young trees and bracken.

●	Stoppers during driving.	∿∿∿	The netting.
○	do. do. flush.	▬▬▬	Beaters stationed during flush.
✚	Keepers stationed back.	⧢⧢⧢	The drivers at different stages of the general advance.
⊕	Flusher moving about.		
☉	Guns placed for flush.	⟵≼	Direction of general advance at different points.

STURSTON CARR.

This is the simplest and easiest form of covert to manage, and is capable of numerous modifications which will not

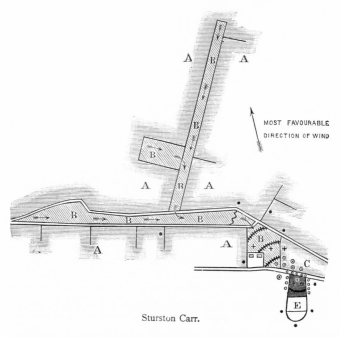

Sturston Carr.

materially alter the method of procedure. The principle is precisely that which yields such remarkable results in the celebrated Scarborough Clump beat at Holkham, *i.e.* driving birds from long ranges of covert into a detached and isolated clump.

CHERRY ROW.

In this plan the flushing point is chosen at D, because there are high oak trees and good under cover at that point. Moreover, as it is the point most remote from the attraction of other ad-

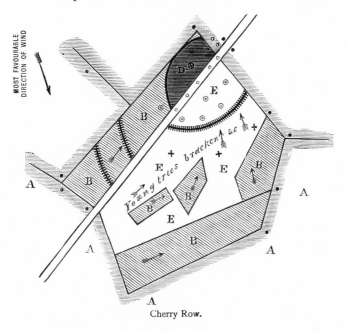

Cherry Row.

jacent woods and feeding-grounds, it best supplies the necessary conditions for providing high rocketing shots. The guns are placed on open ground, chiefly clad with bracken, and behind them this is partly mown to facilitate picking up. As in other cases a screen of hurdles drawn with branches might obviate the necessity for placing a line of stoppers (along the road) at

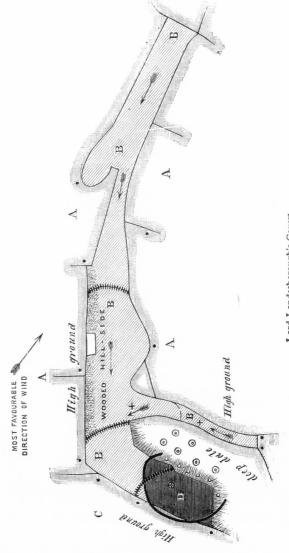

Lord Londesborough's Covert.

the time of flushing : and in the event of high winds from any unfavourable quarter, such a screen would be preferable as less likely to turn the birds. But it would probably be found more advantageous in such case to trust to the wind and to drive to one of the other corners of the enclosure, even although the conditions in other respects might be less suitable for producing high shots.

LORD LONDESBOROUGH'S COVERT.

This diagram, like the others, is reduced from the maps of the Ordnance Survey. The deep dale, where the guns are placed after walking up the long wood on the hillside, insures fine rocketing shots. Stoppers are placed at all points where birds are likely to escape, and these can fall in as the line of beaters reaches them, or remain at their posts if it is intended to repeat or reverse the operation after the first drive. This will depend upon the direction in which it is proposed to take the guns to the next covert, and on the number of birds expected to get away at the flush. The line of beaters stationed during the flush can be contracted, if it is necessary, to concentrate the game, or two flushers instead of one can be employed.

WAYLAND WOOD.

In the case of an isolated wood covering an area of about seventy acres, the pheasants accustomed to feed and roost in the wood will have no natural disposition to leave it, and may be driven to one or other of its corners, with the certainty that on rising they will return towards its centre or thickest part.

The guns may therefore walk in line with the beaters until they approach a corner and are able to form a semicircle, cutting off a sufficient space to contain, without unduly crowding, the whole number of birds that have been driven forward. The guns should then be placed in convenient positions, some perhaps falling back behind the others to secure birds missed or wounded by those in the front line.

The beaters should advance from twenty to fifty paces in front of the guns when stationed, making a slight noise with their sticks, and the flusher should go round and enter the covert alternately from each end of the line, so as to distribute the shooting as evenly and fairly as possible. If the wind is

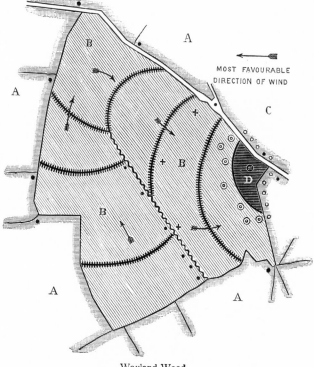

MOST FAVOURABLE
DIRECTION OF WIND

Wayland Wood.

blowing across the front of the line, the down-wind beaters and guns should be slightly in advance of those at the up-wind end, in order to counteract, in some degree, the tendency of the birds to fly down wind to the disadvantage of those who are less favourably placed.

Several points will arise for consideration affecting the plan of action and the choice of a flushing corner.

First, it is important that the place chosen should be sufficiently clothed with under-cover to hide and to separate the birds. In about four years after felling, the condition of the undergrowth will be most suitable for this purpose. If older, it will probably be too high to permit the birds to rise through it, or to allow the shooters to see and move freely when firing.

Secondly, the direction of the wind, especially if strong, will be a cause of success or failure in proportion to the degree to which it may be taken advantage of or ignored. The most favourable condition where this can be secured will be when the centre of the semicircle can be placed exactly facing the wind, but failing this the direction of the wind at the flushing point should be facing, at least, one portion of the line, and that portion should be as near to the centre as is consistent with a due regard to other necessary conditions.

Thirdly, it is probable that in some portion of so large a wood, the undergrowth will be from five to ten years old, and much of this will be difficult to beat through and more difficult to shoot in except where narrow paths or rides are cut. It may thus become advisable to have some portion of the wood driven through by beaters before the guns are brought into the line ; but in such cases nets should be set between the part driven and the part to be shot over, and stoppers should be placed at intervals along the net to prevent birds from breaking back into the heavier thicket. During the execution of such manœuvres, it is often useful to place some guns along the flank of the thicket, where they will usually secure a few overhead shots as well as some ground game which might otherwise escape. There should always be one or two young or energetic skirmishers in every shooting party, who, disregarding brambles and blackthorns, will volunteer for rough service with the line of beaters wherever they may be, on the chance of a few successful snap shots at rabbits in covert. No manager, with a due regard for the safety of beaters or

friends, will send a man who is careless either in handling or
in firing his gun on such an errand, and it will be a wise precaution in case of thick covert to see that rebounding locks
are not made, like the large majority of such delicate pieces of

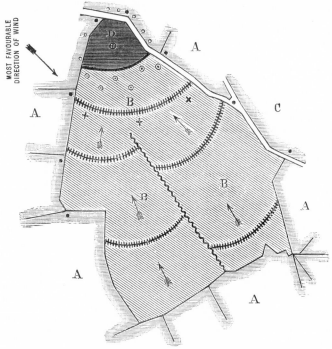

Wayland Wood, about seventy acres.   (Alternative plan of ditto.)

mechanism, so that they can be pulled nearly to full cock by
a catching twig, and when suddenly released can strike the
plunger with sufficient force to fire a cartridge although the
trigger has not been touched.

HOME WOODS.

This plan represents a varied and complicated day's work, and may well be divided into two beats if desirable, although

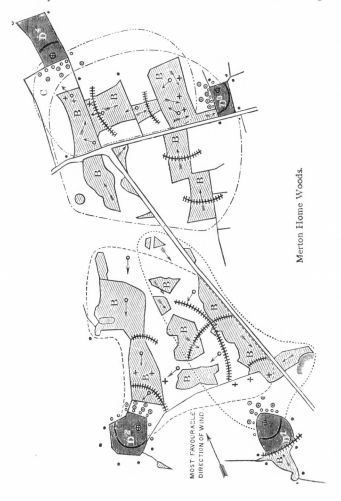

Merton Home Woods.

it is usually taken in one. There are four convenient flushing
coverts : D 1, to which birds are usually driven in the morning
from the area comprised in the line ....; the commencement of the sport consisting of a flush from this covert to guns
stationed in open ground. D 2, into which the birds escaping
from D 1 can be driven on by two separate operations ; the
first extending across the ground traversed in the morning, the
second taking up fresh ground to the north side of it, after
stops and perhaps some guns are placed between the two
quarters of the ground to prevent the game from running back.
This second drive is comprised within the line — — — — —,
and its direction is indicated thus ○→. Later on D 3 can be
made the flushing covert, and all the remainder of the ground,
except the outlying plantation—available afterwards if required—can be driven into it at the same time by separating the
guns and beaters into two parties. This drive is comprised in
the line —.—.—.—. Should there be time for further shooting, the greater part of this ground can be driven in the opposite direction as indicated by ○→ within the line —...—...—,
and D 4 can be rendered a flushing covert by a similar process ;
the guns being placed in the meadow c, to intercept the birds
on their return to the main part of the beat. Not less than
forty or fifty men will be required to beat this ground properly ; and as stoppers cannot be placed in all the necessary
positions in the morning, it must in fact be treated as two
beats, even when taken in the same day.

WOOD PIGEONS.

As connected with the subject of covert shooting, although
not generally spoken of under this head, it may perhaps be
desirable to add a few words about shooting wood pigeons.
There is no kind of sport which tries more severely the
nerve and skill of those who delight to handle the shot-gun.
Many are accustomed to wait for wood pigeons coming into
their roosting places in plantations of spruce or Scotch fir
towards evening. Where the birds are plentiful, several shots

may be thus obtained in a comparatively short space of time ; but the excitement is soon over, whereas by other means it may be prolonged during the whole day.

November, December, and January are the most favourable months. Given a wood where acorns or beech-mast are lying thick on the ground, wood pigeons in almost countless numbers will take up their quarters in the vicinity if undisturbed, and make their appearance soon after daylight to gather their favourite food.

The pigeon shooter should provide himself with three or four stuffed wood pigeons prepared for the purpose, with copper wire, coming from within the body of the bird and passing down the legs, leaving about fifteen or sixteen inches projecting through each foot. He should select a convenient tree on the spot most frequented by the birds, where an active lad can climb high among the boughs and fasten the decoys by means of the copper wire to suitable twigs or branches (No. 1, p. 227)—always placing their heads towards the wind. He should then station himself from twenty to fifty yards off in the direction of the wind, and thus facing his decoy birds—and as well concealed as circumstances will permit—should watch for the pigeons, which, attracted by his decoys, will stoop and wheel in their flight with the intention of settling head to wind.

If pigeons have been already shot at they are very shy of any shelter of boughs or hurdles which could conceal a sportsman, and if no thick hollies or spruce firs are available among which he can stand without being cramped in swinging the gun to the bird, it is best to trust to the colour of his clothing, which should as nearly as possible resemble the bark of the tree against which he places his back.

In snow, which is most favourable if not deep enough to prevent the birds from feeding, a nightshirt put on over the shooting coat and a white flannel cap effect the purpose of concealment admirably. A high wind is almost absolutely essential for this sport. It prevents the gun from being heard at a distance, clears away the smoke which, hanging among the trees on a still day, alarms the birds, and not only makes them fly lower than on calm days, but prevents them from

No. 1. Stuffed decoy pigeon on branch.　　No. 2. Fresh decoy on ground.

seeing so well when flying against it. In such weather they will frequently settle among the decoys or on trees within shot

When to shoot wood pigeon turning.
From a photograph by Lord Walsingham.)

of the sportsman. He who trusts to this chance, however, rather than to a quick eye and ready hand whenever a bird comes within range, will make but a small bag.

It will be found useful to be prepared beforehand with several short sticks pointed at both ends, and when ten or twelve birds are down to gather them quickly and set them up on open spaces beneath the trees as assistant decoys. With wings closed to their sides, resting on their breast-bones, they can be fixed with heads erect or craning forward as if in search (No. 2, p. 226,) of food by passing the upper end of the stick through the lower portion of the beak, the opposite end being stuck into the ground beneath the crop of the bird.

The quantity of acorns which the crop of a pigeon is capable of containing is very remarkable. The writer can vouch for the accuracy of the figures on the next page, taken from birds killed by himself.

A pigeon shot before feeding in the morning has the crop invariably empty.

Stuffed decoy pigeons should never be left on the trees unwatched. Twenty minutes will suffice for their almost certain destruction by grey-backed crows, if there are any in the vicinity.

The writer is indebted to Mr. J. E. Harting for the illustration on p. 229 of an excellent method of mounting dead wood pigeons as decoys. By cutting a number of pieces of wire netting in the shape indicated, the fresh-killed birds can be at once set up with wings clasped to their sides and heads erect, either on short sticks fixed in the ground, or on branches of trees. By means of jointed rods they can also be elevated to any reasonable height without the necessity of climbing.

The feathers of stuffed birds are easily ruffled and spoilt by wet. This wear and tear can be avoided by using the birds only as they are shot.

Another kind of pigeon shooting can be enjoyed in a few places along the coast. In Sutherland and Caithness and on other rocky coasts where blue rock pigeons breed in considerable numbers, exciting sport is to be had by rowing to the mouth of any caves which they frequent, and making a noise to frighten them out.

CONTENTS OF CROPS OF PIGEONS SHOT AT MERTON, NORFOLK.

Date	No.	No. of Acorns	Other kinds of food	Weight of contents of crop
Dec. 8, 1885	1	33	44 beech-mast	These were not weighed
	2	39		
	3	31 (large)		
	4	33		
	5	33		
	6	40		
	7	34		
	8	37		
	9	42		
	10	24	A quantity of barley	
Dec. 30, 1885	1	50	. . . . .	3·25 oz.
	2	36	. . . . .	2·75 ,,
	3	46	17 haws and some turnip-tops . . .	
	4	19	. . . . .	3·25 ,,
				2 ,,
Dec. 31, 1885	1	32 (large)	. . . . .	3·75 oz.
	2	29	. . . . .	2·50 ,,
	3	60 [1]	. . . . .	3·75 ,,
	4	47	. . . . .	3·25 ,,
	5	51	. . . . .	4·50 ,,
	6	49	A quantity of barley .	3·75 ,,
	7	41	A quantity of barley .	3·25 ,,
	8	13	A quantity of barley .	1·75 ,,
	9	—	194 holly-berries .	2·25 ,,
Jan. 30, 1886	1	—	Turnip-tops . .	1 oz.
	2	—	Turnip-tops . .	1 ,,
	3	43 and a quantity of pieces of acorns	Turnip-tops . .	4·50 ,,
	4	20 (very large)	Turnip-tops . .	3 ,,
	5	40	. . . .	2·75 ,,
	6	43	. . . . .	3·25 ,,
	7	13	Turnip-tops . .	2·25 ,,
	8	7	Rush-seeds, barley and turnip-tops . ,	1·75 ,,
	9	3	Clover-leaves . .	1·25 ,,
	10	63 [2]	. . . . .	4·50 ,,
	11	—	Buds of oak and turnip-tops . . .	1·75 ,,

[1] Not common acorns, perhaps from evergreen oak.   [2] Common acorns.

There is no more difficult shooting than to kill a good right and left over head as the flock of birds come rushing out.

The rolling of the boat, the twisting flight of the pigeons, and the distracting noise of the breakers as they dash against the rocks, combine to try severely the skill of the best of shots.

A gun may be posted on the cliff above the caves, and to him the birds dashing out far below will offer scarcely less difficult chances.

Between Caton and Flamborough, on Lord Londesborough's property in Yorkshire, such shooting is sometimes practised,

Net-wired decoy pigeon.

Net-wire for decoy pigeon.

but invariably from above, as the cliffs are too high to enable the pigeons to be reached from a boat. Looking down 200 or 300 feet is in itself sufficiently trying to the nerves and head—and to make the proper allowance for pace and to judge the distance of birds far below the gun is no easy matter.

Those who have travelled along the coasts of Albania or of Portugal will probably have had some experience of this exceptionally difficult shooting.

W.

The following is probably a record for wood-pigeon shooting, and is an instance of the effective use of live decoys in this attractive and beneficial form of sport.

PUTTERIDGE, NEAR LUTON, BEDS.

				Wood Pigeons
Dec. 23, 1895,	Thomas Sowerby	.	. . .	. 220
,,　,,　,,	Harry Sowerby	.	. . .	. 119
,,　,,　,,	Hubert Sowerby	.	. . .	. 106
	Total .	.	. . .	. 445

The bag was made on a bright day with a strong wind blowing, and the guns were placed about three-quarters of a mile apart. In the previous year (1894) the same three guns killed 3,199 wood pigeons, but the best day's bag was only a little over 300.

W. *July* 1899.

CHAPTER X.

REARING.

As directly affecting the question of sport, we have to consider after each shooting season what is to be done in preparing for the next. This portion of the subject is one with which sportsmen do not as a rule specially concern themselves. They leave such matters, for the most part, to the discretion of their gamekeepers, and are satisfied to regulate the amount of confidence they place in them by the results achieved.

However true it may be that the proof of the pudding is in the eating, it is nevertheless desirable that all owners of land on which game is preserved, as well as others who possess sporting rights, should be at least so far acquainted with the duties of a keeper as to enable them to exercise a general superintendence over his work, with a view, not only to efficiency, but to economy. There are many who, almost regardless of expense in pursuit of the pleasures of sport, exercise little or no control over the ways and means by which such sport is produced, and are content to pay the bill and ask no questions.

Unless keepers are a very exceptionally honest class, it is obvious that such a system must offer a strong inducement to imposition and robbery. There are many ways in which it has been endeavoured to guard against this objection. On some estates keepers are paid only in proportion to the results produced ; either at the rate of so much for every bird reared, or so much for every bird killed in the course of the season. Both these methods appear to be open to some objection.

If the price per bird reared is not unreasonable, this plan would seem to afford a sufficient assurance that the sport obtained will be proportionally equal to the cost of providing it ; but as in every other system, so in this also, confidence must be accorded in some manner and to some one person at least.   Some one must count the birds and see that the right number are charged for, and even if the owner should do this for himself, what assurance can he have, if his keeper be not honest, that the number he sees on one day will be there the next ?   The alternative plan of paying so much for every bird killed is provocative of much bitterness of heart in the event of bad shooting.   It is not pleasant to feel that, whenever you or your friends allow birds that come within shot to escape unscathed, the person chiefly interested in the performance is audibly growling his displeasure.   The same system also inevitably leads to great jealousy between neighbours, com-mencing with the keepers and not unfrequently communicated by infection to their employers.   It is not conducive to good feeling between country neighbours to offer any extra induce-ment to a keeper to condescend to artful devices to attract or secure the birds which frequent a boundary.   In every way it will be found preferable to engage the services of the most trustworthy men obtainable, to give them their orders as to what is expected of them, indicating the amount of sport you are justified in looking forward to, and the expense you are prepared to incur in enabling them to provide it.   After this understanding is arrived at, the test of merit may well be the degree of success which attends their efforts, but in any case a very elementary knowledge of the subject will help an em-ployer to detect the causes of failure or to check extravagance in his servants.

So soon as the shooting season is over, a little regular feed-ing in the coverts will enable a keeper to judge what stock of birds he has left. He will soon see how many hens come to the feeding-places, and by listening at the time when the birds go up to roost he can soon determine the proportion of cocks to hens remaining on his ground.

Should he require to take up hens for his mews, if he has any, this is the time to do it, and there are many ways of catching the required number.

One very simple method is to feed in and around an ordinary hencoop, leaving the sliding door elevated by means of a light stick, which would be displaced by the bird in entering. If the proportion of cocks to hens should seem to him to be too large, he may well exchange, with the consent of his employer, a certain number of cock birds for hens or eggs from another locality; the object being to secure a change of blood, which, if obtained from a pure source, is always beneficial to the stock. Care should be taken in making such exchanges not to introduce birds crossed with other breeds, still less such as are likely to be weak or unhealthy. There is no better breed among pheasants than that of the true *Phasianus Colchicus,* commonly known as the old-fashioned dark variety, without a white ring on the neck. These are free layers and good mothers—straying less from home than the paler plumaged varieties more recently introduced. They are quite as hardy, and fly at least equally well. There are few places in England now where some traces of a cross with *P. torquatus,* the ringnecked Chinese bird, are not to be met with, but in the opinion of the writer the cross-bred bird is not so worthy to be encouraged and propagated as are those of the old dark pure breed.

Before discussing the construction of mews or pheasantries, it may be well to consider the advantages and disadvantages of their use in providing the eggs required for rearing.

According to the statements of experienced keepers, hen pheasants kept in a mew, where many are together, cannot be relied upon to produce an average of more than twenty to twenty-five eggs each in a season. Where small numbers only are kept, from thirty to forty eggs per hen are said to have been obtained. But such numbers are not at all likely to be reached where rearing is conducted on a large scale.

A cold dry time does not conduce to free laying ; warm showery weather is more favourable. Wild birds will average from twelve to fifteen eggs each in good seasons ; but they will do well indeed if they bring six birds to the gun if left at large to encounter all risks. Where eggs are gathered from wild birds a good keeper should bring to the gun from seventy to seventy-five per cent. of the birds hatched. The loss through accidents and bad eggs cannot be fairly put at less than twenty per cent., and this will be greatly increased in case of exposure to frost. At Wretham, in Norfolk, out of 8,500 eggs gathered in the year 1885, 7,500 young birds were hatched— giving an average of over 88 per cent.—but the keeper states that this proportion has never before been obtained there in his experience of over twenty years. The opinion of a keeper who has had more experience than almost any other in rear- ing—James Mayes, of Elveden—is that he cannot count upon bringing more than ten birds to the gun out of every twenty eggs gathered from his mews.

Although undoubtedly a larger number of eggs will be obtained per head from healthy hens kept in a mew if well fed and cared for, it is notorious that the proportion of such eggs likely to be infertile, or to produce weakly birds, is considerably larger than that of eggs laid by hens left at liberty. Moreover, a larger number of cocks will be required in proportion to the hens where these are kept in captivity. Whereas a wild cock will probably secure fertile eggs from eight or even ten hens at liberty, the number placed with each cock in confinement should not be more than five or six. The expense attend- ing the system of shutting up the birds is of course con- siderably in excess of that required to feed them at liberty. Where many foxes are to be found this expense is probably almost unavoidable, and certainly the outlay would in such case be justified. But where the dangers to which wild birds are likely to be exposed are not exceptional, the system of gathering the required eggs from the first nests of wild birds will probably be found to yield the best results, at the smallest cost.

The first eggs that should be gathered are those which are laid in the fences of public roads and other similar situations, where they are exposed to the danger of being taken by passers-by. Next it may be necessary where adjacent ground is not preserved to remove those which lie near the boundaries; but where a neighbour is a ·careful preserver, it is scarcely fair to take up the eggs from his boundary, nor is it advisable to do so, as the effect is to diminish the stock in the outlying coverts, which in such a case should be almost as productive as those towards the middle of the ground. If sufficient eggs be not procurable from these sources, as many as may be required may be taken up in the coverts; these should always be the earliest eggs, that the birds may have the chance of laying a second time, and thus bringing up a wild brood of late birds.

In gathering eggs, whether in a mew or in the open, one or more should be left in each nest so long as the bird will continue to lay to them, or if all are taken, a common hen's egg should be put in their place. It will be easily understood that if, say eight or nine eggs are taken up and the nest left empty, the bereaved bird will probably deposit the small remainder of her clutch elsewhere and perhaps commence sitting, and thus the chance of a full second brood will be lost.

In some places it is the custom to take up all the eggs that can be found, but where no wild broods are allowed to get off, it is difficult to prevent the shooting from becoming somewhat tame, partly owing to the proportion of weak birds likely to be found among those reared by hand, and partly from the fact that hand-reared birds are apt to have a certain tendency to tameness. Where mews and pheasantries are required, they can be constructed in many different ways. The best system is probably that in which a piece of ground is enclosed by a high boarded fence, and divided into partitions from twelve to twenty feet square. The more space that can be afforded the better it is for the birds. The pens may be separated either by screens of reed fastened together with splines, or by string netting; the whole being usually covered in with a coarse-meshed string net, well tarred to resist the weather.

Square-meshed netting with a two-inch mesh, although somewhat more expensive, will probably be found more durable than the commoner kinds. In any case string is better than wire, since it inflicts no injury on the birds, if, when alarmed, they dash themselves against it. Strangers should never be allowed to enter a mew; their appearance instantly frightens birds which are perfectly tame in the presence of the keeper who feeds them. Their habitual attendant should even be careful always to wear the same kind of clothing. Any conspicuous change in his dress will be likely to cause a disturbance often resulting in injury. Pheasants in a mew should not be pinioned in the strict sense of the word, but should have the pinion feathers of one wing cut off short to prevent them from flying against the net. When this is done the birds can either be turned out after the moulting season, and thus exchanged for others if desired, or their feathers can be cut again at will. In some places, notably at Elveden, in Suffolk, whole coverts are wired in; a large number of hens are pinioned, not merely clipped, and these enclosures being open above, the wild birds have access to them at all times. From twenty to one hundred acres have been taken in in this manner, and the system undoubtedly conduces to great economy of time and labour in gathering the eggs; it is also probably less expensive in the long run than keeping up a large number of small enclosures. Even in small pens the plan of leaving them open above, to allow the access of wild cocks, has been strongly advocated on the ground that by this method a larger proportion of fertile eggs are secured than where the birds are entirely shut in. In any case it is not safe to trust entirely to the access of the wild male. There should be a pinioned cock in each division with the hens, even if the top be left open, but no bird should ever be pinioned beyond the terminal joint of the wing. Eggs, whether taken from a mew or from the open ground, should be placed under sitting domestic hens with as little delay as possible, and a good keeper will lose no time as soon as the shooting season is over in replenishing his stock of fowls for this purpose, until he has made up the required number of healthy

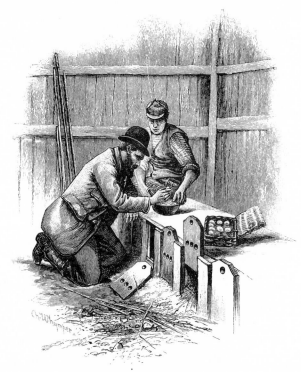

Keeper testing eggs.

birds. Great care should be exercised in selecting fowls for foster-mothers. They should be in all cases free from disease. Pheasants and fowls belonging by nature to the same family group are liable to the same diseases, and these are easily communicated from one to the other. When a keeper has got his

R 2

hens he will do well to remember that every egg they lay will be of value at a later date for the purpose of feeding his newly hatched birds. He should collect the eggs carefully and store them in a cool place on shallow trays—not forgetting to set them up on their small ends, in which position they keep good for at least eight or ten weeks without further attention. A wash of lime water over the surface of each egg has been recommended as a good preservative, but this is found to be unnecessary. When required they can be boiled hard, and the contents chopped up small form a most excellent and almost necessary substance to mix with the food of the young pheasants during the first few days of their existence. A good warm shed should be provided for the fowls to roost in, but they should be left at liberty to roost on the trees if they prefer it. The most important matter to be considered is the provision of suitable coops in which to place the eggs under the foster-mothers. Many different systems have been adopted in the construction of enclosures or sheds for this purpose.

The object generally kept in view has been economy of labour in feeding the sitting fowls. This is not the only consideration to be regarded. Nearly all enclosures are open to one serious objection, which is that they interfere too greatly with the natural habits of the birds. During the period of incubation all birds not prevented from following their natural instincts are accustomed to leave their eggs for the purpose of feeding in the early morning, when there is dew upon the herbage. By thus wetting the feathers of their breasts they are enabled to increase the amount of warmth imparted to the eggs throughout the day's sitting, and it will be found that in all cases where birds are deprived of the power of thus artificially adding to the natural heat of their bodies, the percentage of unhatched eggs left in the nest and of weakly bantlings struggling into a brief or uncertain existence will be much larger than under the unrestricted conditions of a wild life.

In rearing pheasants, as in many other things, the simplest system will probably be found to be the best in the long run.

With a view to accustom the fowls to the new quarters in store
for them, it is well for a keeper, before the pheasants begin to lay,
to put out a number of coops conveniently near his house, and
to make in them false nests of hay, taking care to scrape out
the earth to a sufficient depth to secure plenty of warmth.   By
putting nest eggs in these he will induce his fowls to lay in
them, and when their eggs are changed for those of pheasants,
they will the more readily continue their maternal duties than
if moved to new quarters.   Most keepers prefer to retain the
eggs until they can put down ten or twenty hens at one time,
owing to the convenience secured by the hatching of many eggs
on the same day.   So soon as the eggs begin to hatch a keeper
should shut the sliding door of the coop, and, placing a low
board against it to prevent the escape of the young birds
through the bars, should leave them till the following morning,
when he can take out the whole brood, and put them, together
with their foster-mother, under another coop on the ground
selected for rearing.   This second coop should for about a fortnight be supplied with a small enclosure made by three boards
with some string netting over the top, into which the little birds
can run without danger of being lost or chilled by wet in
high grass.   There is always some danger of the hens crushing
or smothering a certain percentage of the first hatched birds.
Where incubators are available, the first hatched nestlings should
be removed as soon as seen, and placed, together with the unhatched but good eggs from the same coop, in an incubator.
About twenty-four hours after all are hatched the brood may be
returned to the hen.   Incubators may be usefully employed, not
only in this manner, but also whenever the supply of sitting hens
is insufficient.   However many hens may be kept, there is often
some difficulty in getting them to sit at the time when they are
most wanted, and in this case an incubator is a valuable aux-
iliary.   It may frequently be necessary to take up eggs that are
already partly incubated, and if these be not placed under a
sitting hen without delay they will be inevitably spoilt.   Here
again, if hens be not ready at the moment, the incubator may

prove extremely useful. It is also of great advantage for such birds as, when first hatched, are weaker than the remainder of the brood, and seem to require more warmth than the hen can supply. A few hours in the incubator will usually set such birds on their legs. Nevertheless, an experienced keeper will always prefer to place his main reliance on a good supply of hens, and no artificial mechanical system, however perfect, will justify him in entirely dispensing with them.

Having drawn attention to these points, it may be well to give some description of the sitting-houses most generally

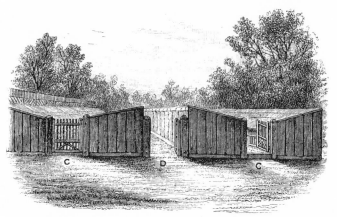

Hatching-pens, as lately in use at Bradgate and elsewhere.

found in use where pheasants are largely reared ; but the writer must guard himself against recommending any such method, having a strong conviction in favour of the more primitive plan already indicated.

The primary outlay required to provide pens for pheasants and hatching-boxes for hens will vary considerably, according to the price of labour and materials and according to the details of construction. If elaborate and luxurious quarters be desired, the expenses incurred may be easily made to reach a large excess as compared with the economic advantages secured. Where simplicity of construction and cheap materials have been insisted upon, the results may possibly be made to justify the expenditure, but any calculation based upon figures not carefully verified would throw but doubtful light upon the subject. Having regard to the very wide divergence which is found between the statements of experienced keepers as to the

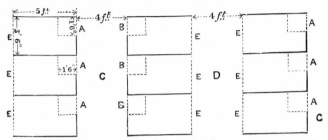

Ground plan of hatching-boxes and pathways to same.

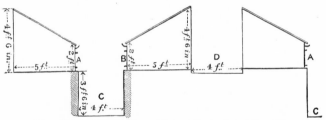

Ground plan of hatching-pens lately at Bradgate and elsewhere.

A and B show positions of slides opening nest boxes. c. Lower pathway by which boxes are reached. D. Upper pathway on same level as floors of hatching-boxes. E. Lattice-work front of boxes.

economy of different systems, it is desirable to avoid all risk of publishing figures which might tend to mislead, and merely to point out the advantages claimed for hatching-boxes as compared with coops.

By having a number of enclosed hatching-boxes in long parallel lines, a keeper can quickly see from either end of the line if one or more of his sitting hens have left their eggs, when he can at once change the hen. One man can also attend to and feed a much larger number of hens in a short time than where these are in separate coops. Having first placed the food in readiness by walking along the line of boxes, he can move all the hens, in turn, off their eggs into the feeding-yard, and let them back by reopening the dividing doors when they are fed. A man can move 300 hens in from twenty to thirty minutes without difficulty under these conditions, and on the principle that time is money there is a certain gain in securing such expedition.

Bearing in mind the advantage already alluded to of an early morning run in wet grass for damping the breast feathers of a sitting hen, the best substitute for this where hens are kept in closed yards is to sprinkle the eggs with tepid water at the time of the morning meal.

Illustrations are here given of the kind of sitting-boxes used at Elveden, and of the system formerly adopted on the estate of the late Lord Stamford and still in use on some other estates where pheasants are largely reared (pp. 240, 241). These illustrations in great measure explain themselves.

Separate portable hatching-pens are also much in use where it is found convenient to change the position of the rearing establishment.

Next in progressive order we should perhaps consider the choice of ground for rearing the young birds and the necessary supply of coops.

Ordinary hencoops can be easily and cheaply constructed. They should cost not more than 4s. each if made of foreign deal, or 3s. if made of rough English wood. The middle bar should be inserted through a hole in the top, and fitted with two cross-pieces grooved or pierced to fit the nearest bars on either side, forming a sliding door which can be raised as required. The small temporary boarded yard can be placed against the coop or removed at pleasure. The number required will of course depend upon the number of broods it is intended to put down. A Dorking or cross-bred hen of ordinary size will hatch and comfortably brood from fifteen to eighteen young pheasants ; but the number placed in each coop must depend

ELVEDEN RANGE OF FIXED HATCHING-PENS

in some degree upon the size of the foster-mother. Turkeys have frequently been used for this purpose, and will cover and hatch thirty or thirty-five eggs each ; but they are too heavy for the young birds, which should be removed and placed under the care of a common fowl as soon as hatched. This is a cause of additional trouble and expense, and constitutes a forcible objection to the use of turkeys.

Grass land which has been closely fed off during the winter, on a sandy soil if possible, is the best which can be chosen for placing the coops. Rough heaths or commons not encumbered by high gorse bushes—which form a holding-place for vermin— nor tainted by being too much overrun with rabbits, are also suitable for the purpose. Fallow lands are usually too cold and shelterless for very young birds, and the drip of trees should be avoided. Old layers of clover or cinq-foin, if close fed, are almost equal to grass. It is a common belief, and by no means unfounded, that it is not well to rear pheasants for many successive years on the same piece of land. Most keepers will be found to advocate a change at least once in every three or four years. Few would think of using the same ground for more than six or seven years if this could in any way be avoided. Nevertheless it is within the writer's experience that at least one thousand young pheasants have been successfully brought up on the same forty acres of poor pasture every year for at least fifteen successive seasons. The question whether a particular locality is suitable or unsuitable for the purpose will depend mainly upon the amount of natural insect food which it provides, and the exhaustion of such food forms probably the chief reason against rearing birds for many years in succession upon the same ground. Where ant-hills are abundant, or where the condition of the soil is especially favourable to insect life, the supplies are not likely to be so rapidly exhausted as on stiff clay or burning chalk. Where ground is well sheltered it harbours more insects than are to be found in bare exposed situations. At the same time it should not be too much shut out from the sun, and for this reason a south or south-west exposure is preferable.

The coops should be arranged in rows from twenty to twenty-five yards apart, and in close proximity to each a few rough thorns with spruce or Scotch fir branches should be laid down to afford temporary shelter for the young birds in case of sudden alarm. These are a great protection, especially against small hawks. In situations where the natural drainage is imperfect and the ground is liable to become saturated with surface water, thick straw mats can be obtained which afford great protection against wet if placed beneath the eggs in each coop; but prevention is better than cure, and such situations should always be avoided if possible. The coops should be moved every day; twice—morning and evening—is better than once only; a yard or two will suffice when the birds are very young, but as they become more advanced in growth, from five to ten or twelve yards should be passed over at each shifting. The move can easily be made, by dragging the coops slowly along the ground by means of a hooked stick placed between the bars, without letting out the hen. The effect of this is that the hen does not brood the birds on ground which has been rendered foul by her excrement, and danger to the health of brood and foster-mother alike will be avoided.

If it should be necessary to move the coops to a different locality, this can be done by slipping a bag net between the coop and the little enclosed yard attached to it, so as to catch the young birds; each brood can thus be removed in an old rice bag or padded basket, but the birds should never be handled.

When the hen has been caught and re-cooped elsewhere, the small attached yard can be put down if required, and the little birds let out again. When it is desired to allow these to have more liberty, it is not well to remove the yard at once, but rather to separate it from the coop by a small space at one corner, so that a few can escape at a time. These will always be attracted back by others left at home, and thus gradually the whole brood will learn to use their liberty discreetly.

When pheasants' eggs are gathered they may be kept for three or four days without danger of spoiling, provided always

that the process of incubation has not commenced ; but from
the moment any change has set in from this cause, their
vitality is in danger of perishing if they are not placed under a
hen or in an incubator within two or three hours of being taken
from the nest. Before coming to the question of feeding young
pheasants from the time of their birth, it should be remembered
that provision must be made for the proper watching and guarding of the ranges of coops during both night and day. A small
movable wooden shepherd's house, built on wheels, is a convenient means of providing shelter for a keeper or watcher ; in
it he can light a small fire and store the various utensils required

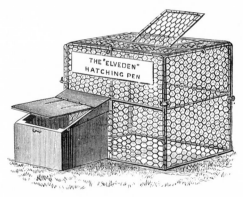

THE "ELVEDEN" HATCHING PEN

Portable single pen.

for his work. If two men are employed for night work, one can
sleep while the other is on the alert ; in any case, a good watch
dog should be at hand, always tied up, to give the alarm if strange
dogs, foxes, or poachers are about. A light temporary shed
is also useful in which to store coops not in use, or under
shelter of which to prepare and mix the food. Some keepers
keep lanterns or fires lighted at night in the neighbourhood
of their birds to scare off vermin, but this is a poor substitute
for constant personal supervision. The vermin chiefly to be
guarded against where birds are reared are stoats, weasels, and

rats, crows. hawks, jackdaws, and some owls. The best way to keep rats in check is by poisoning, after feeding with barley-meal for three or four successive days beforehand in the mouth of their holes, care being taken that the poison is buried very early on the following morning ; stoats and weasels must of course be trapped. Kestrels will attack very young birds, but scarcely any after three weeks old. Sparrow-hawks usually begin to kill only after the broods are three weeks or a month old. These are therefore to be watched chiefly after the kestrels have left off mischief. The common barn owl attacks young game birds only in very exceptionable instances ; but the long-eared brown owl is an enemy to be more decidedly taken into account. The writer has no reason to doubt the strong and unanimous evidence of his keepers that they have frequently seen these owls alight upon the coops at night, flapping their wings and cracking their beaks that they may seize upon any unfortunate nestling driven out by the disturbance. Crows and jackdaws will alike take many eggs and also very young birds. Jays will take eggs but not young birds. A stray dog arriving among the coops at night is often most destructive. He will not only kill a number of young birds, but will overturn the coops and destroy the foster-mothers, and no mercy must be shown to such a marauder ; he is an enemy to the sheepfold as well as to the game-preserve.

When we come to the important question of food, it is impossible to summarise in a short space all that has been published on the subject. Innumerable advertisements are in circulation recommending various patent pheasant foods, containing a great variety of ingredients ; granulated meat, spices, meat graves, rice, rangoon, ground oyster shells, &c., and accompanied by the highest references and testimonials. We are not concerned to discuss their merits here. It will be sufficient for the purpose to indicate a few of the best ingredients, and to describe what should form the basis of a healthy system of feeding.

Mr. Carnegie (' Practical Game Preserving,' p. 34) gives the following table of food for young pheasants 'as an example of a course of feeding . . . not of necessity to be followed exactly.' It has the merit at least of pleasing variety, and may be found useful by those who are not afraid of encouraging epicurean daintiness among their pampered chicks.

Table of Food for Young Pheasants.

Age of Pheasants	Morning Feed	Midday Feed	Evening Feed	Remarks
Up to 3 days	Custard	Custard	Custard	A slight sprinkling of oatmeal may be added if thought advisable
3 to 7 days	Custard and meal	Custard and meal	Custard and meal	The meal to be gradually increased
7 days to 3 or 4 weeks	Custard, crushed wheat, millet seed, chopped lettuce, bruised hemp, chopped potatoes	Custard, barley meal, boiled rice, onion, Dari seed, chopped artichoke	Custard, oatmeal, groats, buck wheat, rapeseed, dry dough	But two of these need be added to the custard, or the separate diets can be alternated day by day or every three or four days
1 month to 2 2 months to 6	Wheat and (or) barley Maize, barley, beans, green food	Custard and meal Dari, oats, maize, green food	Wheat and (or) barley Maize, peas, wheat, green food	These can be given on alternate days, or changed week by week

No food whatever should be given to young birds for at least the first twelve hours after they are hatched. For the first ten days at least the chicks must be fed five times a day, afterwards four times, say at 6 A.M., 11.30 A.M., 2.30 P.M., and 6 P.M., until they are about six weeks old. It is not necessary to place the food in any vessel.

The preservation of a sufficient number of hens' eggs has already been alluded to. These, when hard boiled, should be finely chopped up, or, still better, rubbed through a wire sieve and mixed with a little dust of oatmeal.

After a few days a little finely dressed barley-meal and what is commonly known as 'scrap cake,' finely ground, may be added. We are informed that scrap cake consists of the membrane and tissues of animal fat. When the fat is melted it is pressed through a bag, and the scrap is what is left in the bag. The best scrap cake is from perfectly clean fats used in making butterine. The present price ranges from 12s. to 24s. per cwt.

Greaves by themselves, when finely ground, will be found to answer the purpose perhaps equally well for mixing with the barley-meal. Maggots are also very good food for young pheasants, especially in dry weather, when insects are scarce. But these should be properly purified by being made to drop into rough barley-meal ; unless so purified they will cause the birds to scour and will kill them very fast.

Many keepers are so firmly convinced of the advantage of

'The Foster Mother.'

using maggots, that a visit to their rearing-grounds is often anything but pleasant. When on a warm summer's day the ladies go out to see the 'dear little pheasants' fed, it is a sad shock to their unsuspicious minds if they stumble across the maggot factory ; a dead horse or cow carefully elevated on a wooden rack, with pans of lively barley-meal below it, is apt to be not only high, but almost unapproachable.

Scrap cake is best given after being scalded by having boiling water poured over it. Sometimes it is even boiled in a cauldron.

Rice (and this is a good useful food) should also be boiled. At Elveden, the writer is informed by Mayes, the head keeper, that he considers rice and greaves the best food for young pheasants when about three weeks old. The greaves are chopped up small and both are boiled together ; when cold the mixture will cut like a pudding. He then

'A Night Alarm.'

works some barley-meal into it with a stick, but adds no more water. Rabbits boiled and chopped up small also form an excellent food for young pheasants.

Those who may desire to make themselves acquainted with the views of other authorities on the subject of feeding, may refer with advantage to Mr. Tegetmeier's 'Pheasants,' which contains much valuable information ; to Mr. Bartlett's experiences detailed in Elliot's ' Monograph of the Phasianidæ,' and quoted by Tegetmeier, who, by the way, expresses a preference for canary seed over grits and meal ; to Mr. J. Bailey's ' Pheasants and Pheasantries,' and to many interesting letters scattered through the columns of the ' Field ' and other sporting news papers. But it will be well to bear in mind that the methods adopted by owners of aviaries are not always exactly suited to the requirements of gamekeepers who have to rear birds on a large scale in the field ; and that it is necessary to exercise some discrimination as to what is or is not sound practical advice applicable to the particular case for which the information is desired.

After the first three weeks some old lettuce finely chopped, or a few chopped onions, rue or garlic, should be added to the food, and continued until the birds are old enough to pick a little corn, which should always be steeped for twelve hours. Steeped maize, wheat, or barley is the most suitable food for the hens in the coops. When the food is given in a sufficiently moist condition there will be no necessity to leave pans of water near the coops, nor indeed to give either the birds or the hens any water at all, and many keepers have a strong prejudice against its use, believing it to be the cause of diseases, especially of gapes.

In all cases, if given, it should be first well boiled, and should never be left to stand too long. A few bitter herbs are sometimes added to the water to give it an appetising effect. In speaking of gapes it may be interesting to mention that a paper has lately been read by Dr. Walker, of Franklinville, U.S., before the Buffalo Microscopical Society, of which the following notice appeared in an American local newspaper :—

At a late meeting of the Buffalo Microscopical Society, Dr. Walker, of Franklinville, detailed the results of some experiments upon the ' gape-worm of fowls.'

Before the present investigation was begun, a little more than a year ago, it was generally supposed some intermediate host was required, but what that was no one had any definite idea. That the earthworm is the original host is proved by eight separate experiments with as many different chicks, by feeding them on earthworms from a locality where chickens had the gapes. In every instance the gapes was produced in seven days. The earthworms were examined, and the parasite found coiled up in the structure of the worm in the same manner as trichinæ are coiled up in their cysts. That all earthworms do not contain the parasite was proved by feeding chickens on earthworms from a locality where they did not have the gapes. The disease was not produced. On examining the worms with a microscope the parasite was not found.

The life history of Syngamus trachealis is as follows : Earthworms containing the embryos are eaten by the fowl. The embryos are liberated from the earthworm and force their way through into the air sacs, thence work their way through to the lungs, where they pass through the nymph stage and acquire sexual maturity. The male and female then unite, and attach themselves by their sucker-like mouths to the mucous membrane of the trachea. Between six and seven days are required from its entrance into the fowl until its attachment to the trachea. In seven days more the eggs within the body of the worm become mature ; they are coughed up, swallowed by the fowl, and pass through into the soil. In three weeks these eggs, exposed to the moisture and sun, hatch the embryos, find their way into the earthworm, where they remain until picked up by some bird, when the above process is repeated.

Some years one-half or two-thirds of the young fowls, in some localities, are destroyed by the gapes. This investigation proves that, if young fowls are kept from earthworms, that terrible scourge of poultry, the gapes, will be prevented.

If this gentleman's observations are correct, the danger arising from the use of water insisted on by Dr. Megnin (see p. 159) and others has been possibly overrated. But, on the other hand, the theories of these two scientists are not necessarily inconsistent with each other. Dr. Walker can scarcely be said to have proved conclusively that the embryonic parasite cannot, or does not, live in water at any stage of its existence.

It is difficult to arrive at any exact estimate of the cost of

rearing pheasants, the system, as well as the scale on which
it is done, varying so greatly in different instances, and necessarily affecting the question of economy.

After the birds are cooped, one man can well feed and
look after about forty coops. If we allow three men, or two
men with a boy, to assist in preparing food, this will be an
amply sufficient staff to rear 1,000 pheasants. Their services
would be required for about sixteen weeks—say up to September 1—and if we take their wages at an average of 15s. a
week, the cost is 36l. A peck measure of chopped food will
be about sufficient for each feeding round, and during the
whole time 50l. should be amply sufficient to provide the necessary food. This sum allows 1s. for the feeding of each
pheasant. Hens may be bought in February or March at
about 2s to 2s. 4d. each, and should be sold again in August
at 1s. 6d. to 1s. 8d. ; allow 30s. for wear and tear of coops, and
without calculating anything for the rent of the land occupied,
the cost of each pheasant when turned off into the covert will
be about 1s. 7d. from the time of hatching.

It will be found in many places that this estimate is much
exceeded. There may be special circumstances which justify
the excess, but in the absence of unfavourable conditions we
see no reason for it. Much will depend, as in all cases, upon
the care and attention of those to whom the rearing is entrusted.
There are keepers and keepers. It is absolutely necessary to
find a man who will take some pride in his work. An indolent
keeper is like a field of poor land ; you must be always digging
at him to stimulate his energies, harrowing him if he fails in
his duty, and manuring him with approval if he has produced
good results and is required to produce them again. This
is uphill work, and those employers who, to save themselves
the trouble of finding a better man, continue to put up with
indifferent service, cannot expect a satisfactory measure of
success or economy.

When the young birds are finally turned off into the coverts
to shift for themselves, it is desirable over and beyond the

ordinary hand-feeding to provide some permanent store of food to which they can at all times have access. Rough wheat or barley rakings taken from the harvest field after the crop is gathered can be carted into the woods and heaped in some convenient and central place. A light deal roof erected on four posts to keep off excess of moisture will preserve such food in good condition for a longer time than if it be left uncovered. The birds will soon learn to scrape around it to pick up a few grains, and the heap will be soon brought low and thoroughly ransacked. Rats are greatly attracted by these temporary stacks, and an inspection of such reserves of food will afford a good indication of the efficiency with which the keeper performs his duty in keeping down vermin. Nothing is so distressing to the eye of a sportsman as to see the food-stack full of small round rats' holes, and to find their tracks running to and from it in every direction. He knows, if he knows anything, that for every ear of corn the rats have eaten they have also probably robbed him of an egg or a young bird during the breeding season. Wage war against rats, or you may expect but a poor stock of winged game.

The plans to be followed for the successful rearing of partridges differ in one respect only from those necessary in the case of pheasants : they require somewhat more careful feeding. Where ants' nests are abundant there is no difficulty in supplying the young chicks with their favourite food, but the pupæ of ants, commonly known as ants' eggs, are almost absolutely essential to good results during the first fortnight after hatching. Where these are not to be obtained, many substitutes have been suggested. Mr. Carnegie (' Practical Game-Preserving') recommends bruised wheat soaked and then fried, or Spratt's patent 'Crissel.' He adds :—

About the third or fourth day some custard may be given mixed with lettuce, chickweed, plantain (the unripe flower), groundsel, rice broken small and boiled, and small quantities of any small bird seeds. The best way is to make a thinnish custard, and mix some of the other food materials with it, always giving preponder-

s 2

ance to the green food. Any insects which may be obtainable may also be given in addition to the ants' eggs, which, it is necessary to remark, ought not to be offered the chicks till the other food has satisfied their appetites.

Boiled rice, custard, or hard-boiled eggs well bruised will certainly ensure the saving of a fair proportion of the chicks; but these alone are by no means equal to the same with the addition of ants' eggs. It is a good plan to sweep the rough herbage in the borders of some neighbouring field or wood with a coarse bag net made of canvas or calico on a stiff iron hoop fixed in a strong handle. By this means a large number of insects of various kinds are easily collected, and can be conveyed in a bag to the coops and thrown down for the birds.

When the birds are three weeks or a month old the same food that is given to young pheasants may be provided for them, but grain should in no case be given unless first soaked and crushed. In moving the coops the direction of the open fields should of course be taken rather than that of the covert. There is really very little to be written specially about the artificial rearing of partridges. A good keeper will save himself unnecessary trouble and expense, and devote his attention to protecting the wild birds during the nesting-time, rather than to any substitution of the artificial for the natural process of rearing.

Circumstances may not unfrequently occur which render it necessary to take up eggs. Nests are often exposed by mowing green fodder crops, and the old birds are either killed or permanently frightened from the spot. Two hen birds often lay in the same nest, and sit side by side, or quarrel for the privilege of exclusive attention. In these cases, as also when eggs are laid in dangerous or exposed situations, it is desirable to put them under a hen, especially if there is any reason to fear that the process of incubation has already commenced. If it is certain that the eggs are fresh they can be divided among the nests of other birds which have not yet begun to sit, and provided the number in each nest be not

made up to more than twenty there is every chance that they
will be duly hatched. The usual number of eggs laid is about
fifteen, but if the first nest has been robbed or destroyed the
second clutch laid by the same bird does not usually amount
to more than eight or ten.

As many as twenty-five eggs have frequently been found
where there has been no reason to suppose that they belonged
to more than one bird. Even when eggs are hatched under
hens it will save trouble and produce better results to put the
young birds down as soon as possible with other broods of the
same age if such can be found. The parent birds will not
resent such additions to their families within the reasonable
limits of their brooding capacity, and all the risks attendant
upon artificial feeding and rearing will be dispensed with.

Provided always that the ground be suitable for partridges
and that due care be exercised to protect them against all
enemies, there will be no difficulty in getting up a stock of
such birds where they are scarce.

A few imported birds turned down every season for a few
consecutive years, and fed at least for a time near the spot
where they have been set at liberty, will in all probability attach
themselves to their new quarters without further trouble. It
is a good plan when turning down any wild birds in a new
locality to make a small wire or string netted enclosure and to
confine them for a while, letting out only a few at a time at
intervals of a week or ten days, always being careful to feed
only around the enclosure so long as it contains any birds.
This prevents those which are let out from straying away from
the spot. They remain near their companions which are
unable to follow them, and thus gradually become accustomed
to the haunt. The writer has had some success in introducing
the Virginian Colins in this manner in Norfolk. Although
nearly thirteen years have elapsed since they were first turned
down, an occasional brood is yet to be found about the place,
and at one time they had spread themselves somewhat widely
in the county.

If birds cannot be obtained, eggs can be begged or bought, and thus the nucleus of a stock created ; but it should always be remembered that to buy eggs anywhere except direct from the owner of preserved land is a dangerous incentive to poaching of the worst kind. Many a man has bought his own pheasants' and partridges' eggs, and some men have bought the same eggs twice over, convinced by their keepers that the first lot were all bad and had to be thrown away. Those who may not buy their own can in no way secure themselves against buying their neighbours', unless they take the trouble to deal directly with someone who possesses a stock of birds. Exchanging with a friend is the best system of getting eggs whether for stock or for a change of blood, and many are glad to have the offer of such a chance ; but to do this one must of course have some equivalent to offer, and few game preservers will accept pheasants' eggs in exchange for partridges'. There are other ways of increasing the stock where partridges are not entirely absent. An admirable plan is to sow buckwheat along the furrows of every turnip-field. The seeds of this plant are most attractive to all game birds. On rough waste-land rough barley, wheat refuse, or buckwheat may be scratched in with a harrow, but this is only necessary where no stubbles are adjacent.

The late Lord Stamford used to make his keepers scatter hemp seed along the hedgerows — an expensive but very effective plan of attracting birds. Other preservers have been known to net the coveys on outlying portions of their ground and transport them to the centre, that their places might be taken by immigrants from other quarters. This has been done only in very exceptional cases, and will be generally condemned as an unneighbourly proceeding.

If good breeding-places be provided for the birds, and keepers attend properly to their duties, there should be no difficulty in getting up a stock of partridges on any suitable ground. Light sandy soil with plenty of natural insect food—

a little furze or broom seed sown in old rabbit-holes or along the hedgerows—double thorn fences or young larch and fir belts conduce greatly to success. Heavy stiff clay soils and close-clipped single thorn fences are unfavourable.

The worst enemies to partridges next to foxes are dogs, if allowed to hunt the fences in the breeding season. Foxes comparatively seldom disturb birds on their nests, but will constantly catch them on the open fields, where a covey sit closely

An intruder.

huddled together at night. From the beginning of May to the middle of August it is most important to keep dogs away from any ground on which you may want to get up or maintain a stock of partridges.

The proportion of cocks to hens being almost always in excess in each covey, it is a good plan to let the keepers (or rather those only who have licences to kill game) shoot a certain number of cock birds as soon as they begin to pair. When this thinning process is much required it will be noticed that wherever a pair of birds is to be seen a single cock is in attendance at a respectful distance, having been worsted and beaten off in a fight on account of the hen.

It is not unusual upon land which has long maintained a large stock of birds to find their numbers diminishing in each successive season. If a general condition of ill-health should be found to prevail on any particular farm, the ground should be at once cleared by killing throughout the season every partridge that comes on to it, and if possible keeping it entirely free from birds for a whole year. After this has been done, the same ground should be treated as a sanctuary for a single season. At Holkham by this plan Lord Leicester succeeded in re-establishing a healthy stock on land where for several years he had lost large numbers of birds from disease.

W.

A day with the ferrets.

CHAPTER XI.

RABBIT SHOOTING.

OF the various beasts or fowls of chase or warren which have been treated of in this work, there is none which affords more universal sport and amusement than the common rabbit—common enough, nay, almost ubiquitous as he is ; and there are few sportsmen, however poor, who cannot command during the year a day's outing after the rabbits on some neighbour's farm, or on the preserves of some landowner by favour of the keeper. The first essays of the schoolboy newly entrusted with his light single barrel are sure to be directed against the coney feeding in the park on a balmy summer's evening, well away from the covert. The last resource of older sportsmen, when all the partridges are shot, and all the game in the woods sufficiently thinned, is to 'have out the ferrets' and try to kill down a few more rabbits; while there is no gunner, however deadly at tall rocketers, or at grouse driven down wind with the velocity of bullets, who will not hail with joy the prospect of a good day's shooting among the little white-tailed rodents whose only fault was once defined by a distinguished statesman as being 'six inches too short.' And very much too short he sometimes is, when he darts across a narrow ride like a little brown shadow, and quick must be the eye, and ready the hand, that can get the gun to the shoulder and discharge it in the brief second that elapses between the appearance of a tiny brown nose on the one side of the path and the vanishing of a little snow-white patch of down on the other. Or again, where rabbits lie on thick heath, or dying fern, beneath which they have innumerable runs and highways, smooth as glass, but concealed from sight, and along which they dart with as much rapidity as when in the open, there is no artist with the gun who need be ashamed of himself if he finds at the close of the day that there has been an alarming expenditure of cartridges in proportion to the slain. But the variety of the haunts of rabbits and of the different ways of pursuing them is endless. We will, however, try to describe a few of them.

Perhaps the commonest way of killing rabbits is to employ ferrets to bolt them from their holes, and either to shoot them as they dart forth, or else set purse nets, into which they rush, over the exits. When rabbits can be induced to bolt freely very good sport may be obtained in this way, but unfortunately they are apt to be most capricious in this respect, and waiting for an hour or two while a ferret 'lays up,' without the chance of a shot, is not an exhilarating pastime. Ferrets differ very much in their habits; some, very good ones, can be depended upon never to lay up, but either to drive a rabbit out or else leave him. Opinions differ much as to the best variety of ferret to use. For ourselves we have a preference for the white species over the brown or 'polecat' kind. It is said that these latter are a cross between the ordinary ferret and the true British polecat, and probably this is the fact ; but we think the pure bred white ferret is apt to be more docile, better tempered, and at the same time keener and more bloodthirsty than the brown variety. A cross between the two will often produce an excellent animal, and most ferrets are now bred in this way indiscriminately. Ferreting is perhaps the least exciting form of rabbit shooting, and may be dismissed without further comment than that it requires a windy day for ferrets to bolt well ; they bolt better before midday than after.

Very good sport can be obtained where rabbits frequent hedgerows or banks, especially among old pastures. If a ferret, muzzled, be run through all the holes about two days beforehand, most of the rabbits will be found sitting out, either in the hedge itself or in the long grass close by. With a couple of well-broken spaniels and one gun on either side of the hedge, a most excellent morning's sport can be obtained ; the hedge must be worked very closely, and if it be a thick one the spaniels must be good hard bitten ones to force the rabbit into the open. Once driven out he flies like the wind to some other shelter which he knows of, and affords the most excellent practice even to shots of high skill. Here we would recommend good spaniels as being superior to terriers, beagles, or any other breed, for use with the gun. Terriers, though good in their way, are far too excitable, and will range too far ; besides which, they are of the hound species, and once settled on the line of a rabbit which has been shot at and missed, will follow it as long as they can own the line. Worst of all, when they can mark the rabbit to ground they cannot resist the temptation of following him there and working away under the surface perhaps for half an hour, just when their aid is most needed above ground, to emerge with coat and eyes full of sand, half-suffocated, and more tired and exhausted than if they had roused a dozen rabbits from the covert to afford nice shots for their master. The same objections may be made to some extent to rabbit beagles, which, although they do not go to ground, are yet worse than terriers in their way of sticking to a line and following a missed rabbit far away from the proposed beat. In fact, both of these two breeds of dog, being of the hound kind, are bent first and foremost upon catching the rabbit for themselves. Now the spaniel fully recognises the fact that he is a mere adjunct to the gun, and it is to this latter weapon that he must look in order to realise his quarry. Therefore, when a rabbit is started he is content with one wild rush, and if after a couple of barrels are fired at it the creature escapes, he is willing to fall back into his place and is ready to find another rabbit in the thicket or hedgerow—aye ! and perhaps has done so three or four times, ere the terriers return panting from the fruitless pursuit of the last one that escaped unscathed by the shot. Worst of all, neither beagle nor terrier can resist the temptation offered when the line of a fox or hare is crossed, and either scent may carry them off a long way from the scene of action where their services are needed; while if by chance a vixen with early cubs be found while rabbiting in spring, and she should pop into an earth just in front of the terriers, irreparable damage may be done in a very short space of time.

For all these reasons, then, we recommend spaniels for use with the gun ; and now the question arises, which of all the numerous breeds is the best? The most popular and almost the commonest is the ' Clumber,' a lemon and white variety, too well known to need description. Very good, no doubt, Clumbers are—very steady, but apt to be sulky, and carefully bred to be mute. For many purposes, such as working for snipe or for partridges—and there is no prettier sport in all the world than shooting partridges in high turnips with a couple of guns and a team of Clumbers—this is an immense advantage. Many good sportsmen affirm that the mute spaniel is even more 'killing' than his noisy brother, yet for the particular sport of rabbit shooting we confess to a strong leaning in favour of those spaniels which use their tongues well. In strong covert, such as gorse brakes, it is of no little service to the gunner to know when a rabbit has been freshly roused and may be expected to show himself at a moment's notice, while the tongue of some breeds of spaniel is very eloquent and will serve to warn the shooter not only of what is going on inside, but even of what sort of game he may expect to appear.

There is a good old-fashioned breed of large Cocker, liver and white in colour, strong in bone, and short in the leg, somewhat short in face and wiry in coat, that is, we think, typical of all that is best for this sport. Such dogs are to be found in Devonshire, in the New Forest, and in other similar places where rough shooting is carried on; they are of an old-fashioned breed, having existed long before dog-shows and the various points of coat, &c. were established: free with their tongues, keen of nose, and full of sagacity. Such a one we have often shot with; he was a strong untireable dog and entirely unbroken till two years old, but his natural sagacity and fondness for the gun were such that after a few days' sport he needed no more breaking, but would always work in the best way for the 'bag.' This dog would invariably throw his tongue—a very deep melodious note it was—on the line of anything as soon as he could own it, but he had a different note entirely for winged game from that which he used for rabbits. Rarely did he speak to the latter until on the point of rousing them, and then the short sharp 'yap' left no doubt as to what was going on. On the other hand, on the line of a running pheasant every time a hit was marked by a deep bell-like note, and often we have seen the old dog turn his head to look for his advancing master, for whom he would wait steadily if, as was often the case, the shooter had been outpaced on a hot scent, till he saw that the gun was in reach before darting off again, knowing as well as possible that it was by the aid of his master alone that the quarry could be brought to bag. Then the cheerful burst of cry as the bird was flushed, so characteristic of the Cocker breed, and the merry bay over the game if it fell to the shot, were all delightful, and thoroughly in keeping with the rough single-handed shooting, for which alone spaniels are really suited. For rabbit shooting, then, we would recommend dogs of this breed; strong, sturdy, 'tonguey,' and not too fine in the coat, and we are sure that they will be found thoroughly useful, both for that and for any other work to which they may be put.

It would be difficult to describe a pleasanter day's sport than one which two guns, aided by three or four spaniels such as we describe, may enjoy, either among the dense furze-brakes of the New Forest or on the open heaths and commons in other parts of England where there is a fairly good stock of rabbits and plenty of covert to shelter them. Arrived at the spot the two guns separate, and take up positions whence they can command such small stretches of open ground as are to be found. At a single word all four spaniels are out of sight in the dense thicket, and in another minute the voice of each may be heard proclaiming that the game is afoot. Soon a shot resounds, then another, and another, as the pursuit renders even such a stronghold as a couple of acres of thick furze too warm for its usual occupants. Then a rabbit tries to make away straight over the open hill up to the burrows on its crest, and is handsomely stopped by a fair good cross shot at forty-five yards; next a quick snap is taken at a rabbit that bolts across a single yard of green turf between two patches of gorse that would hide an elephant, and anon the easiest of shots is offered by an all-too-careful coney, who bolts to the very edge of the brake and there pauses, listening to the eager voice of the foe that is pursuing him, regardless or heedless of the more deadly enemy in front to whom his life presently pays forfeit. Then a rapid change of position has to be made by the artillery according as the voices of the spaniels show the game to be travelling in some direction contrary to that which was expected. And so all hands are kept busily employed for an hour or more, until the whole patch of covert is thoroughly explored and the spaniels emerge panting, tired, and bleeding, when perhaps some twenty-five rabbits may be shown as the result of the beat. Then, if at the close of the day some eighty or ninety head of

game encumber the cart or the backs of the beaters who have
to convey it from the ground, the two guns who have been
employed will have no reason to complain that they have not
been kept very actively engaged, or that they have not had a
most excellent day's sport.

For such work as this, dogs—especially spaniels—are of the
utmost service, but we do not recommend their use when more
than three or, at the outside, four guns are employed, nor
where many beaters are made use of. In such cases the only
method that will be found really effective is to form a good line
and to maintain it, sending all rabbits well forward and keeping
them in front. Spaniels, of course, make one rush at a rabbit
as they rouse it, regardless of the direction it may take, and
if used with a line of guns and beaters they will be found to
drive nine out of every ten rabbits back through the line, when
it will be very doubtful if a shot can be obtained at the object
of pursuit, still more if it can be safely fired. For large parties,
then, where a great number of rabbits are to be killed, it will
be wisest to leave the dogs at home and to trust altogether to
a well-kept line of human assistants. Such a day as this is a
different affair altogether from what has been described above.
This is a real ' battue,' if the popularity of the word will render
it for once permissible, as the collection of some twelve or fifteen
steady beaters, the anxious looks of the keeper and his assistants,
and above all the presence of some six or eight well-known
good shots, testify: men who would not be here unless there
were real work in the shooting line to be done. But, as is
often the case in matters of sport as well as in those of more
importance, the essence of success lies in the arrangements
that are previously made to ensure it, rather than in the actual
working of the day itself. So in rabbit shooting, that keeper
will have the best day's sport placed to his record, irrespective
of the skill of the guns employed or of the weather which
may have favoured him, who understands best the art of
'showing his rabbits.' This art lies merely in inducing the
rabbits to lie outside their burrows and in the open or in

the covert, as the case may be, on some given day; and let the stock of rabbits be ever so large, let the damage done by them be ever so conspicuous, or the complaints thereof ever so loud, still unless the rabbits be well 'shown' all this counts for nothing, and failure and disappointment reign supreme.

But the question is how the success should be achieved? There are various ways of making rabbits temporarily forsake their burrows, and one, perhaps the commonest plan, is to bolt them therefrom with muzzled ferrets, when they will not return to their holes till all scent and trace of the ferrets have passed away. This plan answers well enough where the rabbits are few in number, but time would fail ere anything like the multitude needed for a 'big day' could be driven forth. Some other methods must in such cases be adopted, of which one of the best is to lay a little handful of tow or of rags in the mouth of each hole, well soaked in paraffin oil or some other strong smelling fluid, and after the rags have laid there a few days, to loosely stop the earth with a spade. Of all chemicals, however, the most efficacious is spirit of tar, a few drops of which will work better and last longer than any other compound. The best manner of using it is as follows. Cut a considerable number of short sticks or pegs some six inches long, and in the head of each make a slit or notch ; in this place a piece of paper folded four or five times into a square of about an inch. In the mouth of every burrow let a peg with a square of paper be placed by boys, and it will be found that they show up most conspicuously, so that the keeper can walk round his coverts and tell almost at a glance if one single burrow has been overlooked. Then let him take a bottle of spirit of tar and with a brush or stout feather sprinkle every square of paper well, but not moisten the soil with a single drop. Two days afterwards let him set his boys to work to pull up every peg and to loosely stop every hole. Again, when on his rounds the tell-tale and conspicuous paper will reveal where a burrow or a single hole has been neglected. On the day after this has been done the

coverts are fit to shoot. Every rabbit in them will be above
ground, fresh and well, not half frightened to death by ferrets,
but sitting out of his own free will and ready and willing to run
as only rabbits can at the least provocation. Moreover, not a
burrow has been spoilt or polluted, the offensive smell has dis-
appeared with the little pegs and their squares of paper, and in
a few days the rabbits, such of them as may perchance survive,
will be as much at home in their residences as ever. Any devices
such as 'smoking' or 'stinking' out earths will probably lead to
the abandonment of those abodes for a more or less lengthened
period, to the construction of new burrows to the detriment of
the property, or, if it be small in extent, possibly to the emigra-
tion of the whole colony to the adjoining lands of some more
sensible neighbour. If the extent of ground be large and time
be an object, the removal of the pegs and the stopping of the
earth may be omitted. The rabbits will all be above ground,
and will not be so very anxious to return to their burrows, and
the pegs can all be collected and taken up after the day's
shooting is over, when the rabbits can make use of the same
burrows as before, without finding in them a trace of the means
which were adopted to expel them.

Let it be supposed, then, that all these matters have
been satisfactorily arranged, that weather is propitious (and
very much depends on this, for in some weather, especially
when a fall of snow is impending, nothing that can be done
will induce rabbits to sit out), that the party is assembled,
and all is ready to begin. The scene is a large 'wild grassy
chase,' or park covered in parts with vast masses of high
bracken, in others with long tussocky grass, and here and
there with a patch of heather; huge boulders of stone crop
up at intervals through the covert, and the open ground described is on three sides surrounded and sheltered by plantations old enough to withstand all attacks on the part of
the coney. Through the large bracken patches are cut numerous rides, one for each gun, dividing them systematically
into a fixed number of beats, and the same is done where

the gorse brakes are large enough to admit of it. The *modus operandi* is merely to walk in line, but it must be *really* in line. Every beater must be an equal distance from his fellows on the right and on the left, and the guns should be an equal distance apart and in line with the beaters. The object is, first, to pass over no rabbit without rousing him from his seat; secondly, to drive every one that is so roused forward in the direction towards which guns and all are looking, and not to let him run back. It is the fixed idea of the rabbits, as of most other wild animals, to lie as closely as possible in the concealment which they have adopted and to allow their enemy to pass, perhaps within a few feet, but as soon as he is well past them to steal away behind his back. This will show what mischief is done by a man who will not keep line but *will* walk a few yards ahead of the rest. If he kick up a rabbit himself possibly it may go forward, but far more probably it will dodge round him and go straight back through the line, for when once started it is not readily turned. But for one rabbit which is actually moved by the badly drilled culprit he has passed five or six close at hand which have, unnoticed by him, watched him keenly out of their great brown eyes and noted well his presence. Each of these when moved by the beaters in the advancing line will bolt back if he possibly can, rather than run forward to face a second enemy which he knows has gone in that direction. The worst offenders of all in this matter are often the guns themselves. Over and over again have we seen men who seemed as if they could not, or would not, keep in line, but would walk persistently about five yards ahead of the beaters. The consequence is that at least half of the rabbits put up near them will go back, not only affording a much more difficult shot than if they went forward, but also adding greatly to the danger, for if shot at all it must be through a gap in the advancing wall of beaters, and a stumble, a trip, or some trifle of the kind will bring the head of the man between the muzzle of the gun and the retreating coney. Above all, let us entreat every man who goes a-shooting ground game never to adopt the dangerous practice of firing at a rabbit over the body of a man who has crouched or flung himself down to get out of the way, and invites the sportsman to shoot over his head. Perchance the shooter does so, and misses. The crouching beater, who cannot see from his position what is going on, hears the report and starts up again, just in time, it may be, to bring his head level with the muzzle at the moment the trigger of the second barrel (about which he never for a moment thought) is involuntarily pressed by the gunner. Well! we need say no more about the sad result, but let it be remembered that such things have occurred, aye and frequently too, and that too much care and precaution cannot be taken when it is recollected that every shot during the day's rabbiting is fired at such a level that it will wound a man if one should happen to be in the line of fire.

If, however, all precautions are observed and the line well and steadily kept, there is no finer day's sport to be had than a good day's rabbit shooting of the kind described. Every variety of shot is obtained, from the chance taken at a rabbit flitting beneath the bracken concealed almost entirely from view, to the fair long cross shot at forty-five yards aimed at a rabbit darting with the speed of thought across the open sward levelled like a bowling-green by the grazing of generations of his ancestors, or from the quick snap taken ere the gun reaches the shoulder at a rabbit darting between the boulders of rock either of which will amply shield him, to a fair steady 'pot' at one stealing slowly over the ride thirty yards away. There is endless variety, and many shots will be difficult enough to satisfy the most exacting. Above all, where, as is not unfrequently the case, 600 to 1,000 rabbits are killed in one day, there is enough shooting to content anyone. Where the ground and the surroundings lend themselves well to it, the stock of rabbits is a mere question of breeding and feeding. Under circumstances of this kind, such monster bags as 3,000, and even on one occasion 5,000, in a single day have been obtained. But this is a matter rather concerning the warrener than the sportsman, and hardly comes under the head of rabbit shooting proper. Given the stock of rabbits in an enclosed space, it is merely a question of expediency whether the gun or some other means is adopted for reducing them into possession (as the lawyers say) and bringing them into a marketable form.

We have now followed the sport of rabbit shooting in all its details, from the modest hour's sport with a ferret and a couple of guns, to the systematic shoot with its multitude of beaters and crack shots, and have pretty well exhausted all the forms in which the sport may be enjoyed during the legitimate season for shooting. Yet one very pleasant pursuit remains, by which the rabbit may afford amusement at a time of year when there is little else in the way of sport to be had. During the summer months hundreds of rabbits may be seen sitting out in the meadows surrounding every covert and in thousands in many a park. Take a stroll around these localities on some lovely summer evening, say in June or July after a rainy day, and take as your companion one of the exquisitely finished little pea rifles which are turned out by many a firm at the present time. You must know the ground well, and choose the point from which you approach the rabbits with some care, so that there may be a hillside or a dense wood or some similar background to check the course of the bullet should it glance off hard ground or miss its object. Safest of all is the shooting of this description where there exist old sand-pits or stone quarries well frequented by rabbits ; any number of perfectly safe shots can be fired in such places, and the most beautiful practice obtained among the most charming surroundings. Much skill too is needed in the way in which the rabbits are approached, and the direction of the wind, the lay of the ground, and many other things have to be considered. But when a successful stalk has been made, and a fair bead drawn upon a rabbit at sixty good yards distance, with the satisfactory result that he instantaneously turns over and dies with hardly a struggle, as he will do if the little conical bullet strikes him in the right place, the shooter cannot but feel an inward glow of satisfaction not merely at his prowess with the weapon, but at the triumph of woodcraft which has resulted in the successful shot. Easy as it sounds, it should be tried by those who doubt the difficulty. A rabbit at anything over fifty yards in longish grass is a very tiny object, and is almost entirely concealed even by the delicate sights which are affixed

to the rifles turned out by Messrs. Holland and similar professors of the art of gun-making. A straight eye and a steady hand are essentials even to this somewhat tame form of rabbit shooting, but an evening's walk may be enlivened and made enjoyable by the skilful obtaining of some dozen or so of such shots as we have described, and the sportsman's eye loses none of its cunning by being kept in practice by such means as this during the close season, when most forms of his favourite sport are denied to him.

Good work might also be done with the pea rifle at hares upon downs, in large parks, and in those few places or manors

in which these animals are allowed to survive under the legis-
lation which has affected them of late years. In the early
spring troops of jack hares may be seen following the does and
fighting with one another. From time to time, as they stand on
their hind legs opposing each other, they afford the fairest
possible mark for the rifle, and there is no way in which hares
can be better preserved or the stock more efficiently increased
than by systematically thinning down the superabundant jack
hares in the spring. This work is usually left, where indeed
its necessity is understood at all, to the keeper ; but if the owner
of the shooting can obtain an evening or two of sport, and at
the same time improve both his stock of game and his shooting
powers by undertaking it himself, he had far better do so and
not leave it to be either neglected altogether or insufficiently
done by his servants.

With the description of rifle shooting concludes the list of
modes in which the rabbit can be pursued with the aid of
firearms of one kind or another. Enough we hope has been
said to convince the reader that this humble form of sport need
by no means be despised ; that the rabbit, destructive as he may
be to crops or trees, is yet capable of affording much amusement, and that too at a small cost if he be restricted to those
places which are most suitable for him and in which he can do
but little harm. 'Be to his faults a little blind'; remember he
is as it were the staff of life to foxes, and, as well to stoats and
other noxious vermin, that he serves as a 'buffer' between
those destructive forces and game of more value than himself,
and that no shooting will be so profitable, so pleasant, and so
varied as that in which a fair sprinkling of ground game be
allowed to mix with the feathered 'fowls of warren.'

G. L.

THE BLACK LIST

CHAPTER XII.

VERMIN.

THE definition of 'vermin,' according to the game-preserver's view, includes every living creature, four-footed or winged, which can by any possibility, or even by any stretch of imagination, be deemed to interfere with the rearing of game, or destroy one single head thereof when full-grown. In this list, as it is ordinarily accepted by the average, and therefore ignorant, game-keeper, are included many animals which are perfectly harmless, and the persecution of which benefits in no degree the cause which it is desired to promote. On the other hand, there are certain creatures whose very presence on a manor is noxious to the 'beasts and fowls of warren' which may frequent it ; and such creatures form a class of vermin against which every man who desires to see game thriving and increasing on his property will endeavour to wage war to the utmost of his power.

We propose briefly to describe these classes of vermin, and to give a very few hints as to the best method of exterminating them. Every keeper, however, who is worth his salary, will have his own system for destroying vermin, which he has, no doubt. learned as a boy, and it is in most cases the best plan to leave him to himself within certain limits, only restricting his superabundant zeal, if it be directed against those birds or beasts which are of special interest to sportsmen other than game-preservers, or to the naturalist.   On every side we see birds and beasts, once common in this country, gradually becoming extinct before the spread of population and the prevalence of cheap firearms in hands governed by an unthinking head.   Every game-preserver who aspires to be a sportsman also should think twice before he consigns any rare or interesting creatures to the black list of vermin, nor should he do so until he has thoroughly satisfied himself that his sport is really suffering some serious injury from their presence on his manor.

We would, then, divide vermin into three classes : First, those which do nothing else but harm, and a good deal of it. Secondly, those which do some little harm but also some good, and should only be killed to such an extent as to keep their numbers down, and under certain circumstances.   Thirdly, those animals which undeniably destroy a certain amount of game, but which afford sport themselves, or are creatures of such rarity or beauty that we would entreat every game-preserver to pause and reflect ere he destroys one of them ; and whether he spare it for its own sake, or for the sport it may afford to his brother sportsmen, he will act a far better part than that of the man who indiscriminately destroys every living creature which can possibly interfere with his one chosen amusement.

In the first list may be placed crows, magpies, sparrow-hawks, stoats, weasels, cats, polecats, rats.

The second schedule would include jays, jackdaws, kestrels, hedgehogs.

While in the third should come foxes, badgers, peregrine-falcons, buzzards, harriers, ravens, owls.

To begin with the first or 'black list,' we would say at once that not one bird or beast named herein should be allowed to draw the breath of life on any manor where game-preserving is carried on at all.   The two first—the crow and the magpie—are the worst and the most inveterate of egg-poachers, and in this way will do more damage than most of the vermin, which only prey upon game in its full-grown condition. Both varieties of the crow—the black, or carrion crow, and the grey-backed or scaul crow—are equally mischievous, but the latter is not commonly found in England at the nesting period, when most harm can be done. In autumn or in winter the 'greyback' is common enough, especially in the Eastern counties, and it is particularly troublesome, from its habits of following up and mutilating wounded or dead game, which may not have been gathered during the day's shooting, and which if left out for one night only is generally so spoiled by these marauders as hardly to be worth the trouble of taking home. The carrion crow is, however, common enough in every county in the spring, and is one of the worst pests possible. The old birds should be destroyed at once, and not allowed even to form a nest; and here let us at once caution all owners of manors against the practice of rewarding their keepers for destroying vermin by a payment of a fixed sum per head. Such a practice is apt to induce the keeper to allow birds, such as crows, magpies, &c., to breed and rear their young, and then, as soon as the young birds can fly, to shoot them and their parents together, so as to be able to produce the greatest possible number of heads at the annual count. By this practice the worst of poachers are positively encouraged during the only period of the year—viz. the nesting season—when they can do harm. When once this season is over, it matters comparatively little whether the egg-stealer is destroyed or not; probably by next season he will be miles away, if alive at all. But for this one year he and his young brood will have been supported from off the manor where he has bred, and he will have done all the harm which it was possible for him to do for a twelvemonth. Let every crow and magpie then be destroyed as early as possible in the year, and if a reward be paid at per head for such service, let the sum be treble as much for one bird slain before May 1 as for one which is allowed to survive beyond that time; and let this same rule be applied to the destruction of all the egg-stealing birds as well as to sparrow-hawks, which nurture their young to a great extent upon young or half-grown game.

These birds come next upon the black list. To them no mercy should be shown. The powerful female is a most deadly enemy to all immature game, while the male supports himself and his family entirely upon the 'feathered songsters of the grove'; and both of them, from their activity, their dash, and their marvellous accuracy in whipping up their prey, either from among the long grass and covert, or even from the midst of the thickest blackthorns or bushes, are the most formidable adversaries to all of the feathered race which they are enabled by their size and strength to attack.

But of all the pests which the gamekeeper has to contend with, none can be more fatal than the stoat. A more lithe, active, crafty, bloodthirsty foe to all animals in creation of a size equal to itself has never been constructed. With the ferocity of a tiger, the swiftness and activity of a greyhound, and the nose of a bloodhound, nothing is safe from it, and its skill in hunting must be watched to be believed. Rabbits, young pheasants, partridges, and leverets, are all of them its prey in turn, while it has no difficulty in scaling easy sloping trees or low bushes to destroy broods of young birds whose nests have been placed in such positions. The blood only of each victim is sucked and the body left to perish, and we believe that there is no creature alive which destroys so great a number of animals, in proportion to its own bulk, as does the stoat. Let the careful keeper then leave not one alive on his beat, or he will assuredly rue it.

The remarks made on the stoat will apply (but in a lesser degree) to the weasel. There are, however, in this case some extenuating circumstances, in that this latter quadruped is a deadly foe to mice and to rats, and does much, very much, to keep these pests under. Yet it is a creature of indomitable boldness and courage, and is therefore a scourge to every. beast (or bird which frequents the ground instead of the trees) which is in size not more than twice or three times its bulk.

A gamekeeper should show no mercy to the weasel, though the farmer may perhaps have a word or two to put in in its favour.

The true wild cat still exists in portions of the Highlands of Scotland and in Cumberland, but even there it is now very rare. It is practically extinct so far as ordinary game-

A real Poacher.

preserving is concerned, but an almost equally destructive pest is to be found in the shape of the common house cat, when, as is frequently the case, it relinquishes either entirely or in part its domesticated habits and takes to the coverts and fields in order to gain its livelihood. Not unfrequently it breeds in the woods, and it is curious to see how quickly it reverts to the original type and grey-tabby colour of the wild cat. The wild-bred house cat also increases enormously in size, and is not seldom in such cases mistaken for the genuine *felis catus*, but it never quite attains to the huge limbs and great strength of the real wild cat, and its tail remains always long and somewhat tapering. In the true wild species the tail is short, very bushy, and even in size to the end, and this peculiarity alone should always prevent the two varieties from being confused. From the gamekeeper's point of view there is not much choice between them, and he should ruthlessly destroy any cats he finds not merely inhabiting, but even occasionally visiting, his wood. Such animals as have once taken to poaching become perfectly useless so far as mousing is concerned, while, being fed at home, many of their depredations are wrought, not from the pressure of hunger, but from their sporting instincts ; and thus they will do even more harm than the animal which preys merely to support its life, and which, having devoured one victim, will seek for no more until its appetite again stimulates it. But of course the semi-wild cat with a family laid up in some burrow is the worst plague of all, and the quantity of young game which she and her young ones will consume is almost incredible, for so long as game and rabbits are obtainable (and if any exist in the wood at all, the crafty active cat is sure to have them) she will trouble herself to catch no other kind of food.

Polecats or foumarts are now very rare, but a few are killed annually in England. They are most destructive to all sorts of game, but not difficult to trap ; their habitat is generally in an old burrow, or in the clefts of rocks or even of stone walls, into which they can sometimes be marked by terriers, and summarily destroyed.

The common brown rat can hardly be omitted from the black list, although it is well known to all besides game-preservers, as 'vermin.' It is, however, an inveterate egg-poacher, and is also very destructive to young partridges or pheasants, especially the more weakly of the brood. The keeper should explore the old banks and fences among which his partridges breed, and should take care that no colonies of rats exist in them, and if any such be found let them be well ferreted out, and the rats destroyed. Especially he must be careful to see that there are no rats in any old buildings, stickheaps, or stacks, near to which he may be rearing his young game, or he will assuredly find havoc played amongst his coops, and perhaps as many young pheasants destroyed by the hens in the struggle to drive off the marauder as would be taken by the rat himself. Nothing is so ruinous to the perfect quiet which is so necessary to the welfare of newly-hatched game as the presence of vermin of this kind among the hens and coops. With the rat, the list of vermin which cannot upon any consideration be tolerated may be closed. A preserver of game, who can be certain that none of the animals here named exist on his ground, must attribute to some other cause than the presence of 'vermin' any scarcity of game which he may have to complain of.

We now take the second list, that of creatures which do harm, but are not so hurtful to game that they need be persecuted in the same ruthless manner as those animals which we have been writing of above. First upon this list we have placed jays. That these pretty birds are egg-stealers to some extent cannot be denied, but it is very questionable whether they often attack the nests of either partridge or of pheasant. Smaller birds, no doubt, suffer much from their depredations, but we think the keeper need only trouble himself to keep these birds within reasonable limits. One good purpose they certainly fulfil, that of sentinels. No living creature can stir in the woods undetected by the ever-watchful eye of the jays, and if the intruder be of a dangerous nature their repeated screams will serve as a warning to the keeper that something unusual is going on. If he follow the discordant notes with care and circumspection, he will very possibly find that they will lead him to some spot where his presence is, to say the least of it, very desirable at that moment.

Jackdaws may be classed in the same category as jays. As a rule they are not very mischievous, but they are not birds of which it is desirable to have a great number in the woods, and it is as well to keep them within bounds.

As a rule there is no more harmless bird than the common kestrel, or windhover, commonly confused by ignorant and unobservant keepers with the sparrow-hawk, and ruthlessly destroyed by them. Very different are the habits of the two species, and while little or no good can be credited to the sparrow-hawk, the kestrel may lay claim to being one of the best 'farmer's friends' in existence. Its principal food consists of the common field-mouse, and of the numerous beetles and larvæ which it can glean from the face of the land. Grass-hoppers are a favourite food, and it has frequently been seen to destroy the slow-worm, while there are also instances on record of its taking the adder. Very rarely indeed does it seize a bird of any kind, and then only if they are crouching on the ground, but its weak foot and lack of courage render it quite unable to hold even a three-parts-grown partridge.

There is one occasion, and one only, when the kestrel should be killed without mercy. It is when an old bird, having a brood at home to bring up, finds out the coops where a number of pheasants or partridges are being reared. Having once discovered with what ease she can take any of the tiny, half tame, wholly foolish little creatures, she will return again and again, till she has destroyed the entire lot. Let that kestrel be killed without an hour's delay, but let not that be made an excuse for killing, in future, every individual of a species which does so much good. All animals resemble human beings in one respect, namely, their proneness to contract evil habits. The unfortunate bird that had taken to paying visits to the coops has paid for its iniquities with its life, but it does not follow that every other kestrel need do the same. As an instance in point, the following fact may be mentioned. In 1883, about three hundred pheasants were being reared by a keeper, in a field partly surrounded by a wood of ancient trees of considerable extent. In this wood were the nests of no less than six pairs of kestrels, none of which was more than three-quarters of a mile from the coops. The keeper had been strictly ordered not to molest the kestrels in any way, and

The Poaching Kestrel.

ere long he came with a piteous tale as to the birds which had been carried off before his very eyes by these hawks.

He was at once ordered to conceal himself with his gun, close to the coops, and to shoot any hawk he found in the act of skimming down to them. Ere the day was out he triumphantly produced both the male and female of a pair of kestrels which he had shot in the very act of taking his birds, and wanted to know 'what we had to say to that,' and if we still believed that 'kestrels did no harm'? 'Very well,' we said, 'keep your gun handy and shoot any hawk you can catch within range of your coops, but let them come to you—do not go to them.' Not another kestrel was killed that year; though the other five pairs all reared their broods, and their nests were no further off than that of the pair which fell into bad habits and died in consequence. Let the keeper use his discretion, then, and while he will do well to kill any individual kestrel that does harm to him, he should be restrained from killing down too closely such useful birds.

There is not very much to be said in favour of the hedge-hog, who is, we regret to say, a most arrant little egg-poacher. A trap baited with an egg will generally lead to his destruction, and it is only fair to conclude that the egg without the trap would have attracted the hedgehog equally well. At the same time this unfortunate animal is accused of numerous crimes of which it certainly is not guilty, from sucking cows downwards. We do not believe that it is capable of doing any harm to game, worth speaking of, after the egg stage is past. We have, in-deed, heard a most excellent keeper, trustworthy in all other respects, solemnly declare that he had discovered a hedgehog in the very act of taking one of his old hens out of a coop! What the poor hedgepig was about to do with her, or how he meant to take her away, he did not say, and it is to be feared that in this case his zeal and hatred for vermin of all descriptions rather outran his discretion. However, this animal must be written down as dangerous, though it is not one of the most destructive or pernicious class. With the hedgehog ends the list of vermin which must absolutely be either destroyed, one and all, or else kept down within narrow limits if it is desired to preserve game. Other considerations must, however, be taken into account as regards the 'vermin' named in the third of our schedules, and concerning each of them much may be said on both sides of the question.

First on this list comes the fox. Now it is idle to pretend that foxes do no harm to game. There is no doubt that they do kill a certain quantity thereof, nor do we think that the interests of fox-hunting are well served by those who seek to make out that the presence of foxes does nothing at all to injure the sport of those who depend upon an abundance of game for their pleasure. It is surely far better policy to admit that a fox does undoubtedly take for his own use, and otherwise destroy, some game of all kinds during the year; but, on the other hand, the sport which foxes themselves afford, the benefit of fox-hunting, socially and pecuniarily, to every neighbourhood where a pack of fox-hounds exists, the amusement afforded thereby to all classes of society, and the churlishness of putting a check to it for the purpose of adding slightly to the pleasure of the owner of the coverts they frequent and a mere handful of his friends, are all considerations which should induce a man to pause long and often ere he allow the fox to be included in the list of 'vermin' under any circumstances whatever. Besides all this, the mischief foxes do is very greatly exaggerated. Where rabbits abound they will molest little else, and a great head of game can be killed in coverts which are full of foxes if the keeper really understands his business. We ourselves have, during the year in which these remarks were penned, seen over eight hundred pheasants killed in one day in coverts in which no less than six foxes were seen during that day's sport. Few game-preservers can beat such a day's sport even if every fox be ruthlessly and selfishly exterminated, and we heartily trust it will be many years before the fox's claim to the care and protection of every covert-owner ceases to be regarded throughout the length and breadth of England.

The poor badger is in somewhat the same position as the fox, except that he affords but little sport to the public generally.

He is, as regards game, of but little account one way or the other, though it may too certainly be alleged against him that he will eat fox cubs. He will also, no doubt, occasionally rob a pheasant's nest of her eggs if he comes across it in the course of his nocturnal rambles, and he will sometimes dig out a 'stop' of very young rabbits. But, on the other hand, he is an interesting beast, now becoming rare in England, though not so rare perhaps as many suppose, for badgers are common and were numerous in many English counties ; still we would put in a plea for him on the ground that the amount of mischief done by him does not warrant the destruction of so curious an animal, unless he should happen to exist in too great numbers in any particular locality.

The peregrine falcon, like the fox, is too noble a creature to be properly included in any list of 'vermin,' but as he also is guilty of occasionally destroying grouse or partridges on very open ground, he meets with but short shrift from many an unthinking, narrow-minded keeper. Small indeed is the harm he does, for he strikes his prey only on the wing, and game in an enclosed or a wooded country is absolutely safe from him. Only on the moors or on the downs can he do any mischief at all, and even there he is here to-day and gone to-morrow; for what are the boundaries of the largest extent of shooting in the whole kingdom to a bird with the power of wing of the peregrine? On the other side of the account, too, there is much to be said. In the first place, this hawk is an active agent in keeping down that disease which will nearly always follow over-preservation of game. As already remarked, it is on the wing alone that he seizes his prey, and as he does so simply in order to obtain food for himself, he naturally chooses the bird out of the covey which he can most easily overtake. Will it then be the fresh active young cock bird, which flies at the head of the pack as they scud from the hillside across to their feeding grounds, that the hawk will overtake first and seize as he swings over the shoulder of the hill in full pursuit, or will it not rather be some unsound or wounded bird which feebly lags behind,

and which the hawk would have to pass by ere he could reach
the sounder and swifter birds? Naturally, like every hungry
wild animal, he will take that which he can most quickly and
easily reach, and by thus persistently killing off weakly and
unhealthy birds, he will do more to check and stamp out disease
than any device which can be adopted by man. Again, suppose
that, to the consternation of the ordinary gamekeeper, a pair of
peregrines, which he is not allowed to molest, should establish
themselves in some cliff or beetling crag upon his beat. He
will, of course, imagine that every brood of grouse on the moor
will be attacked by these marauders. But what is the result?
If he observe the eyrie with care, he will see that gulls, wood-
pigeons, sea birds, crows, &c., form the staple food both of
parents and of the young brood, because the birds are to be found
upon the wing instead of crouching for three parts of the day
among the deep heather and boulders which effectually protect
the grouse. But most of all, if he will watch the actions of the
peregrine at this season, he will learn that no animal can be
more intolerant of neighbours than this hawk. Not a raven,
crow, jackdaw, or hawk of any kind, dares to show his face
on the wide tract overlooked by the eyrie of his powerful and
tyrannical congener. If, indeed, he should do so, he will find
himself harried and hunted for miles, and lucky will he be if he
escape with his life. It is certain that the presence of a pair of
peregrines will keep the ground round their nest clear for miles
of every egg-stealing bird, and the benefit that they do in this
way will far more than atone for the loss inflicted by them of
the few brace of grouse which they may fall upon from time to
time. Last of all, let it not be forgotten that it is upon the
peregrine that falconers rely, in order to maintain the ancient
and interesting sport of falconry, and it is perhaps not too much
to ask of the game-preserver that he should spare this beautiful
bird for the sake of his brother sportsmen, and sink the thought
of the few head of game which it may perchance cost him to
do so, in the reflection that he has not only assisted to stay the
destruction of one of the most interesting creatures of the British

fauna, but has also done what he can to promote what is to its devotees the most fascinating of all the sports now practised.

The beautiful little merlin, the male of which is hardly larger than a blackbird, and the still more beautiful and almost entirely insectivorous hobby, have not been included in any list of vermin, because it is not to be supposed that any rational being will really believe that these poor little birds, whose only offence it is that they belong to the genus *accipiter*, can possibly do any harm to game of any sort or kind. We would entreat every owner of a manor to insist upon his keeper showing some discrimination in the kind of hawk he destroys, and while no mercy should be shown to such of the tribe as really interfere with his preservation of game, let nothing else be destroyed for the mere sake of killing.

Buzzards, harriers, and similar birds of prey have now become too rare in England to need more than a passing notice. That they may perhaps do some little harm in cases where they are breeding in some wood adjoining an open partridge manor must be conceded, but here again the question arises whether it is expedient to destroy every specimen of a rare and beautiful bird, on the chance of their doing some infinitesimal amount of harm to the game of any particular manor. On the same grounds would we plead for the raven, though in England he is so rare a bird that it is hardly worth while to put in a word for him. In Scotland, where he is far more common, he may do mischief, especially where there are many blue hares, for the leverets are a favourite quarry of the raven. In cases such as this too many of these birds should not be allowed upon the ground, but here again let careful judgment prevail over the slaughter.

Owls are now protected by law for the period of the breeding season, since they are included in the schedule to the Wild Birds' Protection Act 1883. No doubt the benefit which the farmer derives from their presence on his ground is the reason why such protection is accorded them, but the game-preserver need not complain of this, for except by the loss of a few half-grown rabbits, and perhaps of an occasional leveret, no injury worth speaking of is inflicted on him by these birds. With them the list of vermin of all kinds closes, and while we would urge upon every gamekeeper the necessity of destroying every head of those animals which we have set down as being most destructive to game, yet we trust we have convinced him that the list of his foes is a much shorter one than that which he has perhaps been in the habit of composing for himself.

Naturally the question arises, how are these animals which are so hurtful to game to be destroyed and kept down ? The gun is one method, and it is not a bad one, where winged vermin are concerned. A 'braxey' sheep or other piece of carrion, laid within easy shot of some favourite covert in which the keeper may be concealed, will prove a good method of attracting to their death carrion crows and magpies, and if the bait be removed often enough to different spots every bird of the kind within miles may be destroyed. Poison is a thing that should seldom, almost never, be used, yet, in the case of a pair of egg-stealers that can be approached in no other way, the use of an egg impregnated with *nux vomica* is allowable. It should be placed in the fork of a tree well out of the reach of all other animals, and if laid in a conspicuous place near to the usual haunts of crows or magpies, it will generally prove fatal. In open ground, where crows are very difficult of approach, a cat tethered beneath a tree will infallibly lure them up. Stooping at her and mobbing her, even perching upon the tree, they will afford an easy mark to the concealed gunner and so fall victims.

For stoats, weasels, and even cats, by far the best and simplest trap is the old-fashioned 'dead fall,' consisting of a large heavy stone, or block of wood, set with the well-known 'figure of four' trigger or support. Many are the advantages of this trap. In the first place it is most inexpensive and simple, every keeper who knows anything of his trade can prepare it, and if it is well set, in or near the runs, with a good bait, such as the entrails of a freshly killed rabbit, it will prove most killing. But above all it is the most merciful of traps, for the creature captured is flattened out then and there, and there is no lingering in pain, to be disposed of when the keeper next goes his rounds. Open wire box traps, if well set on the runs and in dry ditches used by weasels and stoats, are very effective, especially that kind which is open at both ends when set, and can be so arranged as to remain open for many days until both weasels, stoats and rabbits use them as a regular run. Then when they are well accustomed to the traps the bait is placed and the trigger set, and the first carnivorous creature entering the trap is sure to become a prisoner. These are merciful traps, and we wish that the destruction of vermin could be brought about by such means. But this can hardly be accomplished. There is in existence an engine called a 'gin' or steel-trap, which is necessarily cruel and, by the careless manner in which it is employed, almost diabolically so. But if properly set it is the most effective of all traps, and as it can be used in places where no other device can be worked, and is equally serviceable for all kinds of vermin, it is not likely to be discarded. Its nature and appearance are well known to all. Every village iron-monger sells it, but few who purchase the machine know the amount of suffering which can be inflicted by its use ; and, in fact, it is such a cruel engine of destruction that we cannot advocate its use. Vermin must no doubt be killed, and where gentle means fail harsher ones must be employed ; but let any thinking person consider the effects of capturing any animal in one of these traps ; let him picture the suffer-ings of the creature held by a fractured limb in an iron grip, with sharp teeth lacerating the flesh, and a powerful spring drawing the hold tighter and tighter, until by some happy fortune, it may be, that limb is severed and the tortured animal escapes, maimed, bleeding, yet with its life left in its body. Above all, let him realise the agonies endured when no such lucky chance liberates the victim, but when the trapper neglects to visit his gins with proper regularity—the lingering death from thirst and hunger, hastened, but far from mitigated, by acute pain, and we feel sure that no steel traps will be allowed in future on the property of any humane man save under the strictest regulations. For ourselves we could wish that the use of these terrible implements might be declared illegal; but, if the necessity for their employment be granted, and if vermin cannot be kept down without their aid, let every game-preserver only permit their use upon the express condition that each trap of the kind is visited regularly at least twice a day. If this rule be insisted upon, the number of traps set (the setting, by the way, is illegal above ground) will be limited, and the suffering inflicted greatly diminished. Of all the forms in which the gin appears, none is more cruel and more useless than the 'pole-trap,' or steel-trap, perched on a high pole in some open space. Nothing ever falls a prey to this device except owls, which are frequently thus trapped, and an occasional kestrel; and often, too often, these unhappy victims are left by a careless keeper to hang head downwards till death brings a tardy relief to their sufferings. There are many other dodges and devices by which a clever keeper can outwit his subtle foes, winged and quadruped, but it would occupy too much space to enumerate them, and, as has been said, the keeper who knows his business is best left to himself (under certain restrictions) to carry it out. The destruction of vermin is a most important part of that regulation of the balance of nature which is the secret of what is called game-preservation. It is essential in the interests of game that it be done well, but it is also essential in the interests of sport generally that it be done with discrimination and not to excess. If the rules laid down in the preceding pages be well carried out, the owner of shooting may rest assured that his game is thoroughly protected as far as 'vermin' is concerned, while naturalist and fellow-sportsman will alike bless the thoughtful consideration with which their pursuits have been treated. By such mutual courtesy alone can sport continue to thrive, and to be enjoyed by all classes in this country.   G. L.

The Keeper's Cottage.

CHAPTER XIII.

KEEPERS.

ON keepers the prospects of sport greatly depend. They are the non-commissioned officers of a shooting field, and their duties are as necessary as those of the same rank of men in the field of war. The principal tasks a keeper has to perform consist in rearing game, destroying vermin, and protecting the birds from poachers ; and he must also have a knowledge of the habits and haunts of game and of the best methods of obtaining it. Pay your keeper well, and it will be then worth his while to stop with you and take care of your interests ; and before engaging a man it is desirable to ascertain that he comes from a manor similar to that for which you propose to employ him. A head-keeper accustomed to an estate whereon he has had some dozen under-men, though he was as good as could

"OLD" WATSON.

Died 1834.

From a sketch by the late Sir Robert Frankland, Bart.

be in such a position, will never answer if he comes down to a manor requiring the attention of only himself and one assistant. The keeper who gives himself airs, loudly roars his commands in the field, and is generally noisy and talkative, is never to be trusted.

We remember overhearing such a man remark to one of his fellows when about to place the guns (an act that should

'Sovs. and half-sovs.'

never be left at the discretion of a keeper), 'Put the sovereigns at the wood end, Bill, and the half-sovs. can walk with the beaters and stop back,' which showed that this man made a distinction in giving favourable places to the shooters according to the 'tips' they were able to afford him. For this reason, in some large houses, it is the custom to place a money-box, marked 'Keepers' fund,' in the hall—a very excellent plan for several reasons, and as every shooter likes to give something to a keeper, it is not a 'tax,' but merely the best and pleasantest method of meeting a difficulty. We often think it is very hard that a head-keeper should usually pocket all the donations, when there are under-keepers as well who have probably had just as much trouble and responsibility, and who, by preserving the game on their own particular parts of the estate, contribute towards the day's sport as much as does their senior in command.

It is difficult to say what amount of 'keepering' a manor requires, as this depends upon its size, position as regards towns, footpaths, and poachers; its amount of covert or arable, as well as the number of head hand-reared or naturally sustained ; also whether the estate is compact—and so easily protected— or the reverse.

A good head-keeper and two under-keepers will easily look after an estate of about 3,000 acres, if favourably situated for protection and night-watching. A bad keeper can scarcely manage with the same number of assistants half as many acres. But, as already remarked, a really good keeper, competent to manage the shooting under his charge, is invaluable, as far as sport is concerned, and it is better to give such a man 25*s.* a week, or even more, than be ill served by one at 20*s.* It is only the best men with the best characters who can obtain high wages, and the difference of 5*s.* a week that exists between a first-class man and an ordinary one is repaid over and over again by his better preservation of the game.

A good keeper, and one who knows his work, is quiet and civil, but never obsequious ; he talks but little in the field, and does more with a wave of the hand than does the noisy fellow by means of loud oaths and constant commands of 'Keep in line, will you!' The good keeper, too, may be told by his dogs, as well as by the cheerful willingness or the reverse with which his men serve him. His success in trapping vermin, and his constant attention to this duty, also mark a good keeper and save the game. A clever keeper is usually a good rearer.

It is true he often has curious notions of his own about curing gapes, distemper in dogs, and other ills connected with his duties —notions to which he will stoutly adhere, and which nothing will put aside ; but this cannot be helped, for he is sure to be a careful, watchful man with his game, and kind and constant in his care of his dogs—two qualities of the greatest value.

A good keeper will take a natural interest in his avocations; unless he be born, so to say, to his work, and the love of it

Keeper with field-glass.

is inherent in him, he cannot be taught, nor will he properly regard, his duties. We would much sooner choose for a keeper an ignorant man, so long as he was interested in 'keepering,' than a man, however much he knew, who was bored with it. The former will improve daily ; the latter will become more and more careless and valueless as years go by.

A head-keeper, as well as any intelligent assistant, should be provided with a small pair of field-glasses, such as can be bought for a couple of pounds, and taught how to use them. When the glasses are once focussed to suit the man's vision, as used on an object a few hundred yards away, they should be fixed from further movement, so as to be instantly available. We recollect a netting case being tried, in which it appeared that two poachers, caught after an assault on a keeper in the dark, managed to escape with their booty ; but as dawn was breaking the keeper spied them making off in the distance, out of eyesight, though not beyond the powers of the field-glass he carried. He, though badly wounded, managed to get home, and at once despatched a messenger on horseback to the adjacent town, with a note to the police-inspector, giving the names of his assailants. The constables proceeded to the respective homes of the poachers, and took them red-handed ; in fact, waited for them to return, which they presently did. The evidence was too strong to be rebutted, and the men pleaded guilty, one remarking to the other as they separated at the dock, ' It's them cussed spectacles (i.e. field-glasses) as did us, Bill '—a broad hint that was at once acted upon by the local game-preservers to their great advantage, and to the confusion of the poachers in that neighbourhood.

As soon as a keeper gets a new situation, it is his duty to make the acquaintance of, and so be able to swear to, all the poaching characters of the locality, but on no account ever to drink with them. Doing so is the first downward step a keeper takes, and a very fatal one.

It is most necessary that keepers should be acquainted with the game laws and the laws of trespass, so as not to commit mistakes, nor overstep the law when taking it into their own hands. Few keepers, for instance, know that they may not kill a strange cur when hunting in a wood, or that they cannot apprehend a poacher in a road (unless they have followed him there from their master's land) if the road does not adjoin their master's property ; or that they can apprehend and take before a justice of the peace (without waiting for a summons) a poacher found in the act of poaching if the delinquent refuse his name and address, give an obviously incorrect one, or continue his misdeeds at once after being first caught. For these reasons it is both useful and advisable to have printed on a large card the chief clauses of the poaching and trespass laws, that it may be framed and hung up in gamekeepers' cottages for ready reference.[1] A head gamekeeper certainly requires a gun ; if he cannot be trusted with one he is assuredly not fit for his position. A gun is often a necessity to a keeper, especially when he is 'rearing,' as by its means he can put an end to all marauding birds that beset the young game. Less responsible men, such as under-keepers, should not, in our opinion, have the use of guns, as they are thereby often encouraged to lazy practices, such as endeavouring to shoot four-footed vermin instead of trapping it.

As to keepers defending themselves against night poachers by carrying guns, it is a mistake to think they do so. A poacher will much sooner shoot a keeper than a keeper a poacher, should both be armed, and so the former gets the first chance of using such a deadly means of defence. It is far better that keepers should carry revolvers,[2] as these weapons are a great deal more effective than guns when a hand-to-hand struggle for life takes place, and poachers are more afraid of a revolver hidden, or supposed to be hidden, in a keeper's pocket, but yet ready for use, than they are of a gun. However, to fight and risk his life to secure some few pounds' worth of game from poachers is not a keeper's first duty, but to identify and afterwards convict, and for this latter reason a dark lantern, that can be made to instantly flash a man's countenance into his memory, is one of a keeper's most useful weapons. On no account ought a keeper to call a man by name in a poaching affray should he recognise him; many a

[1] Every game-preserver, shooter and keeper should obtain an excellent little pocket-book called *The Game Laws of England, for Gamekeepers*, published at about one shilling by Van Voorst, Paternoster Row, and written by Mr. H. Neville, M.A., barrister-at-law.

[2] Revolvers, however, require considerable care in their handling, or they are liable to cause accidents to their possessors. The only way to carry a revolver safely in the pocket, so that it cannot explode by a fall or jar, is to take out one cartridge and let the hammer lie on the uncharged chamber. Above all things avoid a cheap revolver, such as is sold by ironmongers for about 1*l.*

keeper and watcher have been shot dead by a recognised poacher for doing so, the man determining to commit a murder rather than face certain conviction afterwards. Long and heavy oak sticks have been found more effective for keepers than guns or pistols, and always will be if their owners use them the right way, which is to *thrust* with them at close quarters, and *not* to strike, the latter being usually a wild and useless form of attack.

Health and strength are enjoyed by keepers, probably from the outdoor nature of their avocation, and many an old keeper of seventy is a match for a man, whether friend or poacher, of half his age. A good keeper is rarely on the sick list, or, if ill, is so to an extent that would half kill a weaker man ere he will confess himself unfit for work. The ailments of a keeper are few, or, at all events, he conceals them if he has any. A keeper pleading illness to escape hard work is almost an un-heard-of occurrence. We have, however, had experience of one such man, and as the affair amused so many friends at the time we record it.

We had lately engaged a new head-keeper. The first day he accompanied us out shooting we were alone with him, and as the day was fine and partridges plentiful we shot till a little past two o'clock, or the usual luncheon hour. About 1.30 he began continually to pull out his watch, so much so that we inquired if it had stopped. 'No, sir,' he replied, 'but is it not the luncheon hour?' This aroused our suspicions. The next day several friends came to shoot with us. We were all waiting near the gun-room, both guns, keepers, and beaters, but the hungry chief of the previous day did not appear to lead the way. At length messengers were despatched to his lodge hard by, who returned saying Mr. —— was ill. Sorry for this, we all proceeded to see what was the matter, as our route led near his house. On knocking at the door our half-hearted henchman appeared, and, lolling out a long and very ugly tongue from his mouth, exclaimed in plaintive accents, 'How can you, sir, expect me to go out shooting with a *tongue*

No. 2.

ISRAEL BUCKLE.

Died 1873.

From a sketch by the late Sir Robert Frankland, Bart.

like that ?' That we soon parted company need scarcely be remarked, but we must add that this man was the only example of a really poor-spirited keeper we ever knew of, for though a keeper be an arrant poacher, or otherwise of bad character, a want of pluck, as far as health goes, he rarely exhibits.

One of the best qualities of a good keeper becomes apparent when it is found that he causes all the farmers and labourers on the estate he protects to take an interest in his work and his master's game. If a judicious, friendly man, he will usually succeed in doing this, and the assistance keepers can obtain in a quiet way from labourers and farmers is incalculable.

The portraits of three generations of keepers on a Norfolk estate are inserted in this chapter. Watson, the acting head at the beginning of the present century, lived until about 1837, and was nominal head until the formal deed of appointment of Israel Buckle in 1835.

This document, witnessed by the clerk of the peace for the county, gave him authority to take from any poacher among other 'engines' 'cross-bows.' Although these weapons could scarcely have been in general use at so late a date, there was lately exhumed from an old rabbit warren on the same estate, the stock of a crossbow which from its condition could not have belonged to any very remote period.

Watson was famed in his day for being a dead shot at snipe, which he killed with a very long single-barrelled small-bore gun, of course with a flint lock.

Many stories are told of Israel Buckle's pluck and cleverness in catching poachers. He was a small active man. On one occasion, when chasing a poacher along the furrow of a ploughed field, the man sloped his gun back over his shoulder and fired, blowing the brim off Buckle's hat. Buckle at once drove his head between the poacher's legs, and having upset him, sat on him until assistance arrived.

John Buckle, who has been acting head for more than twenty years, although a son of the last keeper, is of a different type. His brain is more actively useful than his legs. No one knows better who everyone is, or what everyone is doing, within ten miles of his place. Devoted to his duties and to his employer, and possessed of tact and judgment in keeping on friendly terms with all his neighbours, he is exactly what a keeper on a large estate should be, especially at a time like the present, when to presume too much upon the authority or privilege of his position might not only create ill feeling, but be prejudicial to the interests of sport.

A story is told of John Buckle that, when faced by a poacher who threatened to shoot him dead if he advanced another step, he handed his own gun to a companion with these words—'If he shoots me, Bill, do you shoot him,' and then walked up and collared his man.

The two first portraits are reproduced from water-colour drawings, by the late Sir Robert Frankland, Bart. The last is from a photograph.   R. P. G.

Head-keeper's Lodge, Thirkleby Park.

No. 3.

JOHN BUCKLE.

Son of No. 2.

Present Head Keeper, Merton, Norfolk.

From a Photograph.

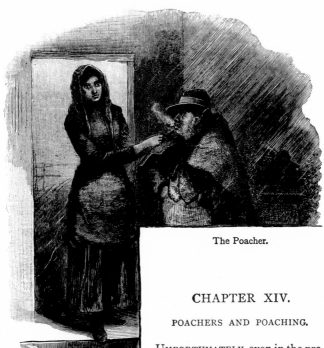

The Poacher.

CHAPTER XIV.

POACHERS AND POACHING.

UNFORTUNATELY, even in the present enlightened days, a poacher is often regarded as a 'bold outlaw,' a sort of revival or descendant of Robin Hood. The feebly sympathetic man who is ignorant of country life will be apt to say, 'Poor fellow, he has a wife and family to support after all, and it must be a great temptation to a starving man out of work to see half-crowns and shillings running about near his cottage in the form of pheasants and rabbits.' There is still something of a halo of romance thrown round a poacher. His silent, stealthy expeditions by night, his risk of apprehension and other dangers from keepers and mastiffs, court a feeling of sympathy in the minds of many

who do not know him as he is, who are inclined to consider
him 'a gallant, clever robber,' a Claude du Val of the preserves.
A magistrate is sometimes heard to say, 'I always let off a
poacher as easily as I can,' and such a justice goes from court
thinking he has done rather a kind and not at all an unfair act,
and maybe whistles the old Lincolnshire poaching air of—

> 'Tis my delight on a likely night
>   In the season of the year ;
> We can run and fight, my boys,
>   Jump over anywhere.

The above is the incorrect and purely sentimental aspect of a
poacher.

The correct and practical aspect is as follows. A poacher
is, with scarcely an exception, a cowardly, drunken ruffian. He
and his wife and children are clothed in rags ; his idleness and
loafing habits are habitual to him, for he will not accept
honest, well-paid work. If he is not poaching, owing to the
close season, he is committing petty thefts, stealing ducks and
chickens, or scouring the country to pick up information for
future nocturnal larceny of game.

As the song says, it certainly *is* his delight to thieve game
on a likely night ; he would not go out on any other, and can
hardly lie quietly in bed if the wind blows, for wind is a
necessity to a poacher, enabling him to conceal his presence
from both game and watchers. He cannot run—he is too
heavy and bloated from drink to do so ; but he can sneak
about in fine ʼstyle under the shelter of walls and hedges or
among shadows, and perhaps he can jump a little—probably
not much—if necessity so obliges him to escape pursuit. He
is, however, a fine fighter (the words of the famous song are not
incorrect in that respect), always provided there be five or six
poachers to one or two keepers, for he has not the courage to
fight unless the odds are greatly on his side. Among a dozen
bad characters the poacher can be detected almost to a certainty. Why? Because he is sure to have the worst-looking

countenance of the lot. His restless, suspicious leer, hollow eyes, alehouse face, and his stooping shambling gait proclaim him at once—not to mention his clothes. Even they tell his

The Day Poacher.

trade: the knee-worn trousers, bloodstained and wide-pocketed coat, with often bits of spare snaring wire coiled round the buttons, the latter an evidence of poaching that may frequently be found if looked for. He drinks and sleeps by day like a great fat cat, and like the cat (who, by the way, is as big a poacher as himself) prowls by night.

The rural poacher, who actually lives amongst the game or in a village close by, who takes his bold walks abroad by day, is the greatest nuisance preservers have to deal with. He knows exactly the rounds and movements of each keeper, and watches him like a lynx; he knows very well that a keeper cannot be in two places at once, and takes care to act accordingly. If the keeper suspects and watches him, a thing the poacher often purposely encourages him to do, in order that an associate may take his chance in another part of the property, the rascal is rarely caught; to take him in the act he must be detected in every way unawares, and when he thinks himself safe. A poacher will often take service under a farmer (for a short time, for he has to change his ground), so that as a labourer he may have a right to tramp an estate, either at his work or to and from it. In such employ he is up at daybreak, and on his way to his work drops a snare here and there, which he picks up when returning home or steals out to inspect by night. Dinner hour with the labouring poacher is commonly a most successful time, for he will very often carry in his food-basket a small ferret and a bit of netting.[1] When retiring to his dinner he chooses a hedgebank as a seat, and that part of it that contains rabbit burrows; then, by means of the ferret and net, he soon bolts and pockets four or five shillings' worth of rabbits.

The poachers from a large town are bolder and more skilful in their depredations than the country thieves, and harder to convict, as they cannot be so well watched; their visits are few and far between, and quite unexpected, for they usually take estates here and there, and do not levy a tax upon one only, as is the habit of the rural poacher.

---

[1] A *white* ferret is always in demand amongst poachers, because they can see to work with such a creature at night on account of its bright colour; white ferrets should not be sold, or indeed brought up by keepers, for this reason.

These men frequently go three or four in a farmer's gig, and sometimes dress up as much like farmers or herds as possible, even fastening a sheep net over the back of the trap, to imply that they are going to market or have sheep or pigs with them, instead of which a couple of 'lurcher' dogs are lying in the straw at the bottom of the spring cart or gig,

Driving Poachers.

whichever is used. These fellows drive very slowly along roads that intersect game preserves (till some one they do not like the looks of comes in sight; they then drive at a usual pace), and select as an object of attack small clumps, on every side of which, and up and down adjoining roads, they can plainly see, and so guard against chances of interference. On selecting the ground, in an instant out come the dogs, animals that will snap up a hare (in covert) or a rabbit, before either animal has gone thirty paces. These dogs do not chase, or only for a very short distance, and never give tongue.

Three of the poachers, one of whom only has a gun, now

drive the wood in a quick but systematic manner, the man with the gun standing inside the wood, as he wants to kill, not to sport, at the very point where the game is likely to break. In ten minutes the whole thing is done, and the poachers, with their spoil and dogs hidden, are again driving slowly and innocently along the road, on the look-out for another bit of covert suitable for their piratical purposes.

The poacher left with the trap is the look-out man; he stands up in the vehicle, and from the height of his position can see for about a mile on all sides. If his suspicions are aroused he whistles shrilly to his confederates, whose ears are ever on the *qui vive* for a signal; they catch the warning note at once, and in a few seconds dogs and men are in the trap as before, continuing their progress along the safe high road.

Sometimes this class of poacher will allow one dog, the fastest and best, to trot alongside the trap. On coming to likely ground, a wave of the hand sends him scouring the fields, not often unsuccessfully, as far as hares and rabbits are concerned. If a keeper or watcher happen to come by at the wrong moment, or just as the dog has killed, there is a great outcry raised by one of the men in the cart, who yells and screams at the dog for leaving the road, makes every apology, handing over the game at once, and says he will never bring the wretched brute out again, as it got him into trouble with Squire ——'s keeper last year just the same way.

The driving poacher also does great execution amongst coveys of partridges sitting near the road. These birds do not mind a carriage, and can be shot from one with ease over the hedges, especially in the snow. Pheasants, too, are very easy to shoot from a vehicle early in the morning, and scarcely walk away when passed close by, if feeding on a stubble on first coming down from the trees they roost in. The poachers who drive do not often go out night-poaching; they would not risk doing so, as it is difficult to manage a night-poaching expedition unless on foot—the use of a horse and carriage increases the danger of identification in such case. The poachers who come from towns are in the confidence of the rural game-stealers. If a wood full of pheasants has to be attacked, they are forced to consult the local men as to the position of the watchers and keepers. The town poachers, who often thus help their local accomplices, dispose of the stolen game.

The town men send out one of their number to confer with a rural poacher as to 'ways and means'; the former then make a descent on the neighbouring villages in the form of tramps, or as men seeking work, and on a certain pre-arranged night all, including the local poacher they have consulted, attack the game in one particular wood upon which they have, for usually good reasons, decided to make their raid. Their first step is to put the watchers and keepers on the wrong track by sending one of their confederates to fire a gun several times near a wood which, though on the same estate, is distant from that they have fixed on, and the poachers, giving the keepers a little time to go in a false pursuit, then set to work with nets or guns, as the case may be.

Poachers usually have confederates on the railway, and a hamper addressed, 'John Smith, Esq.—to be called for,' is a dodge not seldom carried out. Mr. Smith in this case is the poacher himself, or someone whom the poachers send to the station for the package, or a man in some way connected with the disposal of the stolen game. The most extensive system of poaching we ever personally knew of was as under:—

The poachers had in their pay the guard of a luggage train, a train that passed just before dawn every morning through the woods of the estates from which the game was purloined. The poachers having made a good haul, one of their number went up the line to meet the train, and struck a match as a signal to the guard, just as the latter (on the lookout) passed him in his van. The guard then slowed the train a little, and, pulling out a long stick armed with a crook like a salmon-gaff, hooked into his van the hamper of game. The hamper was then dropped just outside the town, and taken away by a man in wait for it, who handed it back to the guard on the next night, when it was taken on and dropped, so as to be once more picked up full of game on the return journey. In the above case it was known that the estates were being plundered, but it long baffled both police and keepers to discover how the game was made away with—a discovery that was not easy when such an artful dodge was resorted to by the poachers, and one that would not have been brought to light had not the thieves quarrelled among themselves, and let the 'murder out.'

It is often said that, on the principle 'Set a thief to catch a thief,' reformed poachers make good keepers ; our experience, however, shows that this latter phrase is quite incorrect. 'Once a poacher always a poacher' is much nearer the mark. A poacher who would be a keeper, though he vows and protests all manner of good things, is not to be trusted ; the instinct is too strong in him, it is but dormant ; the ease with which as a keeper he can poach, tempts him too strongly to let him adhere to his good resolutions. When a poacher-keeper relapses into his old habits, good-bye to the game. He is then looked upon as a 'godsend' by all the poachers of the neighbourhood ; they have him fast. If he tells aught against them, they can tell something about him, quite enough to turn him out of his situation. The following story illustrates the cunning of a poacher and the experiences of a friend who made the experiment of engaging one of this predatory race as a keeper, kindness (and solemn protestations of future behaviour on the poacher's part) outweighing common-sense, as is often the case.

On this gentleman's estate (we will call him Thomas Jones) the game by degrees got less and less, though the keeper vowed he could not account for it, and that day and night he was on the watch for poachers. The owner began to suspect that everything was not right, and in consequence all trains that arrived in the neighbouring town from his direction were watched for hampers or sacks of game—to no good. But one day, by mere chance stopping at a wayside station a hundred miles or more from his residence, the gentleman was addressed by the station-master as follows :—'Sir, I see by your luggage you come from —— in ——shire; can you tell me if I have addressed this hamper correctly, as the gentleman who writes about it must live near you, and is of the same name? Here is his letter.' The letter ran :—

'To the station-master at —— (naming the distant station). Sir,—I have lost a hamper of game sent me by a friend, who has addressed it to the wrong place. If it lies with you, please forward it to —— (the town which had been watched), and put on it enclosed label.'

Now the game being addressed to a well-known person, no less than the real owner of it (marked 'To be called for,' and being also booked through), passed safely by the authorities, and when re-directed was, as per label, sent straight to an accomplice by a train that was not watched, as it did not come from the direction of the pilfered estate. The letter was signed 'T. Jones,' and at its head was the owner's printed address, the paper having been purloined from his study by the keeper as he put by the guns after a day's shooting. When he somehow despatched a hamper, the rascal sent it to a different and distant address every time, afterwards, as above described, writing to have it re-directed and called for by a confederate.

Something may now be said about the actual devices practised by poachers, and we will take each variety of game by itself.

PHEASANTS.

These are obtained when roosting. The poachers know exactly the kind of tree in which a pheasant roosts, which is nearly always one with boughs at right angles to the stem. He therefore goes straight for trees of this kind at once, and with a small charge of large shot and half a charge of powder in a small, very short barrelled gun, picks them off one after another. In doing so he works against the wind, and the more stormy the night, as long as it is not pitch dark, the better for him ; by working against the wind the pheasants to windward do not hear him.   If a poacher by making too much noise set the cock pheasants in a wood calling before he begins his attack, it is as much a signal to a keeper that something is wrong as is the noise of his gun.   It is commonly imagined that poachers have other methods of killing pheasants besides the use of a gun, such as snaring them by means of a noose at the end of a long stick, or shooting them with air-guns.   These rascals nowadays generally use common guns, though air-guns are not altogether discarded, notwithstanding that they make nearly as loud a crack as a lightly-charged firearm, and are not half so effective.   A poacher does not fire unless he is perfectly sure of his bird, as indeed he easily can be, for a pheasant will oftener sit within twenty feet of the ground than not, and at that distance a very light charge will kill.

If half-a-dozen poachers go out together after pheasants, their practice is each to choose a bird; then, after a certain lapse of time, their leader fires, and so do all the others at the same moment.   If after gathering the game there is no sign of inter-ruption or warning whistle from the look-out who is parading the outskirts of the wood, they all proceed to find each another bird, and again all fire as much together as possible, so that instead of a series of shots, only one seems to have been fired, if, indeed, that is heard, which owing to the light loading of the guns is often improbable on a stormy night. The best method of stopping the depredations of these fellows is by means of alarm guns.   The poacher cannot see the wire of an alarm gun, and with his eyes cast upwards to the trees as he searches their branches for birds, plunges right against it.   Whether a keeper and his assistants be near or not, an alarm gun startles a poacher out of his senses.   He fancies the keepers are ready at hand to answer the signal, and so to pounce upon him, and he usually sneaks off at once, unscrewing his gun (for a poacher's gun takes to pieces to go into his pocket) as he makes for home or a confederate's house.

Poachers are great moral cowards, and we have known a keeper, when devoid of assistants (and therefore unable to attack them), put a whole gang to flight by simply sounding

a note on his police whistle—the latter an article, by the way, with which everyone who watches game should be provided.

The only sure way to catch the poachers who drive about, and shoot pheasants near the road, is by means of a man on horseback, who can follow them, look into

The Night Poacher.

their cart as he trots alongside to see what it may contain, and ride on to give information or trace them home as required.

PARTRIDGES.

These birds were formerly taken by poachers by a system of driving, a practice they never now employ. The driving net consisted of a net the shape of the letter **V**. At the point was a tunnel or bag net. This net was staked upright in the ground, and the partridges slowly edged (often by using a horse), without causing them to fly, within the sides of the **V**, and so gradually onwards into the closed tunnel net at its extremity, wherein they were then quickly secured and despatched. This plan, however, the poachers found took too long a time to arrange, nor could the net be quickly removed in case of an alarm, and they now use nothing else but the drag net—a safer, quicker, and more deadly contrivance for the purpose. This instrument merely consists of a net some thirty yards in length by four to five in breadth. The net has a stout cord run through its meshes on one edge with projecting loops at either end to take hold of, and its lower edge, that is, the edge that trails along the ground, is fitted with light lead weights to keep it down. Two men drag the net, one at each end, by the loops, and another follows in the rear at its centre, to disentangle it from sticks and thorns. The net is dragged systematically all over a field, and directly birds feel the rearmost edge of it touch them they endeavour to fly ; the poachers feel the first struggle of the birds, and that moment drop the net and so secure them.

Partridges are also frequently taken with snares set in their dusting places, but not much damage can be done or need be feared by this method. It is the drag net that should be securely guarded against, and protection for the birds can easily be in a great measure ensured by 'bushing' thickly all the meadows and 'after-grasses' on an estate, as it is on these that the birds sleep and the poachers' net in consequence is chiefly used. The best way to check the depredations of the netters is to lay thorns or bushes on the ground, so that on the net touching them they are rolled up in it in hopeless confusion. If the thorns are fixed (as is usual) firmly in the soil, the net can be lifted over them by the poachers, should the latter feel the obstruction when dragging over the ground.

Another excellent plan, to check the operations of poachers who net partridges, is to procure three sticks of thorn, each two feet long, tie them across in the centre, with wire or tarred string, in the form of a cross or star, sharpen their ends, and place one of the points lightly in the ground.

This arrangement cannot be seen at night, and on being touched by a net rolls up in it end over end like a wheel.

The sticks can be kept from year to year ready for use, and be quickly placed in position in the fields.

GROUND GAME.

A poacher will do far more execution at all times among hares and rabbits than he is able to do among pheasants or partridges. With the former, dogs and nets alone come into play, and these make no noise that can alarm a keeper.

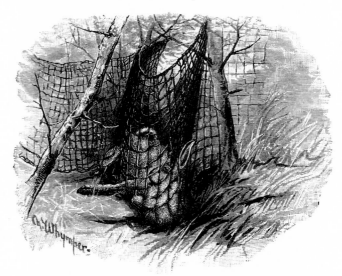

Hare in Net.

Hares are very easily taken by means of gate nets. This net extends the whole length between the posts and is set on the opposite side of the gate from that facing the field to be driven.

The net is hung on pins in loose folds to upright sticks two feet from the gate, with several inches of net resting on the soil. The poacher then steps to one side and sends his dog, one that hunts and ranges well and without a sound, to drive the field. If a hare be put up she makes for the gate, as, when alarmed at night, hares forego their usual runs in the hedges, preferring the more easily seen gate. As she bolts through the latter she goes head-first into the net, which is large and loosely hung, and, the force of contact freeing the pins, the animal is taken and rolled up into a helpless entanglement. The hare is quickly killed and the net reset for another capture. The poacher who employs gate nets can be checkmated by making the bottom bars of gates so close together that a hare cannot easily bolt through, or, a cheaper way, by fixing on its lower bars small upright strips of wood.

Another and very deadly method in use by the poacher is that of taking hares in purse nets. This system is usually carried on single-handed, and resembles in its practice the gate net. For example, a labourer or professional poacher, whilst at his work or on the prowl, will make a mental note of the half-dozen or so regular runs (inlets and outlets) that may be seen in the fence that compasses a small wood—and the smaller the wood is, the more successfully does he poach it. These men will, if not watched, by daytime set wire snares in the runs, and sometimes meet with success thereby,[1] but their usual and more fatal plan is to return at night and cover each run on its

[1] For hares they set a wire noose tied to a stick by strong cord, placing edgeways to the ground a small twig which supports it in the proper position, that being two fists high for a hare, and one for a rabbit. To find these snares, never search close along the bottom of a hedgerow near the runs. If set there, it is by some bungler, and the noose will catch nothing ; though, of course, it may be watched to see if the owner pays it a visit. The accomplished poacher sets it quite two feet from the hedge. He knows that a hare always canters up, pauses a yard or more away from the fence, and then springs into the hedge bottom, as if to look through before passing on ; and it is in the act of jumping that she is taken. If a hare has been thus captured, and the noose and peg removed, a trodden circle will be seen at the spot, should the ground be damp, beaten down by the animal's feet in its violent attempts to escape.

outside with a loosely hanging purse net suspended by easily detached meshes to the twigs near by. One or two men then enter the covert without a dog, the latter not being necessary to drive out the game, and one by one the hares are taken as they bolt through their customary runs, and so roll themselves up in the purse nets that bar their way.

RABBITS.

The long net comes into use for rabbits, a net of from a hundred to a hundred and twenty yards in length and four feet high, usually made of silk, very light and strong, and—what is of more consequence to a poacher—very portable. The poacher notes the parts outside a wood where rabbits chiefly feed in the evening. He then chooses a warm, dry, dark, and windy night, for on warm, dry nights rabbits feed a long way out from shelter, and on dark and windy nights do not see their enemy nor hear footfalls. He now, with an accomplice, sets his net so as to intercept and cut off the animals from their burrows or the wood they have emerged from. This is done in two or three minutes, for the net and the sticks attached to it are previously rolled up, so that all will unroll without a hitch in a very short space of time. As soon as the net is set one man drives the rabbits, who, making instantly for home, run straight into it   They are killed with sticks if not well meshed as they run in, or if well entangled, which, owing to the fineness of the net, is oftener the case, are left till all can be taken out together. Poachers will sometimes get two to three hundred rabbits in a night by this means, and the only way to make all secure against long netting is to lay thorns in profusion on the ground at places where a net is likely to be used.

R. P. G.

The Retriever, the Shooter's Companion.

CHAPTER XV.

ON DOGS AND DOG-BREAKING.

IN the time of our grandfathers nine out of ten men who went shooting were accompanied by either pointers or setters. In those days, and before the introduction of reaping machines that now leave the stubbles close and bare, cutting by manual labour was alone in vogue. This system left not only the stubbles but anything else so treated with good covert or hiding ground for game, as it was not cut short and close to the ground, as is the case with our modern reaping machines ; the result being that the game was tame, and generally rose and was killed at a much easier range than is now the case. If a stubble be entered at the present date, probably every head of game, however numerous, is soon flushed ; formerly, a party might tread over a field again and again without discovering all the game it contained, so good and high was the concealment afforded. Game too, in former days, by reason of the thick growth on the ground which high farming has since destroyed, was comparatively tame and lay close, so much so that it might often be almost trodden on. Pointers were therefore, in the days we write of, admirably adapted for finding the game, and the old sportsman took more pleasure (or said he did) in seeing a brace of well-broken dogs quartering the ground for game, and ' setting ' and ' backing ' when they found it, than in the actual shooting ; for shooting at birds rising under one's nose and flying straight away was, and is, little test of marksmanship, and the lack of variety afforded by the rising game as far as shooting it went, no doubt caused the working of the dogs to be the real centre of interest in days gone by. A shooter over dogs is almost invariably a slow, poking aimer, and rarely succeeds in training his eye and hand enough to meet the difficulties of cross and driving shots. However, in course of time pointers were discarded ; for, with bare fields and little covert for birds, they were found to be comparatively useless, and are now, practically speaking, only used for grouse —rarely for partridges.

Pointers may be said to have been superseded and out-rivalled in favour as sporting dogs by our grand retrievers— animals that are clever, intelligent, and sociable to an extent never found in a pointer, though we may say that in some degree the good qualities of the retriever are perhaps equalled by those of the setter. Before alluding to the different kinds of sporting dogs, it will be well to give some general hints on breaking and management such as may apply to all breeds.

If a sportsman wish to use a dog out shooting for his own purposes, and keep the dog entirely to himself, to accompany him and work with and for him, wherever he goes, he *must* break him himself. This is most necessary. No dog will ever work well for anyone save his own master, whom he knows, fears, and loves, to whom he looks for food, and who has also trained him up in ' the way he should go.' To break a dog properly will require on the part of its owner or keeper an amount of kindness, firmness, and tact, judiciously blended, such as is rarely met with. The gift of dog-breaking is born in the breaker, and cannot be acquired. It is similar to the power some men have over horses. One rider will reduce a wild restless horse to a state of quietude directly he mounts him and feels his mouth ; another, were he to try for ever, could not bring about the same result. So with dogs. To some men dogs take kindly at once, obeying them without hesitation ; to others no dog will be agreeable, whether punished or fondled.

Now every shooter should possess a retriever. He may have a dozen, but by *a* retriever we mean one particular dog of his own that is entirely subservient to his wishes. It is no hard thing to own a fairly good retriever, but to own a perfect one is another affair. A perfect retriever is rarely, very rarely, seen working for his master—usually it is for a keeper, and it may pretty safely be asserted that in the British Islands there are not a score perfectly broken retrievers that work only for and with their masters out shooting. A perfect retriever is one that is *not* led by a string, and does *not* run in, however much game may pass before his eyes ; one that will go direct for wounded game and search the ground *where told* to do so, without even noticing, much less dashing after, unwounded birds or animals that get in his way or that rise or run near him ; one that, if he should on the spur of the moment follow unwounded game under the impression that it is the wounded creature he seeks escaping him, will desist instantly, at first call, on being told to do so. We cannot expect a dog to have as much reasoning power as a man, and in his keen anxiety it is hard for him to discern at first sight, when seeking the wounded, what is, and what is not, a proper object for him to pursue.

The first lessons of a dog should begin as soon as he can follow his trainer about the country (his practical instruction as to game not till he is six to eight months old)—lessons that consist, in the first instance, in the inculcation of implicit obedience ; for obedience is the most important part of a

dog's training. These first lessons should be mainly directed to
making the dog lie down to command, teaching him to return,
if ranging, when summoned by voice or whistle—the latter for
choice, as it is less alarming to game, and the voice may well be
reserved for correction or encouragement. The dog should be
taught to keep rigidly to heel, to leave his master only when
the latter waves his hand, and on no other occasion, even
though he be a retriever and wounded game pass right before
him. A retriever under such tuition will soon learn to look to
his master as the best adviser as to whether he should go after
game or remain at heel ; in fact, he will wait for his master to
tell him whether the game is wounded, and so a fit object of
pursuit and search, or whether the reverse is the case. Giving
a dog a severe beating is cruel and useless at all times ; if a
well-bred animal it breaks his spirit, if badly bred it turns him
sulky. It is not the severity of the punishment that cures a dog
of disobedience or running in ; it is the scolding and correction
(of a light nature) as well as the threatening attitude of his
master, *immediately* after the fault has been committed and
while it is fresh in the animal's memory, which makes the
necessary impression.

How often do we see a dog make a (perhaps pardonable)
mistake out shooting, and for half-an-hour keep at a safe distance from his master, a keeper, the latter remarking as the
poor culprit slinks out of his reach, 'Wait till I get hold of
yer ! I'll teach yer ! ' The dog, after a few minutes, entirely
forgets his original error, the memory of which is lost in the
fear of his trainer, whose threats and wrath terrify him, and
completely absorb his mind. When the thrashing does take
place, the unhappy dog quite forgets what it is for, and instead
of learning to obey and love his master, fears and distrusts him
for the rest of his sporting days.

It is, in fact, a useless and wanton cruelty to beat a dog at
any time, unless the chastiser is well assured the animal knows
why punishment is awarded to him. The dog-beating bully
may always be told by the manner in which his dog approaches

him after making a mistake—if, indeed, he approach him at all.

To a good, judicious trainer, however firm he be, so long as he is judicious, a badly behaving dog will crawl up as if sorry for his sins, will fall down at his feet, and probably evince his contrition by rolling on his side with upturned sorrowful eyes. The intelligent creature knows he has done amiss—his very attitude admits it; he solicits pardon by his eyes and wagging tail; he knows, too, he will be punished (not by having his bones nearly broken, as would occur with an ill-tempered master; he would not come to hand if he thought *that*). When a dog acts thus, holding his ear and scolding or whistling into it meanwhile, is quite enough; he is fully sensitive to the fact that he is being punished and, moreover, disgraced. Of course, some dogs require more correction than others; where a word will do for the one, the other must be treated to the lash of a whip—*never* a stick. A lash, if not severely handled, frightens a dog more than it hurts him, and it is wonderful how useful a small whip is in the field if a dog is in the habit of being chastised with it. By merely cracking it the animal can in a short time be brought to heel. Anything is better than the loud tone of command so often directed at dogs in the field; though it may not actually rise game, it will set it on the alert or running forward, which is just as bad. All game must be approached in silence if it is to be successfully overreached. Cats do not 'mew' when seeking mice or birds, nor, for that matter, does any wild animal seek its prey save in absolute silence. This a dog knows as well as should his master, and will, at all events, soon learn by instinct if he does not. There is no difficulty in teaching a young dog, whether pointer or retriever, to stand or retrieve game; it is the A B C of his education. The difficulty is to prevent the one from running in, to teach him to 'beat' the ground well in a systematic manner, and to make the other understand when and where he is not to 'chase.' A pointer is much more easily broken

from chasing than a retriever. The pointer on no occasion
is allowed to chase even a rabbit scrambling along on three
legs; this is with him a hard-and-fast rule. Retrieving pointers
as well as setters may be seen, but they are as one in a thousand, and except as curiosities are not to be encouraged. With
a retriever it is different, for sometimes he is encouraged to
chase and at other times is punished for doing so. In this
case the decision must rest with his master, and the dog must
be taught to look to his master for advice in the matter. Thus
it is of great importance that the dog's master (especially in
the early days of training) should be most careful never to
send a retriever after game that there is little chance of retrieving, on the principle of ' giving the dog a run,' or ' a try.'

There are some few retrievers, however, who are marvellous
in their ability of telling whether their services are needed. We
once had such a dog, and have seen one other. Our dog would
keep at heel, watch every shot, and go or not after wounded
game just as he thought fit. If the game were palpably struck
he was off like a rocket ; if missed he took no further notice of
it. But his cleverness consisted, first, in marking birds that
dropped at a distance unseen by the shooter, and in going quietly
and directly to the spot, though a quarter of a mile distant,
and finding them ; secondly, in suddenly rushing after a hare or
rabbit that had, to all appearance, not been wounded, but in
his judgment was. After a considerable lapse of time he would
return to heel with the animal in his mouth, flying the gates
and hedges in his course, though it were a 7-lb. hare he carried.
His judgment was rarely at fault. He was the largest yet the
cleverest retriever we ever saw. Large retrievers are not by any
means specially desirable, as they do not hunt with their noses
so near the ground as the smaller ones, nor are they so quick
and bustling, and they sooner tire in hot weather ; besides, now
that hares are not so plentiful as they used to be, powerful retrievers are of less use than they were formerly, and are besides
never able to undergo from their size such a hard day's work
as can a lighter animal.

After returning home from a day's shooting (sport for the shooter, hard work for the dog) a good and kind sportsman or keeper will, before he lays down his gun in the one case or has his tea in the other, attend to his dogs. It is cruel and unjust that the shooters and keepers should be refreshing themselves after a long day, and the equally tired dogs be left out in the cold, wet, hungry, and unkennelled, and trying to lick the thorns out of their feet in some shelterless back yard.

Dogs require clean straw placed on a boarded floor to lie on. If the straw be not frequently renewed the plain floor is better for them ; but of course their beds should never be neglected. The best dog-kennels consist of covered-in houses, with sleeping benches raised above the ground and secured to the wall. Exercising yards, surrounded by railings, should be built in connection with the sleeping departments, with a door between each two divisions, and one in the rear of each house as well.

Under no circumstances should a dog be allowed to sleep on a cold floor of brick or stone; he is sure to get rheumatism and stiffness therefrom. Dog biscuits are all very well for non-sporting dogs, but for retrievers, pointers, or setters animal food is a necessity if they are in regular work. Remember that all dogs, and especially setters, require water throughout the day at intervals ; the best of dogs will not work well or retain their powers of scenting with dry and dusty noses.[1]

GUN-SHY DOGS.

The best-bred dogs, though they come of a long line of sporting ancestors, are occasionally gun-shy. It is therefore advisable to treat all young dogs as if they were gun-shy, before taking it for granted that they are not. In the dog's

---

[1] It is a useful thing to know that a shooter can often create, by stamping with his heel on the ground in a soft mossy place, a small pool of water for his dog, amply sufficient to assuage thirst. This too can be frequently done on a dry grouse moor with no visible water for miles.

CONSIDERATE MASTERS

mind the report of the gun and the finding of the game, if a pointer, the recovering if a retriever, should be connected one with another, so that on firing a gun to accustom a young dog to the sound, it is always well to walk up and let him find, if a retriever, or pick up yourself if using a pointer, a dead bird or rabbit. The dog should be made to imagine that he and the report of the gun somehow obtained the game afterwards shown him.

If a dog shows any nervousness on the report of even a small charge of powder, let him walk with an attendant a

'Off home.'

hundred paces distant, and every time you squib off the gun proceed to call him and pick up a bird, which can be laid down when he is not looking. He will probably overcome his fear in his anxiety to take part in a performance so interesting to him, and can gradually be coaxed and brought nearer and nearer to the shooter, until he at length learns to stand fire without dread, and thinks only of the game the report will produce. Puppies, when first taking the field, should never be taxed with too rapid or close firing, but may, as it were, be broken to the gun by degrees, and with the aid of older dogs that never flinch. A gun-shy dog that trembles and starts away at this or that shot, but does not bolt quite as far as home, and returns when called, may with great care and after some weeks of patience on the part of his trainer be completely cured ; but the really bad case, such as the dog that, though divided by the breadth of the field from the gun, goes off as hard as he can, tail between legs, till he reaches his kennel or hides in a house —one that, if led, nearly pulls his head off in wild struggles— must be considered hopeless : at least, we never saw or heard of a complete cure for such a one that answered when put to practical proof, except a mutton chop served with strychnine sauce.

POINTERS AND SETTERS.

These dogs find their game by instinct, and require, if well bred and keen, but little regular training; if they come of good stock, they are pretty sure to stand any game, if working up wind, that may be within twenty to forty yards, according as the scent be strong or weak. The principal thing consists in teaching them to ' quarter' the ground well, to cause them to 'down charge ' when the shot is fired, and, easiest of all, to break them from chasing. To 'down charge' well is the first lesson given, and the dog may learn so much before ever he sees a bird or gun. He can easily be taught this absolutely necessary duty of a pointer or setter in a yard or garden. Impress upon the dog's mind that every time the hand is raised above the head and the word ' down ' uttered, though he be walking or cantering, down he has to lie. To fix this in the mind of a young dog something more than the voice is necessary, and so a check cord is brought into play. Many people in the first place tell the dog to lie down—and this he will likely enough do so long as his master is standing over him—and then tie him by a string twenty yards long secured to a peg sunk in the ground. On walking away the dog will get up and endeavour of follow his master, to be pulled up short on reaching the end to his tether. But it will be found that a dog learns to 'down ' more readily if the ' command ' and the ' check ' come upon his notice at the same moment. For this reason the trainer would do well to make a hole in the peg, pass a longer and running string through it, and, holding it in the hand, walk away from the dog; then, the instant the dog rises, the jerk against him of the string and the word 'down' occur at the same moment. When the dog has well mastered this, his first, lesson, and lies down as quickly as wished—will scarcely, indeed, get up without being lifted, and will, moreover, remain down whether his master be in or out of sight, engaged with other dogs or upon other occupations—then his further education may be proceeded with.

He may now be taken about an open space with a long cord still attached to the soft collar round his neck, and will have to be taught to 'down' as before at any moment and in any position, as he moves about. After a little time, assuming that firmness and patience on the part of his master are judiciously shown, and the cord is used to check him, and so call his attention to the word 'down' when uttered, he will soon learn to obey and drop at once on being told to do so. When the voice and cord together induce him to 'down,' his obedience will have to be tested in as many ways as possible—by walking round him, looking at him, and leaving him; but he should not be spoken to. At first he will be sure to rise to follow his master, or because he wishes to range at his will as before. At the moment of rising, the voice and check-string come together, and down he goes. After a time he will obey the voice only, and the string can be kept as a 'broad hint' (for it is more or less a punishment) should the dog be inclined to move when down or neglect the word 'down,' and become careless or disobedient. While this training is progressing a very lightly charged gun can be occasionally fired. It will, at all events, be a satisfaction to know that the dog is not gun-shy, and if he is, it may accustom him to the sound.

He may then, if so far perfect, be allowed to run loose, still with a dozen yards of cord to his neck, but without its end being held by his trainer. He must now be regularly practised in 'dropping down,' whether far or near, and if he refuses, or stirs to get up when down till he is called up, the cord should be taken hold of and rather strongly jerked as the command is again given ; and he may be tried several times with the cord in hand to call his attention to the word ' down ' before he is allowed to run free again. The dog may next be practised in ' quartering ' ground (where there is no game), his obedience to ' down charging' being frequently enforced for fear he should forget his previous lessons.

Learning to quarter well is a difficult thing to teach a pointer or setter; as his knowledge of how to beat a field so as to find the game without missing it comes to him very much by instinct, he can only get perfect at it by slow degrees, and cannot become really accomplished in this respect during his first season.

Young dogs should at first be taught to quarter (that is, to range about in search of game) against the wind only. The trainer should walk across the ground and then return to cross it again, moving up wind all the time, and waving his arm as an encouragement to the dog to search about. The dog will have to be carefully taught not to go twice over the same ground or to range too wild, as well as not to turn inwards down wind after having crossed up wind, as this would be not only a useless proceeding but a loss of time. The trainer will have to see that the dog does not work too far from him, and when teaching a young one he will have to walk parallel to the dog, keeping him near or far as desired by a wave of the hand, and ordering him to turn at the whistle, come to heel, or ' down charge ' now and then, to test his memory and discipline.

A dog should not be kept too long at this kind of work, or he will become sluggish and disappointed at not finding game, so that it needs to be got over as quickly, but withal as effectually, as possible. Having now proceeded so far in the dog's training, take him to where you are sure to find some partridges, putting him through his evolutions of ranging and dropping to command *en route.* When near where the birds are likely to be found, work for them against the wind, and keep the dog well

in hand, but do not hold the check-string tied to his collar.
He will not only scent the birds, but if a well-bred dog will
'stand' them too. Go up to him, pat him, and encourage him
to steal slowly and steadily on, and at the same time secure the
end of the string in your fingers. When the birds rise he is
pretty sure to spring forward in his eagerness to try and catch
them. That moment, pull him steadily back with the string,
telling him in a stern voice to 'down charge'! By carrying out
the last instructions patiently and firmly, and repeating the pro-

A Real Treasure.

cess as often as the dog requires it, a young pointer or setter,
if well bred, will usually soon learn to 'stand' birds, and afterwards to drop on their rising, of his own accord ; but should
the dog persistently flush bird after bird, he is simply worth
nothing more than a charge of powder and shot. We like to
see all pointers or setters taught to drop without an order on
the first bird or birds rising to the 'point.' It not only causes
them to be obedient and steady, but prevents them from flushing other birds close by, which would be apt to rise before

the gun was ready for them. To teach dogs to 'back' well, all that is necessary is to compel any others that may happen to be undergoing training at the same time to 'down charge' with the one to whom the order is given, and they will, in consequence, soon learn to copy one another, both in 'standing,' 'backing,' and also in creeping forward to the game when the dog that holds the scent is 'drawing' up to it; but care will have to be taken that the dog who first 'stands' is not passed by others behind, jealously creeping up to him. If one does so, he should be pulled back with a check-string and made to 'down charge'; he will then soon learn to 'back' steadily.

Young pointers are often scolded for flushing game without first pointing or even footing it, but the cleverest pointers and setters will do this on a bad scenting day, as when the air is hot, still, and dry, and dust from the ground, pollen on the turnips, and a parched nose interfere with the dog's power of smell. If pointers are very well broken, they may, as a final and most useful course of their instruction, be taught to gallop off down wind, turn at the sound of the whistle, and then work back home against the wind to their master, so getting the birds, it may be said, between two fires. If the game be wild, they can thus render great assistance. To break pointers and setters from chasing 'fur' the check-string comes into play, just as it does to correct them from springing after rising birds. Chasing is an unpardonable fault, and one rarely seen even in a fairly well-broken pointer; for, unlike a retriever, he is never allowed to even think of such a thing as pursuit. With setters it is a commoner occurrence, as they range wilder and wider, and are not usually under such strict or good discipline as pointers. Indeed it is sometimes found that many setters require a short course of breaking-in at the commencement of every season.

To cure pointers and setters of chasing, let them, when young, see a few tame rabbits about the enclosure near which they are kennelled. They will soon become not only tired of pointing them, but from frequent reprimands will otherwise leave them alone, and before they take the field treat them with indifference. It is those dogs who only see ground game now and then that are most given to chasing. It is wiser to take a young dog out where there are plenty of hares or rabbits when undergoing his first lessons, than to take him, as is often

'Ah-h! you brute!'

purposely done, where there are but few : in the former case he will get accustomed to seeing them and require less correcting ; but, if he only sees 'fur' now and again, he is more likely to be excited at its sudden appearance. Pointers and setters sometimes 'stand' hares and rabbits by nature, but it is a habit

'Ware chase, will you?'

to be strongly discouraged. Dogs, if broken to find 'fur,' will be disheartening animals at finding birds, will not quarter well, will stick to the hedge bottoms, and cause a loss of time and temper to the shooter. The fewer and shorter the words of encouragement or reprimand a trainer employs the better, and the easier and quicker will they be understood by his pupils. 'Ware chase!' answers both to tell a dog that birds have flown and to scold him away from 'fur' or 'feather.' 'Heel!' orders him to walk close behind his master; 'Come to heel, will you?' if he leaves without orders; 'Soho!' to induce the dog to stand stiff at a point, and till his master approaches; 'Have a care!' or 'Steady!' with an upraised hand, a movement of significance to a dog to make him go slowly and carefully forward; and, lastly, 'Hold up!' with a wave of the hand as he follows at heel, will send him off joyfully to quarter for game in front of his master.

Little has been said about teaching a pointer or setter to find, which means to 'scent,' game; for, as before remarked, this part of his training lies more with the dog than his master, and is a gift of nature peculiar to his breed. A good scenting dog will carry his nose high of his own accord (with a retriever the reverse is the case); if he does not do so, teach him to find, when a puppy, previously concealed 'titbits' placed a foot or so above ground. In fact, every pointer or setter may go through a course of seeking for hidden food; it will, at all events, do him no harm, and may do a great deal of good. Make it a golden rule, however, never to let the dog see you throw or place what he has to discover; for it is by scent he has to find it (as afterwards his game), and *not* by sight; make him also, when he does draw up to the object of his search, stand steady, checking him back with a string if necessary should he wish to rush in; then approach him, pat him, and allow him to go slowly forward to the word 'steady' and enjoy the morsel, talking kindly to him meanwhile and giving it him piece by piece in your hand (never throw it him) as he licks and snuffles for it.

Young dogs may even be treated to 'titbits' such as they love when first taking the field. A careless scampering puppy has often been taught to mend his ways in a short time on observing his better behaved companions rewarded with pieces of food for a clever performance on their part, given of course at the moment of its accomplishment.

'HAVE A CARE'

The foregoing hints equally apply to setters and spaniels ; but spaniels, though they require just the same treatment, are by nature so bustling and lively that they are more difficult to manage, and want more time and trouble expended on them to make them perfect, than is the case with pointers and setters.

RETRIEVERS.

A retriever is, to our mind, the king of all sporting dogs. He has none of the heaviness (or stupidity) of the pointer, or the fawning adulation for a master shown by the setter or spaniel. His mien is dignified, his actions show the height of animal intelligence, and he is affectionate and companionable as is no other dog used for shooting. He does not waste his love here and there and on anyone that chooses to fondle him and call him pleasant names ; he keeps his affection for his real master—he who owns, houses, and works him, whether he be gentleman or keeper. If he does a clever act he cares not for the approval of outsiders. He is not, he feels, working for them ; he works for but one, his master, and to him only he looks for encouragement and words of praise. His actions do not run in a groove, as do those of the pointer, setter, or spaniel, for he often has to act, and on the moment judge for himself, what is correct behaviour on his part, and what is not ; and if well broken his thoughtful sagacity rarely fails him, though he be out of sight and hearing of his trainer. Though it is difficult to say what a retriever is or should be, he is, without doubt, a modern invention necessitated by the increase of game, by its wildness, which causes it to be oftener wounded, as well as by the decadence (from their comparative uselessness in shooting nowadays) of pointers and setters. The object of a retriever is, it need scarcely be said, to save wounded game from being lost, and the true sportsman would rather see a retriever find and save one wounded bird than take half-a-dozen pot shots at as many unwounded, found by a pointer and flushed underfoot.

As to the kind of retriever, as just remarked, it would be difficult to say what a pure retriever is; whether he should be short or long, low or tall, smooth or curly-coated. We can merely recommend what is most useful for the field. It is usually insisted upon, that whatever form a retriever takes, he must, at all events, be black as soot from nose to end of tail; and yet some of the very best of the class for work (not show) have not obeyed this regulation as to colour. Many retrievers have setter blood in them, and are often commended for this; but it is difficult to see the practical use of the cross, and the evident disadvantage is, that a dog so bred has a habit of working up wind (as does a setter) and carrying his head high instead of circling in all directions with his nose to the ground when seeking wounded game, as of course he should do.

A mixture of retriever and colley blood has been tried, but this serves no good end; a cross between a small retriever and a large Irish water-spaniel, however, gives a very good dog. A retriever, to be useful, should have legs short and as straight as darts, firm and strong; a full-sized head (a dog with a too small head is rarely a clever worker), a tail that does not curl over his back, but is borne high and light, good loins, a shaggy and yet glossy coat, small ears, large feet with well-planted toes that do not splay outwards, and a deep well-formed chest, which does not imply a broad, massive one—the latter is a disadvantage, as it means a slow and heavy dog, especially in covert; lastly, a coat as black as you can get it. A curly-coated dog is, we have usually found, harder to break than a smooth-coated one, but, on the other hand, is generally the quicker and more dashing of the two, as well as being in our experience the cleverest.

There is no greater nuisance out shooting than a half-broken retriever. To see a retriever bolting about a field, putting up covey after covey that would otherwise have afforded sport, and to hear and see keepers, masters, and men yelling, gesticulating, swearing, and even dancing with rage, all about one miserable dog, not to speak of the sport that is destroyed thereby, is a painful infliction. It is almost worse in covert. Maybe Mr. So-and-so brings out with him what *he* considers a well-broken dog. At the gathering of guns, keepers, and beaters before starting, many admire the dog, for he appears handsome and intelligent, and keeps at heel when not among the game. Mr. So-and-so is proud of his dog. It is probably a recent gift or purchase, or one that he does not know much about, and he wonders how it was he got him, good character notwithstanding, such a bargain. A friend remarks, ' I have not a dog with me, as I dare not bring mine out till I feel he is safe, so if I lose any game I hope you will allow me to borrow yours.' At length the coverts are reached; the owner of the retriever gets some shots, and after a period notices his dog did not follow him over the last fence or out of the brushwood; but he has no qualms; the dog, perhaps, remained behind with some one else, as his nature was, he knew, very affectionate.

Presently, and when all are at a halt before getting in line, pheasants are seen rising in a far part of the covert, a part not yet, but just about to be, beaten, and very likely one reserved till the last as being the best, or that has had birds driven into it, so that the guns may stand outside and get shots at its un-disturbed contents. In a moment the head-keeper's or the host's eyes are riveted to the spot. One or the other turns with furious countenance to the equally astonished group of assis-tants near him, and asks, 'Who the —— is forward in the wood?' They reply as one man, horrified at such a wicked suggestion, ' No one, sir.' A frightened boy pipes out, 'Please, sir, I heard a dog bark!' The other guns who are standing by in a less degree dumbly reflect the anger of their host. Poor Mr. So-and-so with a bold front trembles inwardly, hoping against hope—a hope ruthlessly dispelled on seeing—what everyone else sees too—his own Don dash out of and back into the cover yelping after a rabbit, and so continue his course of sport-spoiling, curses, threats, and whistles being in vain.

The host at length remarks in cutting tone, 'Perhaps, So-and-so, as your dog knows you well, you could go up to him and bring him quietly out.' The unhappy owner of the delinquent takes a wild plunge into the wood; he will get the dog or die in the attempt is his feeling. But the former part of this performance is none so easy. Don is mad with excitement at the amount of game he sees all round him; one moment he dashes at a rabbit, the next tries to 'fly' after a pheasant rising under his nose. The further his master follows him, the more harm is he conscious he *and* his dog are doing. At last, by throwing himself on the animal in a thicket of thorns, the sinner is caught, and has a pleasant time of kicks and cuffs for five minutes, for no stick or whip is handy, and his yelps call forth curt and pleased remarks from the beaters and keepers in the distance, such as, 'He's got hold on 'im!' 'Ey, mon, he is larropping 'im!' The dog is led back with a handkerchief, and is as much an object of loathing as if he were mad. The host looks for the rest of the day as if all his and his friends' sport had been completely spoiled, and the head-keeper audibly and with great gravity and seriousness remarks, 'Folks as 'as dogs as 'as no manners 'as no right to bring 'em out and spoil other folks' sport.' Poor Mr. So-and-so has learnt a lesson which will last him his life, which is, that no gentleman, keeper, or beater should ever on any account take out when sporting in company a retriever that he does not know from personal experience is worthy of absolute confidence.

The above by no means unfrequent incident is given as a warning to young shooters, and as an inducement to them to bestow all possible pains and time in completely breaking in a retriever, and, when broken in, to influence them to thoroughly try and test his discipline at first when out shooting alone, or at all events at home.

Discipline and unswerving obedience are of the utmost importance in a retriever, for the amount of 'sport-spoiling' a wild dog can achieve in a few minutes is incalculable. The power of scent in a retriever is a gift of nature or the result of practice, and is, it may be said, of secondary value compared with the quality of obedience. A bad-scenting dog may improve, and if steady can, anyhow, always be used. A wild, disobedient dog, however good his nose, is practically useless.

The first instruction a retriever puppy should receive is finding, when hungry, pieces of concealed meat about the enclosure where he is kept; these he should be encouraged to seek for and find, and he may (unlike a pointer) be allowed to go straight up and eat them as the immediate reward of his cleverness. Secondly, he should be taught to 'foot' after a 'titbit' dragged some distance by a long string, straight during his first lessons and afterwards in circles or zigzags. The longer he is practised in doing this the more thoroughly will he be trained and the more anxious to find. Make a point of practising him yourself when alone, and on no account let him be disappointed in finding. If after a careful search he does not succeed, lay down a piece of meat near him in the track of the other and let him find that, or else lead him up to the original piece. He will also have to learn to 'retrieve' as well as to find. This will come quite naturally to him if a steady well-bred dog. Begin at short distances, only a few yards and in sight, and lengthen the space by degrees till the object you throw (a stuffed rabbit or partridge with a piece of meat thrust inside it for scent) falls out of sight, first in long grass, then over a hedge or in a thicket. The dog will also need careful training in the matter of 'down charging' with the check-string at home, and as directed in regard to pointers, before he is taken into the field. He may then continue his lessons in some place where ground game are fairly plentiful, and be broken from 'chasing.' The first time he sees game running of course he chases ; he cannot help doing so—it is his nature, he knows no better. At first flog him pretty smartly with a whip (never a stick), and if of ordinarily amenable nature, though for some time he may make frequent attempts at chasing, the crack of the whip, as a reminder of what he may expect on his return, will bring him round to heel again after he has gone a short distance in a half-hearted, doubtful manner. If the above course of instruction fail, then, and not till then, a score yards of check-string may be attached to his neck to pull him up short when he attempts a chase, letting him get half the length of the string before pulling him back. A retriever is however far better when broken from chasing without the aid of a check-string if possible.

Provided the dog is fairly cured of chasing, taught to 'down charge,' find, return, and keep at heel, and is generally docile and obedient, he may be taken out with a well-broken dog and a gun. He should for an hour or so be allowed to watch what goes on, hear the report, and see the other dog retrieve the game. The old dog can then be kept up, and the young one have a try, the shooter being careful to choose an easy shot so as to make sure of dropping the game. At first, lead the dog up to the spot, tell him to 'seek,' cautioning him meanwhile to be steady. If he have a hard mouth he will pounce on the bird and crush it; if not, he will lift it gingerly, as if half afraid of it, especially if the bird can flutter. In the latter case he is all right, and always will be; in the former he will require a little more education in the matter, and should be treated as follows. Have ready prepared a piece of hedgehog skin, and secure it firmly by elastic straps or twine to a recently killed partridge. Give the dog to an attendant, and substitute the bird just dropped for the other. Now let the retriever seek and find, and from pricking his mouth he will soon learn to pick up game tenderly, whether alive or dead; and he can be practised afterwards at home in the same manner. Stuffing gloves or skins with pins is cruel and injurious, and cannot be done in the field to game, where the first lessons of this kind should invariably take place. Puppies intended for wildfowl shooting should be taught to go into the water in summer and autumn, and then in the winter they will not shirk the cold.

R. P. G.

CHAPTER XVI.

PIGEON SHOOTING FROM TRAPS.

To attempt in these days a defence of pigeon-shooting would be considered by many an ungrateful task, yet it is with a full sense of responsibility that we give to this branch of shooting a place in the present volume, nor is it really a difficult matter to dispose of the numerous allegations, most of them wholly devoid of truth, which have been brought forward as the heavy artillery to support the attacks made upon it by sentimentalists. We are inclined to clear the ground by saying that we do not claim it as a 'sport,' but as a perfectly legitimate pastime in which men of all degrees may indulge without discredit so long as the rules of fair play and the ordinary code of humanity be properly observed. That these are observed, and that no form of wanton cruelty is permitted at the leading shooting clubs in London and the country, has of late been amply shown, and it is worthy of note that at the London Gun Club, the head-quarters of pigeon shooting, the committee of which stand in much the same position towards adherents of pigeon shooting as the Jockey Club occupy towards the racing community, the officers of the Royal Society for Prevention of Cruelty to Animals have been cordially invited to attend, without previous notice, in order that they may satisfy themselves of the humane manner in which the birds are treated. They have expressed themselves perfectly satisfied, and we would recommend those who may be concerned in forming a pigeon-shooting club to visit the Gun Club and Hurlingham, and there ascertain for themselves the rules and restrictions, which are imposed upon all engaged, for ensuring the prevention of cruelty and the preservation of fair play for shooters and birds alike. Of course if shooting—i.e. the destruction of birds or beasts with gun or rifle—be cruel, then pigeon shooting is cruel. But we hope to be able to show that it is no more so than any other form of sport ; nay more, that the pigeon slain at the traps has a happier lot both in life and death than most of the animals which minister to the pleasure or necessity of the lords of creation.

We may fairly point to the names of those who have followed with zest the pastime of pigeon shooting, a list spread over four or five generations, and comprising most of the best-known sportsmen of this century, as an answer to the diatribes of ignorant sentimentalists. The leading pigeon-shooters, since the days when the 'Old Hats' at Ealing was the principal rendezvous, have been men noted for their devotion to sport of every kind, and to write down their names in order should be sufficient to convince an unprejudiced person that a pastime to which they were addicted cannot be dismissed as contemptible, brutal, or un-English. Surely Mytton, Osbaldeston, Ross and Anson may appeal to us as the bearers of good English names, giants of sport, men trained to feats of endurance and nerve on foot and on horseback. Later on we find the late General Hall, and Mr. Stirling Crawfurd (one of the best), Mr. Walter de Winton, Lord Leconfield, Lord Huntingfield, Mr. Corrance, Mr. W. G. Craven, the late Mr. Dudley Ward, and a host of others well known at the covert-side, on the turf, or on the moor and stubble ; while to pass to our more immediate contemporaries, the names of Bateson, Hill, Cayley, de Grey, Rimington-Wilson, Shelley, Hargreaves, and many others need no recommendation to modern sportsmen. The jungles of Africa, the precipices of the Himalayas or 'Rockies,' the corries of Inverness-shire, or the wolds of Yorkshire have known them alike in their generation, and we might be safe in assuming that a pastime with which they have not been ashamed to identify their names needs no further defence.

But a few facts are useful to satisfy the uninitiated, and first we would lay great stress upon the circumstance that the pigeon leads the happiest of lives, until the moment when, startled by the fall of the trap and by noise behind him, he flies away for his life. It is a complete error to suppose that he is ill-treated. If he were, he would not be worth the fancy price, sometimes as high as half-a-crown a bird, which the match-shooter pays for him. He is used to being handled, and the writer has often seen birds feeding on stray grains of corn, or comporting themselves in a manner which proved how utterly unconcerned they were, in the hampers within a minute of their being trapped and killed.

They are brought up upon the very best of food and water, and in all things treated as carefully as a race-horse. The best of reasons exists for this : their value depends upon it, and the desire of the pigeon-shooter is to get the strongest and liveliest birds to test his skill upon. As to wounding, no doubt some are wounded ; but suffering is reduced to a minimum by the rapid retrieving, and on the best grounds by the high boundary. For if a bird be strong enough to get over this his struggle for life is short, and he probably drops dead a few yards beyond it. If broken-winged he is retrieved and his neck wrung in a scientific manner in less time than it takes to describe the act. We would urge upon those who may be interested in founding a shooting club special attention to the following points : (1) Let the birds be supplied by some well-known pigeon-dealer who has every interest in supplying the best, and producing them fresh and uninjured upon the ground. (2) Let the Club have spacious and well ventilated baskets, and provision for the birds to be placed in the shade during hot weather. (3) Let the rules be stringent against any ill-treatment or mutilation. (4) Let the trapper be the servant of the pigeon-dealer, and not of the club, that it may be to his interest that all the birds should be healthy and fly strongly. (5) Let the puller have a mechanical appliance for pulling, and let him be the servant of the club, to prevent any collusion as to producing a different class of birds for different people. (6) Let the birds be taken from the dealer's hampers, and mixed into the club hampers in the presence of members or officials of the club. (7) Insist upon the dealer producing good dogs for rapid retrieving. (8) Let the boundary fence, where practicable, be a good height, say 8 feet, and let a person be employed to look after and secure at once any birds which may fall dead or wounded outside the boundary. (9) Let the club always, if possible, have rights over a larger space of ground than the absolute shooting enclosure, in order that the foregoing system may be carried out. (10) Arrange if possible for the traps to be shifted when necessary, so as to shoot always *with* the wind.

The height of the Gun Club enclosure averages 9 feet, and the average distance from the middle trap is 70 yards. At Hurlingham the average distance from traps is 75 yards, and the lower enclosure 8 feet high. There is here a very high fence to protect other parts of the club grounds from shot, but the scoring of a dead or lost bird is determined by the lower fence. We strongly recommend the long distance or 'fall,' as it is termed, from the traps with the high fence, on the score of humanity. At Monte Carlo the boundary is only 18 metres from the centre trap, and the fence about 3 feet 6 inches high, enabling a large proportion of birds to escape wounded. At the Cercle des Patineurs at Paris the birds fall into water. Neither of these is a humane arrangement, but we do not require to go abroad to learn anything connected with shooting.

The handicap should range from 21 yards to 31, but the ground should be so arranged as to afford the possibility of shooting at 35 yards, or even farther. Let the longest distance mark, say at 31 yards, be some way out from the barrier behind which those who are not shooting must stand, and the trap-pulling machine very near the 31 yards mark, that the shooter may not be distracted by the remarks of onlookers, and that the puller and the shooter may hear each other distinctly. A good pulling machine is an expensive thing, yet we should recommend every club to look upon it as a necessity. It should so work that no one, and certainly not the puller, can possibly tell which trap will come over next. ' Si vis pacem, para bellum'; and on the same principle we should insist strongly upon everything being done beforehand to arm the cause of fair-play against collusion of any kind between puller, shooter, or trapper. Every form of dishonesty in pigeon-shooting is preventible excepting one—a man missing a bird on purpose. This, however, is of no great consequence, unless there be betting, and though there generally is betting, more or less, at all pigeon matches or sweeps, it is not within the province of this volume to deal with its abuses. All we can do is to lay before novices who are beginning to shoot pigeons, or forming a new club, the best means of checking dishonesty of any kind.

A few hints will be necessary to those about to attempt pigeon-shooting. In the case of an absolute beginner with the gun this is a very useful way of learning how to handle it in the most safe and effective manner. We would recommend a single-barrelled gun to begin with, and should place the young shooter at 21 yards or even nearer, increasing the distance as he improves. Impress upon him the necessity of not fixing his eyes upon any particular trap, and of not standing in a constrained or set position. He should be as free as possible, the left hand fairly well forward on the barrels, the stock gripped firm in the right, and the whole gun, though below the elbow, sufficiently forward to admit of its being brought smartly to the shoulder without the stock catching either the elbow or the coat. Let him pull trigger at the instant of bringing his gun to bear upon the spot he intends to hit, and not after 'poking' or dwelling on the bird. Tell him to shoot well over the birds, and always (if he be using a double-barrel) to shoot the second barrel as carefully as the first. When you have said this there is no more to be said to a complete novice. Further instruction must be given by the correction of his peculiar faults as time goes on.

To one more experienced with the gun, but shooting at the traps for the first time, we must try and give more detailed advice We will suppose him armed with a gun that suits him, and Purdey, Grant, and a few, though not many, of the other leading gunmakers can ensure this for him. He will take his gun and cartridges from a rack, or from the gun-maker's assistant, only at the moment when he is called on to shoot ; to wait about carrying a gun, apart from the fact that it is probably against rules, is tiring, however imperceptibly, to the wrists or arms. Load when at the mark, not before, lest you should one day arrive there and on pulling trigger find your gun empty and lose a bird. Be careful to cock both barrels, and let the loading and cocking become a mechanical sequence never omitted on reaching the mark. Take your stand facing the traps, with the left foot only a little in advance of the right, and be careful to feel that you are thoroughly firm on your feet. The positions of the feet and body should be practically the same as in boxing, and a steady balance on both feet is absolutely necessary.

Now reflect as to your weak point in shooting. If you are specially taxed by a bird going to the left, face the middle trap, or slightly to the left of the middle. If you are weak at shots to your right, face somewhere about No. 4 trap, but do not in either case fix your eyes upon any particular trap. Stand well upright, for leaning forward is, speaking generally, a fault in style, as tending to depress the muzzle of the gun when firing. Avoid all hard-set or cramped positions, keeping your action free and loose, with one exception—let your hands grip the gun very firmly. Raise your gun, if you like, once or twice, not more, to the shoulder, to ascertain that your left is grip-ping the barrels at the right length. Keep your left as far forward on the barrels as you can, consistently with the gun coming quickly up and down. Do not hurry yourself at all ; give the 'Are you ready ?' calmly, and the 'Pull !' equally so, but be careful to hear the answering 'Yes' of the puller before saying 'Pull.' Shoot quickly, if possible, rather *over* the bird ;

and lastly, *always* until you have gained great experience use your second barrel at the bird, and carefully, even though he be knocked down and apparently disabled. Many a match has been lost owing to a bird presumed to be dead by the shooter rising and getting out.

Should the bird not rise when the trap comes over, but remain seated, take your decision immediately whether to call 'No bird' or to stick to him till he does rise. As a general rule we would advise taking a sitter, and sticking to him ; since you know where he is, and have only to watch intently for his rising. But a very good rule is to be guided by the direction of his head—to refuse him if it be turned away, and take him if turned towards you. Some very experienced shooters invariably refuse sitting birds. But, whichever rule you adopt, stick to it ; and, if you choose to shoot at them, make a study of how to kill them with certainty, bearing in mind that you are entitled to shoot the instant the bird's wings are open and his feet off the ground.

In double-rise shooting (for which the distance is now usually twenty-five yards) the above instructions apply equally. Shoot at the bird which first catches your eye, and should you not kill him, shoot at the same again. If you kill him, above all do not hurry with your second barrel on the other bird. This is the great secret of successful double-rise shooting. You have more time than you think, and in very many instances the second bird will cross as though to join the other one, even though the latter be killed. Of course if only one of the two sits on the trap, kill the one that rises as quickly as possible. If both sit, it is better as a rule to take them ; they are likely to fly across and towards each other, giving easy shots.

In shooting a match, whether at twenty-five, fifty, or a hundred birds each, there are a few points worth remembering. If you win the toss, take the lead ; it is as well not to have to kill to win at the end in case it comes to that. Take a chair, sit apart from spectators and conversation, and rivet your mind entirely upon your own performance, though watching your adversary, as in all contests, with sufficient care to be sure that he adheres to rules. Take no heed of his score, nor of any remarks made to you by anyone, for remember that it is your performance which decides the match. Say to yourself, 'If I can kill so many birds, I win ; ' and work straight away to make this score, leaving all consideration of what your adversary makes out of the question. Do not begin carelessly ; many a match is lost through carelessness at the start, and the first bird counts one on the score as well as the last. If the weather be hot and the match a long one, keep in the shade or have an umbrella, and have water at hand to cool the gun-barrels frequently. No man can shoot his best with a hot gun. If in winter and the weather be very cold, keep warm between the shots, and wear thick shooting boots to keep the feet dry. Eat and drink next to nothing during the match, but if it be a long match, have a cup of beef tea, cold or hot, during the interval. Avoid Dutch courage, and remember that to do your best you must be in perfect health. A match of one hundred birds each will surely try your nerve and endurance, and you ought to be as well and fit to do it as though you were going to fight. The conditions of making a match must be left to the judgment, but we would advise no one to match himself to shoot at one hundred birds until he has tried himself a few times at that number. Such a match lasts three hours and a half, and many a man who is first-rate at twenty-five or fifty birds cannot stay the longer course equally well. Seventy kills out of a hundred, at thirty yards rise, used to be considered good, that is, making seventy kills to thirty misses, or just under five to two, which was formerly almost the invariable bet on the gun *v.* the bird.

This score, however, is not good enough to win a first-class match in these days, and unless a man can be pretty sure of killing 80 out of 100 he had better let the best shots of the present day alone. Captain Ross, many years ago, is said to have killed 96 out of 100, but there is very little doubt the birds were not so good in those days as they are now, and the shooters then used very heavy charges—$1\frac{1}{2}$ oz. to $1\frac{3}{4}$ oz. shot, and heavy guns. Lord Huntingfield also made some remarkable totals, but his best distance was 25 yards. His charge $1\frac{1}{4}$ oz. and No. 6 shot in the first, with No. 5 in the second barrel.

Though pigeon shooting had been in vogue since 1790 or thereabouts, handicaps were never shot, or at least are not recorded until 1856. The first of these was shot at Purdey's ground at Willesden at that date, the handicap varying from 30 to 24 yards, and it is worthy of note that the two first were won by the long-distance men. Not long after this Mr. Frank Heathcote started handicapping at Hornsey Wood, whither the shooters had repaired when the Red House at Battersea was done away with. About this time General Hall, whose shooting at Six Mile Bottom, near Newmarket, became so famous, was in command of the First Life Guards, and, himself one of the best, had in his regiment a whole array of first-rate shots, among them Lord Leconfield, Mr. W. de Winton, and Captain (now General) Bateson. A match was shot between the latter and Sir F. Milbank at Hornsey Wood House for a large sum of money, and before an immense attendance, there being over twenty coaches on the ground. Bateson won the match, which was at 25 birds each, 25 yards rise. Another notable match was between Lord Aveland and Mr. Reginald Cholmondeley. Later on Mr. F. Heathcote founded Hurlingham, and here, under the patronage of the highest in the land and every well-known sportsman in England, pigeon-shooting entered upon that flourishing condition which it maintains to this day. Then came the Gun Club, founded by Lord Stormont and other well-known shots, and it is here that of late years all the best men have competed. Here every modern improvement in guns, powders, or cartridges has been brought to the test, and there can be no doubt that the practical proofs supplied by pigeon-shooting have been of great service to the science of modern gunnery. No better test of guns or charges is necessary than the fact of what first-rate shots will use when shooting for a heavy stake. Some good matches and notable performances have been seen at the Gun Club and elsewhere of recent years, and the arrival of Captain Bogardus, and later of Dr. Carver, two American professional shooters, each professing to be champion of the world, produced some contests of special interest. A match was shot at the Gun Club between Bogardus and Captain Shelley, when the former won easily. His heavy gun and smashing charges of powder, the charge of powder being unlimited at that time, gave him an undoubted advantage. Many English shooters at once adopted the same method, with the result that two years later the charge of powder was limited by Gun Club rules to 4 drs., and the weight of guns to 8 lbs. Too heavy a gun is no advantage, but the contrary, and to prove this the present writer shot a match at 100 birds for 100*l.* a side in which he conceded to his opponent, the late Mr. Bolam, 5 yards on condition that that gentleman used a gun weighing 10 lbs. Before the match was half over Mr. Bolam offered 50*l.* to be allowed to use a light gun, an advantage which was of course refused, and Mr. Bolam lost the match by an absurdly large number of birds. Bogardus was next tackled by Mr. Dudley Ward, who shot a tie with him, each killing 84 out of 100—a very fine score. On shooting off Mr. Ward won easily. The famous match between Mr. Aubrey Coventry and Bogardus at Brighton came next, but here the Englishman was defeated, the scores not being on either side particularly high. Bogardus is reported to have said it was 'no catch' shooting against our best men.

Next appeared Dr. Carver, whose marvellous skill with the rifle had fairly astonished the world. After shooting many matches and never being beaten or approached (excepting in a contest at 25 birds each with Mr. Heygate, one of the best shots at the Gun Club, especially in a short match, the result being a tie), he finally shot against the present writer at the Hendon ground on December 8, 1882, for 500*l.* a side. This match ended in a tie, each killing 83 out of 100. There was much betting on this contest, and it was rendered peculiarly exciting by the fact that it was a tie at the 50th bird, and again eight or nine times during the last half of the match, as at the finish. The writer was unlucky, for his 50th bird fell dead upon a small building within the enclosure, but by the custom of the ground was given a lost bird. Carver did some wonderful things, but though he and Bogardus (who were, it should be remembered, professionals) claim to be better than our best men, they certainly failed to prove it by their public performances.

The best pigeon-shots ot Hurlingham and the Gun Club of recent years have been, or are, Lord Hill, Lord de Grey, Captain Shelley, Mr. Berkeley Lucy, Mr. Dudley Ward, Mr. Aubrey Coventry, Captain Aubrey Patton, Mr. H. J. Roberts, and Lord de Clifford, while a host of others would run any of these very close.

We have not gone into the details of setting traps, of mechanical appliances, pavilions, scoring-boards, or measurements generally, because so long as pigeon-shooting lasts all information of the sort, together with rules, &c., can be readily obtained from the secretaries of Hurlingham or the Gun Club for the benefit of any one wishing to start a new club or ground. The Hon. D. Monson at Hurlingham, or Mr. G. A. Battcock at the Gun Club, both excellent referees and men with wide experience of the subject, would gladly give facts and information which the limits of this volume do not admit of our setting down here.

In conclusion we would advise all young shooters, whether at home or abroad, to shoot pigeons only at recognised clubs, and to avoid promiscuous gatherings, where they might find their experience rather dearly bought.

A. J. S.-W.

NOTE.

WITH regard to the much talked of 'Paradox' Gun, we give the result of some practical trials which we personally undertook to test its capabilities, experiments which convince us of the value of this weapon for large game shooting abroad, as well as for ordinary game shooting, whether abroad or at home. The shooting given here is not chosen from the best of a series of shots, but is simply the result of taking the gun up and using it in an ordinary way. The gun in appearance and weight is exactly similar to an ordinary 12 bore.

Trial of Messrs. Hollands' 'Paradox' Shot and Ball Gun,
May 20, 1886.

1*st series, Ball.*—6 shots; fired right and left, with conical express bullets. Range 100 yards; all in 1½ in. × 4½ in. See No. 1.

2*nd series, Ball.*—6 shots; right and left. Range 50 yards; same cartridges as before, making the extraordinarily fine diagram of 1½ in. × 2¼ in., all being in the centre of the bull's-eye. See No. 2.

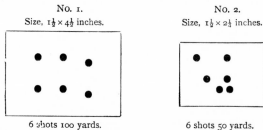

No. 1.	No. 2.
Size, 1½ × 4½ inches.	Size, 1½ × 2¼ inches.
6 shots 100 yards.	6 shots 50 yards.

3*rd series, Shot.*—8 shots; range 40 yards. Charge, 3 dr. No. 4 powder + 1⅛ oz. No. 6 shot, 30 in. circle; making the very good patterns of—right, average 144; left, average 165; with good force and an even distribution of the pellets.

INDEX.

ABB

ABBEY FARM, Thetford, sport
at, 166, 167
Accidents, 34, 38, 101, 134,
174, 176, 196
Ammunition, 99
Ants' eggs for partridges, 253
Automatic cartridge extractors,
52

BADGERS, 283, 284
Bags of game, large, 12–17, 19,
24–26, 45, 179, 180, 211,
212, 213, 269
Battcock, Mr. G. A., 345
Batteries, 164
Battues, 3, 20, 182
Beagles, 261, 262
Beaters, and their duties, 22,
131, 133, 144, 146, 164, 167,
169–171, 187, 188, 190, 193,
196, 201, 219, 220, 265, 266,
268 ; *see* Keepers
Beginners in shooting, hints to,
31 ; caution with loaded guns,
31 ; following game with gun,
32, 33 ; fitting gun to shooter,
33 ; precautions against accident discharge, 34, 38 ; care
in firing, 34 ; too long and

BRA

too near shots, 35, 41 ; on
self-laudation, 35 ; training,
36 ; how to carry a gun, 37 ;
choice of a gun, 38, 39 ; aiming forward, 40 ; where to
strike, 41 ; use of one or both
eyes in aiming, 42, 43 ; scien-
tific shooting, 44 ; shooting
schools, 46, 47 ; further hints
to shooters, 176–178 ; single-
barrelled guns for beginners
in pigeon shooting, 339 ; *see*
Shooters and Shooting
Belgian gun-barrels, 66
Berberis (Mahonia) aquifolia,
190
Bird enemies, 246
Birmingham guns, 55, 66, 74,
86
Biscuit for dogs, 320
Black list, the, 273–289
Blubberhouse Moors, sport at,
24
Blue rocks ; *see* Wood Pigeon
Bogardus, Captain, 344
Bohemia, sport in, 14, 15, [177]
Bolam, Mr., 344
Boots, 342
Bore of guns, 96
Bradgate Park, 214, 240, 241

BUC

Buckenham, sport at, 164, 169, 213
Buckle, Isaac, keeper, 297
Buckle, John, keeper, 297
Buzzards, 286

CAMBRIDGE, sport in, 9, 27, 29, 179
Caps, shooting, colour of, 165
Caps, gun, 51, 112
Cartridges, 52, 53, 101, 108; gas-tight, 109; Joyce's invention, 110; sizes and colours, 110; brass cases, 110; Eley's, 110; Kynoch's, 111; brass *versus* paper, 111
Cartridge-extractors, 52
Carver, Dr., 344
Cases, gun, 115, 116
Cats, 277, 278, 287; *see* Vermin
Cercle des Patineurs, Paris, pigeon shooting at, 258
Chantilly, sport at, 30
Charges of guns, 101–103
Cherry Row, plan of covert, 217
Chilled shot, 104
Choke-bores, 62, 63, 82–85, 104, 105
Chronometer oil for cleaning guns, 118
Cleaning guns, 116–120, [119]
Cleaning-rods, 120, [119]
Clothing, 188, 189, 225
Clumber spaniels, 262
Cocker spaniels, 263
Coops, 238, 242
Copper caps, 51
Coverts, planted, 190; plans of, 215–224
Crops of pigeons, contents of, 228

ELE

Crossbows, 297
Crows, 246, 274, 275, 285; *see* Vermin
Croxteth, sport at, 213

DAMASCUS barrels, 64, 65
Decoy pigeons, 226, 227, 229
Detonating powder, 50
Detonators, 51
Dogs, uses, merits and demerits of, 5, 9, 10, 14, 22, 131, 135, 140, 142–146, 156, 157, 172, 192, 193, 199, 201, 203, 246, 257, 261–265, 303; breaking, 315; points of a good retriever, 316; first lessons, 316; punishment, 317; penitent, 318; use of the lash, 318; kindness to, 320; food, 320; gun-shy, 320, 321; training pointers and setters, 322; teaching to quarter, 324; 'down charge,' 325; backing, 326; curing chasing, 326; words of encouragement, 328; teaching finding, 328; superiority of retrievers over other classes, 329; pure and cross breeds, 330; mischief done by half-broken animals, 331; training retrievers, 333; *see* vol. ii.
Drivers, 162; *see* Keepers

E.C. POWDER, 100, 102
Ejector guns, 55, 59, 60; *see* Guns
Electric light in grouse shooting (a hoax), 21
Eley, Messrs., cartridge-makers, 110

ELV

Elveden, sport at, 28, 174, 180, 234, 236, 242, 248
Engraving, gun, 74

FENCES, 160–165
Ferrets, 260, 261, 302 ; *see* Vermin
Field glasses, 293
Fitting a gun, 85–88
Flags, 171
Flint locks, 13, 48–50, 99
Flushes, 191
Fosbery, Col., 69
Foumarts, 278
Four-barrelled guns, 62
Foxes, 234, 257, 262, 283 ; *see* Vermin
French partridges, 143

GAME accounts, tabulated abstracts of, 209, 211
Game-book, of the Chantilly estate, 30 ; of Elveden, 180 ; extracts from Riddlesworth, 211 ; extracts from the Holkham, 212
Gapes, the, 158
Gape-worm, the, 250
Gate nets, poachers', 311
Gaultheria Shallon, 191
Gilbert, Mr., his 'Shooting Corrector,' 43
Greener's, Mr., method of making shot, 106
Ground game, 200, 311
Grouse moors, the best, 24
Gun-barrels, 64, 75 ; *see* Guns
Gun-cases, 115, 116
Gun-cleaning, 116–[119]
Gun-locks, 68, 117 ; *see* Guns
Gunmakers—Beesler, Mr., 93 ;

GUN

Bland, Messrs., 73 ; Boss, Messrs., 91 ; Cogswell & Harrison, 55, 56, 94 ; Fullerd, 66 ; Gibbs & Pitt, 57 ; Grant, 55, 74, 77–81 ; Greener, 54, 57, 62, 75 ; Holland, Messrs., 55, 57, 60, 61, 69, 74, 87, 271 ; Lancaster, C., 62, 78–81, 94 ; Lang, 51 ; Manton, 50 ; Murcott, 56 ; Needham, 56 ; Pape, 62 ; Purdey & Sons, 49, 50, 53, 55, 57–59, 74, 75, 89, [119] ; Rigby, 55 ; Westley Richards, 53, 57, 135 ; Woodward, 55 ; *see* vol. ii.
Gunpowder, black, 99 ; chemical powders, 99 ; Schönbein's discovery, 99 ; Schultze's invention, 99 ; E.C., 100, 101 ; varieties of nitro-powders, 102-103 ; *see* vol ii.
Gunpowder making, the Explosive Company, 100
Guns and gun-making, Purdey's ancient and modern, 49 ; Manton's flint-lock, 50 ; muzzle- and breech-loaders, 51 ; Lefaucheux pin-fire, 51, 52 ; central fire, 52 ; Westley Richards' snap-action, 53 ; Purdey & Son's bolt improvement, 53 ; Greener's top-extension, 53, 54 ; Cogswell & Harrison's ejector, 55, 56 ; Henry Rifle Co., 66 ; Needham's, Murcott's, Gibbs' and Pitt's and Westley Richards' hammerless, 56, 57 ; Anson and Deeley's invention, 57 ; Purdey & Son's hammerless, 57 ; ejectors, 59 ; Holland's ejector, 61 ; four-barrelled, 62 ;

GUN

choke-bores, 62 ; choke-bore
v. cylinder, 63, 84–88 ; gun-
barrels, 64 ; 'Damascus,' 64,
66 ; steel barrels, 64 ;
barrel-making, 66–68; 'action-
ing,' 68 ; the stripper's and
finisher's work, 68, 69 ; shot
and ball gun, 69 ; prices
and values, 71–81 ; London
versus Birmingham workmanship, 74 ; engraving, 75 ;
Mr. Greener's account of
make and cost of a good gun,
75–77 ; prime cost of best
class of gun, 77 ; Grant's hammerless, 77 ; the Lancaster,
78 ; Lancaster ejector, 80 ;
the choice of a gun, 82 ; fitting
gun to the shooter, 85–88 ;
balance, 86 ; well-shaped, 87 ;
bad-shaped, 87 ; Try guns,
88, 89 ; hammerless *v.* hammer, 90 ; single-trigger, 91–
96 ; weight, bore, and
charges, 96–99 ; powder, 99–
103 ; shot, 104–108 ; cartridges, 108–112 ; caps, 112 ;
wads, 112 ; proof of guns,
114 ; cases, 115 ; cleaning,
116–120 ; locks, 117 ; cleaning-rods, 120, [119] ; for
pigeon shooting from traps,
339 ; 'Paradox,' 346 ; *see*
vol. ii.

HAMMER guns ; *see* Guns
Hammerless guns ; *see* Guns
Handicap pigeon shooting, 338
Hares, 10, 17, 135, 201, 214,
271, 304, 311, 312, 319
Harriers, 286

KEE

Harting, Mr. J. E., his method
of mounting dead pigeons as
decoys, 227
Hatching-pens, 240, 241, 245
Hawks, 284, 285 ; *see* Vermin
Hedgehogs, 282 ; *see* Vermin
Herod, Samuel, keeper, 179
Heron Court, sport at, 44 ;
game and fowl shot in thirty-
nine seasons at, 45
Hobbys, 286 ; *see* Vermin
Holkham, sport at, 16, 17, 180,
189, 190, 205, 217
Hornsey Wood, pigeon shooting
at, 343
Hurdle batteries, 164
Hurlingham, pigeon shooting
at, 335, 338, 343, 345
Hypericum calycinum, 190
Houghton, sport at, [178]

INCUBATORS, 239
Ireland, sport in, 27
Irish water-spaniels, 330

JACKDAWS, 246, 274, 279 ; *see*
Vermin
Jaggard, Jerry, keeper, 141
Jays, 246, 274, 279 ; *see* Vermin
Joyce's absolutely gastight car-
tridge case, 110

KENNELS, 320
Keepers, and their duties, 119,
125, 126, 131, 132, 140, 146,
153, 155, 156, 158, 159, 162,
165, 168, 169, 172, 183, 185,
186, 201, 203, 204, 206, 207,
214, 215, 231, 233, 234, 236,
237, 239, 241, 243, 245, 248,

KEE

252, 254, 257, 265, 273–284, 289 ; qualities and characteristics, 291 ; taking tips for placing shooters, 292 ; 'keepers' fund,' 292 ; good and bad, 292, 293 ; supplying with field glasses, 293 ; dealings with poachers, 294 ; acquaintance with the game laws and laws of trespass, 294 ; head-keepers to be furnished with guns, 295 ; attacking poachers, 295, 297 ; use of revolvers, 295 ; use of sticks, 296 ; good health enjoyed by, 296 ; skulkers and malingerers, 296 ; three keepers on a Norfolk estate, 297 ; a deed of appointment in 1835, 297, 302, 304, 317, 320 ; *see* vol ii.
Kestrels, 246, 280–282, 289
Kites, 154

LANCASTER gun, 78
Lefaucheux pin-fire gun, the, 51
Loaders, positions of, and instructions to, in handling guns, 173–175
London Gun Club, 335, 338, 343–345
London gunmakers, 74, 89

MAGGOTS, 248
Magpies, 274, 275
Malmesbury, Lord, grand total of game killed by, in forty seasons, 45
Matches, pigeon-shooting, 342
Mayes, James, keeper, 234, 249
Megnin, Dr., quoted, 159, 251

PAR

Merlins, 286
Merton, sport at, 174, 214 ; home woods, plan of coverts at, 223, 229
Mews, 233, 235
Monson, Hon. D., 345
Monte Carlo, pigeon-shooting at, 258
Muzzle-loaders, dangers of, 174

NEATSFOOT oil, for cleaning guns, 118
Netting, 200, 309–313
Neuropterus lenticularis, 215
New Forest, sport in, 263, 264
Norfolk, sport in, 9, 27–29, 44, 51, 143, 155, 170, 176, [178], 207, 212, 213, 223, 229, 234, 255, 207 ; *see* vol. ii.
Norfolk shirts, 189

'OLD HATS' at Ealing, pigeon shooting at, 336
Ormerod, Miss, 208
Owls, 246, 286, 289

'PARADOX' gun, 69 ; result of trials with, 346
Paraffin, for cleaning guns, 117–119
Partridge shooting, popularity of, 139 ; driving, 140, 148, 155 ; knowledge of the ground, 140 ; keepers interested in sparing the birds, 140 ; anecdote of Jerry Jaggard, 141 ; working with pointers, 141 ; walking in line, 143, 148, 149 ; introduction of the

PAR

'French bird,' 143 ; 'mark over,' 143 ; inferiority of the 'red legs,' 144 ; cause of the abandonment of dogs, 144 ; working with retrievers, 145 ; good and bad dogs, 146 ; marking, 146–148 ; the line *en échelon*, 149–152 ; a bowed line, 149–153 ; out-manœuvring a covey, 151 ; the shooting and the flushing point, 151 ; working down wind, 153 ; use of kites, 154 ; shooting over dogs, 155, 156 ; match between Mr. William Coke and Lord Kennedy, 155 ; the selection of the fittest, 155 ; rewards for bringing in cock pheasants, 156 ; abuse of driving, 156 ; planning and execution of a day's driving, 157 ; where to find the birds, 158 ; partridges few where pheasants are many, 158 ; the gapes disease, 158, 159 ; remedies for, 159 ; a favourite holding cover, 160 ; height and position of fences, 160–165 ; conduct of the guns at the fences, 163 ; battery made with hurdles, 164 ; pits, 164 ; wooden shields, 164 ; distances between batteries, 165 ; colour of hats or caps, 165 ; order and succession of drives, 165 ; beginning at up-wind end of beat and driving down wind, 166 ; scattering the birds, 167 ; driving and walking combined, 168 ; James Woodrow, of Buckenham,

PHE

169 ; use of fresh ploughed land, 169 ; placing the beaters, 169 ; assignment of colours to various divisions of beaters, 171 ; the use of flags, 171 ; economy of time, 172 ; picking up dead birds, 172 ; placing the shooters, 172 ; dangers of muzzle-loaders in driving, 174 ; instructions to loaders in handling guns, 175 ; changing guns, 176 ; hints to shooters, 176–178 ; 'traversing,' 177 ; match between Mr. Crawford and Mr. Osbaldeston in 1850, 178 ; large bags, 179, 180, [181]–[183], 304, 309; reply to critics on driving, [182]

Pea rifles, 270, 271

Peregrine falcons, 284

Phasianus Colchicus, 233

Phasianus, Lin., 185

Phasianus Reevesii, 185

Phasianus torquatus, 233

Pheasants, inimical to partridges, 158 ; pheasant shooting, [180] ; diverse literary opinions on battue-shooting, [180], 181 ; killing with sticks in Persia, 182 ; management of covert shooting, 182 ; placing shooters, 183 ; genera of birds, 185 ; their running powers, 185 ; best direction to beat a covert, 185 ; placing stoppers, 187 ; bramble beating, 188 ; clothing for men who beat in brushwood, 189 ; character of covert, 190 ; flushing, 191, 203, 206, 217, 219–221 ; 'high side shot,' 192 ; method of pursuit advocated by oppo-

PHE

nents of the use of beaters, 193 ; 'straight over,' 194 ; how far to hold in front of a bird, 195 ; following birds with the gun at the shoulder, 196 ; shooting positions, 197, 198 ; 'mopping up,' 198 ; in the presence of ground game, 200 ; netting the covert, 200 ; 'sewin,' 200 ; co-operation of subordinates, 201 ; use of dogs, 201 ; tricky keepers, 201 ; fees to keepers for best places, 202 ; picking up dead birds, 203; retrieving wounded birds, 203 ; sparing hens, 203; counting the bag, 204 ; keeping individual scores, 204 ; question of the domestication of the pheasant, 205 ; whistling at feeding times, 206 ; thinning the cocks, 206 ; proportion of cocks to hens, 207 ; number of birds sent to London markets, 207 ; increase of birds in present century, 207 ; consumption of worms and grubs, 208 ; proportion available to general consumer and prices, 208, 219 ; cost of preservation, 210 ; abstracts of game accounts, 210 ; extracts from the Riddlesworth gamebook, 211 ; extracts from the Holkham game-book, 212 ; a big bag with muzzle-loaders at Bradgate Park, 213 ; the largest bag ever made in one day (at Croxteth), 213 ; excellence of sport not dependent on quantity of game killed, 214 ; feeding in covert, 215 ;

POA

natural food, 215 ; plans of coverts at Sturston Carr, 216, Cherry Row, 217, Lord Londesborough's, 218, 219, Wayland Wood, 219, Merton home woods, 223, 224 ; poaching, 304, 307

Pheasantries, 233, 235

Pigeon shooting from traps, 335 ; position of clubs, 335 ; leading shooters, 336 ; care bestowed on birds before shooting, 337 ; club rules to prevent ill-treatment, 337–339 ; single-barrelled guns for beginners, 339 ; advice to advanced shooters, 340 ; match shooting, 341, 342 ; handicaps, 343 ; notable matches, 343 ; Dr. Carver and Captain Bogardus, 344 ; best shots at Hurlingham, 345 ; sources of information respecting, 345

Pin-fire guns, 54

Pinnock, James, beater, 189

Pits, for shooters, 164

Poachers and poaching, 294–297 ; sentimental views about, 299 ; practical aspect of poaching, 300 ; the poacher's physical appearance, 301 ; rural, 302 ; town, 302 ; driving, 303 ; use of dogs, 303, 304 ; collusion between town and rural, 305 ; confederates on railways, 305; reformed poachers as keepers, 306 ; a cunning scoundrel, 306 ; at pheasants, 307 ; use of alarm guns, 308 ; at partridges, 309 ; netting, 309, 310; at the ground game, 311 ; hares, 311 ; gate nets,

POA

311 ; purse nets, 312, wire snares, 312 ; at rabbits, 313 ; the long net, 313

Pointers, use of, 5, 22, 27, 141, 144, 145, 193, 314, 315, 318, 319, 322–330

Poison for destroying vermin, 287

Polecats, 261, 278

Pole-traps, 289

Powder, 99–104 ; proof of guns with nitro-powders, 114

Prices of guns, 71–81 ; of pheasants and other game, 208–210, 252

Purse nets, 260, 312

RABBITS, and rabbit shooting, 11, 12, 85, 131, 210, 213, 249 259 ; popularity of the sport, 260 ; a difficult shot, 260, 271 ; use of ferrets, 260, 261 ; purse nets, 260 ; use of spaniels, 261–265 ; terriers, 261–262 ; beagles, 262 ; preference for the employment of Clumbers and Cockers, 262, 263 ; shooting, 264 ; the line of beaters, 265 ; 'showing,' 265, 266 ; the sport in detail, 267 ; keeping the line, 268 ; caution in firing, 269 ; use of the pea rifle, 270 as vermin, 304, 311, 312, 313

Rats, 18, 246, 253, 278 ; *see* Vermin

Ravens, 286

Rearing, 231 ; paying keepers by results, 231 ; proportion of cocks to hens, 233 ; crossing, 233 ; the Phasianus

REA

Colchicus, 233 ; P. torquatus, 233 ; advantages and disadvantages of the use of mews, 233 ; weather favourable for laying, 234 ; proportion of eggs hatched, 234 ; gathering eggs, 235 ; construction of mews and pheasantries, 235 ; precautions in attendance on the birds, 236 ; pinioning, 236 ; enclosures open above, 236 ; fowls as foster-mothers, 237 ; preservation of eggs, 238 ; suitable coops, 238, 239 ; use of incubators, 239 ; hatching pens, 240, 241 ; sitting-boxes, 242 ; construction of ordinary hencoops, 242 ; number of eggs to a sitting, 242 ; objections to the use of turkey hens, 243 ; choice of soil for the coops, 243 ; ant-hills, 243 ; arrangement of the coops, 244 ; guarding the coops at night, 245 ; vermin destructive to eggs and young birds, 245, 246 ; bird enemies, 246 ; dogs among the coops, 246 ; best kinds of food, 246 ; hours of feeding, 247 ; hen's eggs as food, 247 ; scrap cake, 247, 248 ; maggots, 248 ; Mr. Carnegie's table of food for young pheasants, 248 ; rice and greaves, 249 ; authorities on feeding, 250 ; use of water, 250, 251 ; Dr. Walker, of Franklinville, U.S., on the gapes disease, 250 ; proportion of men to coops, 252 ; estimate of cost of rearing and

REA

selling prices, 252 ; good and bad keepers, 252 ; permanent stores of food and their inspection, 253 ; perpetual war against rats, 253 ; partridges, 253 ; ants' eggs for partridges, 253 ; Spratt's patent ' Crissel,' 253 ; collecting insects for food, 254 ; taking up eggs, 254 ; imported birds, 255 ; caution in buying eggs, 256 ; use of buckwheat and hemp seed in attracting partridges, 256 ; good breeding-places, 256 ; dogs the worst enemies to partridges, 257 ; thinning off cock birds, 257 ; re-establishing healthy stock on land, 258

Rendlesham, sport at, 16

Retrievers, use of, 5, 145, 315–319, 321, 329-334 ; *see* Dogs

Revolvers, 295

Riddlesworth, sport at, 184, 211

Royal Society for Prevention of Cruelty to Animals, 335

SCHÖNBEIN, experimenting chemist in gunpowder, 99

Schultze, Captain, inventor of the ' sawdust ' gunpowder, 99

Scotland, sport in, 6, 27, 144 ; *see* vol. ii.

Setters, 144, 181, 314, 319, 320, 322-330

Sewin, 201

Sharnton, Richard, winner of prize for shooting in 1811, 17

Shields, wooden, 164

Shooters, 121 ; the best kind, 121, 123, ; mistaken notions respecting, 122 ; qualities of,

SHO

124 ; bad unsporting kind 124-127 ; wrong sort, 127 ; bad shots but excellent fellows, 128 ; jealous, 128 ; ' wiping another's eye,' 129 ; anecdote of the general, the parson, and the lawyer, 129 ; schoolboys out shooting, 130 ; the anxious host, 131 ; the host who gnawed the turnips, 131 ; the martinet, 131, 132 ; the excitable host, 133; dangerous shooting companions, 134 ; the old-fashioned shooting host, 135 ; marking, 137 ; ' Woodcock Brown,' 137

Shooting, modern methods of, 2 ; driving, 3 ; a battue, 3, 4, 20 ; cheap pheasants, 3 ; ignorant critics, 3, 4, 20 ; use of dogs, 5 ; grouse, 6 ; phenomenal marksmanship, 7 ; hasty firing, 8 ; judging distance, 8 ; partridges, 9 ; shooting over dogs, 9 ; hares, 10 ; rabbits, 11 ; old style, 14 ; sport in Bohemia, 14, 15 ; in Suffolk in 1807, 16 ; at Holkham, 16 ; analysis of yearly bags at Holkham, 17 ; a prize winner in 1811, 17 ; increase in pheasants, 18 ; a big bag at Lord Stamford's, 19 ; trapping a critic, 21 ; pointers, 22 ; Bromley Davenport on sporting critics, 23 ; increase in grouse, 24 ; the best grouse moors, 24 ; six days' shooting at Wemmergill, 25 ; average bags in Ireland, Wales, and Scotland, 27 ; skill of the Maharajah Duleep Singh, 28 ;

SHO

the game book of the Chantilly estate, 30

Shooting-coats, 136

Shooting corrector, 43

Shooting schools, 46

Shot, soft, 104, 105 ; chilled, 104 ; hard, 105 ; manufacture, 105 ; Greener's method of sizing, 106 ; number of pellets of hard and soft to ounce, 106 ; sizes suited to seasons and game, 106, 107 ; quantity to gun, 107, 108

Shot and Ball Gun, 69, 346

Six Mile Bottom, sport at, 179

Snares for wood pigeons, 226, 227, 229 ; for partridges, 310 ; wire, 312

Sore-finger, [119]

Spaniels, 181, 193, 261–265

Sparrow-hawks, 246, 276, 280

Sportsmen and game-preservers, past and present — Ashburton, Lord, 164, 179, 180, [179], 213 ; Baring, Hon. A., [179] ; Baring, Hon. F., [177] ; Bedford, Duke of, 212 ; Birkbeck, Mr. E., 180 ; Bromley Davenport, Mr., 132 ; Brooke, Sir V., 12 ; Brown, Mr. Gilpin, 24 ; Buckley, Col., 176 ; Cambridge, Duke of, [177] ; Campbell of Monzies, 26 ; Chesterfield, Earl of, [178] ; Coke, Col., 180 ; Coke, Lord, 180 ; Coke, Hon. W., 155, 180 ; Coke, Mr., 28, 178 ; Corbett, Sir V., 28 ; Corrance, F., 7, 336 ; Crawford, Mr., 178 ; Deerhurst, Viscount, [178] ; Devonshire,

SPO

Duke of, 24 ; Digby, Col. E., [177] ; Downe, Lord, 24, 27 ; Duleep Singh, Maharajah, 7, 18, 26, 28, 174, 180 ; Duleep Singh, Prince Victor, [179] ; Edwards, Sir H., 6 ; Elcho, Lord, [178] ; Eversleigh, Lord, 69 ; Fellowes, Mr., 18 ; Forbes, Mr., 180 ; Fosbery, Col., 69 ; Fryer, Mr. F., 7 ; Grey, Earl de, 7, 28, 174, 213, 336, 345 ; Gurney-Buxton, Mr., 180 ; Hall, Gen. J., 24, 141, 146, 169, 179, 336, 343 ; Hawker, Col., 1 ; Heathcote, Mr., 343 ; Heygate, Mr., 344 ; Hill, Lord, 18 ; Huntingfield, Lord, 7, 18, 155, 343 ; Ilchester, Lord, [177]; Kennard, M. T. [178] ; Kennedy, Lord, 28, 155 ; Lathom, Earl of, [179] ; Lavington, Lord, 15 ; Leconfield, Lord, 180, 336, 343; Leicester, Lord, 16, 18, 184, 212, 258 ; Londesborough, Lord, 18, 28, 219, 336 ; Low, W., [178] ; Lyttelton, Lord, 180 ; Macdonald, Gen. J., 141 ; Malmesbury, Lord, 44, 45 ; Milbank, Mr. Ralph, [177] ; Milbank, Sir F., 7, 24, 26, 343 ; Mildmay, Capt. E. St. J., [177] ; Newport, Lord, 7, [179] ; Normanby, Marquess of, 37, 38 ; Osbaldeston, Mr., 28, 156, 178, 336 ; Pembroke, Earl of, [179] ; Price, Mr. R. J. Lloyd, 213 ; Pryor, Mr., 180 ; Rimington-Wilson, Mr., 24, 26, 27, 336 ; Rendlesham,

SPO

Lord, 16, 18 ; Ripon, Marquess, 24, 26; Ross, Capt., 342; Roxburgh, Duke of, [177] ; Rutland, Duke of, 69; Sefton, Lord, 18, 213 ; Shelley, Capt., 344, 345 ; Stamford, Lord, 18, 19, 169, 179, 214 ; Stonor, Hon. H., [178]; Stuart-Wortley, Mr. A., 7 ; Sutton, Sir R., 156, 167, 178 ; Tyssen-Amherst, Mr., 18 ; Vane-Tempest, Lord H., [178] ; Wales, Prince of, 18 ; Walsingham, Lord, 7, 18, 24, 26, [177], [179] ; Ward-Hunt, Mr., 7 ; Ward, Mr. D., 344, 345 ; Wharncliffe, Lord, 12 ; Wenlock, Lord, 180 ; Wood, Mr. A., [177] ; York, Duke of, [178]

Stoats 276, 287, 288 ; *see* Vermin

Stoppers, 187, 191, 200, 206, 219

Studley, sport at, 44

Sturston Carr, plan of covert, 216

Suffolk, sport in, 9, 17, 27–29, 51, 143, 155, 170, 180, 207, 212

Sutherland, sport in, 227

Syngamus trachealis, 159, 251

TEGETMEIER, Mr., quoted, 205, 208, 250

Terriers, 261

Traps for vermin, 287

Traps, pigeon-shooting, 338–341

Try guns, 88, 89

Turpentine as a cure for gapes, 159

VAMBÉRY, Arminius, quoted, 182

WOO

Vermin, destructive to eggs and young birds, 245, 246 ; definition of, 273 ; animals and birds which do great mischief and must be destroyed, 274–279 ; folly of allowing keepers so much per head for destroying, 275 ; creatures which do harm but have some few redeeming points, 279–282 ; creatures which destroy game but possess qualities which should prevent their indiscriminate destruction, 283–287 ; use of poison in destroying, 287 ; traps, 287 ; unnecessary cruelty in trapping, 288 ; the pole-trap, 289

Virginian colins, introduction into Norfolk, 255

WADS, 112–114

Wales, sport in, 27, 213

Walker, Dr., of Franklinville, U.S., quoted on the gapes disease, 250

Watson, keeper, 297

Wayland Wood, plan of covert, 219–223

Weasels, 276, 287, 288; *see* Vermin

Weight of guns, 93

Wemmergill, sport at, 24, 25

Wild cat, 277 ; *see* Vermin

Willesden, pigeon shooting at, 343

Windhover, 280

Wire snares, 312

Woodcock, 12, 137, 213

Wood pigeon shooting, 224 ;

WOO

most favourable months for, 225 ; decoys, 225–227, 229 ; colour of clothing for shooter, 225 ; high winds favouring, 225 ; shooting blue rocks on rocky coasts, 227, 229 ; contents of crops, 228

Woodrow, James, keeper, 169

Works quoted—Bailey's ' Pheasants and Pheasantries,' 250 ; Blaine's ' Rural Sports,' 193, 212 ; Bromley Davenport's ' Sport,' 23, [180], 181 ; Carnegie's ' Practical Game-Preserving,' 253 ; ' Curiosities of Civilisation,' 207 ; Daniel's ' Rural Sports,' 143, 214 ; Elliot's ' Monograph of the Phasianidæ,' 250 ; ' Field,' The, 25, 30, 207, 250 ; Forby's ' East - Anglian Vocabulary,' 215 ; ' Gapes Disease in Gallinaceous Birds,' 159 ; Greener's ' Gun and its Development,' 14, 75 ; Johnson's ' Sportsman's Cyclopædia,' 195, 212 ; Jullien's

YOR

' La Chasse, son histoire et sa législation,' 181 ; Manley's ' Notes on Game and Game-shooting,' [184] ; Megnin ' On the Syngamus trachealis,' 159 ; Neville's ' Game Laws of England for Gamekeepers,' 295 ; Nimrod, 39 ; ' Oakley Shooting Code,' 192 ; ' St. James's Gazette,' 207 ; Stevenson's ' Birds of Norfolk,' 19, [180], 207 ; Stonehenge's ' British Rural Sports,' 4 ; Tegetmeier's ' Pheasants,' 250 ; Thornhill's ' Sporting Directory,' 193 ; Waterton's ' Essays on Ornithology,' 205, 207 ; White's ' Natural History of Selborne,' 178

Wretham, Norfolk, sport at, 234

Wynter, Dr., cited, 207

YORKSHIRE, sport in, 6, 24, 25, 28, 44, 229

Yorkshire moors, 6

PRINTED BY
SPOTTISWOODE AND CO., NEW-STREET SQUARE
LONDON